BUILDING AN ADIRONDACK GUIDEBOAT

Wood Strip Reproductions of the *Virginia*

MICHAEL J. OLIVETTE and JOHN D. MICHNE

Nicholas K. Burns Publishing
Utica, New York

Nicholas K. Burns Publishing
130 Proctor Boulevard
Utica, New York 13501

First Edition

ISBN 0-9713069-9-0

Photographs by the authors except as noted.
Drawings by Dick Millet and Rob Axelson where noted.
Cover photograph of the *Virginia* by Eric Borg courtesy Adirondack Museum.
Book design by Alyssa Krill/Little Utopia, Inc.

Both authors contributed equally to the development and writing
of this book. The appearance of the author's names on the cover
and elsewhere in the book is random and does not denote the
prominence of one author's contribution over another.

Library of Congress Cataloging-in-Publication Data

Olivette, Michael J., 1957–
    Building an Adirondack guideboat : wood strip reproductions
of the Virginia / Michael J. Olivette and John D. Michne.—1st ed.
    p.   cm.
    ISBN 0-9713069-9-0 (pbk.)
    1. Adirondack guide-boats—Design and construction. I. Michne,
John D., 1937- II. Title.
VM355.045 2005
623.82'9—dc22   2005007144

DEDICATION

Dedicated to the memory of those builders
who have gone before and left the fruits of their labors
to inform, instruct, and inspire us who would follow.

CONTENTS

CONTENTS

FOREWORD

If you buy anything from The Adirondack Museum, cruise its website, or read one of its publications, you will inevitably come across its logo. It looks like a man with a canoe on his head. Like most logos, this one is reduced to its most basic elements and can be confusing. People have been known to attach it upside down, so that it pictures a person standing on his hands in a canoe. But if you are among the cognoscenti, or if you have paid attention when you visited the museum's boat exhibit, you  know which side is up. You know that the little figure neither has his boat on his head, nor is that boat a canoe. The boat is resting on a carved yoke supported on his shoulders, and it is an Adirondack guideboat.

The Adirondack guideboat is pointed at both ends, and many people unfamiliar with small craft call it a canoe for that reason. It is well known among boat scholars and boat fanciers, however, for what it is—a rowboat, and one of the finest types of traditional boats that has evolved anywhere in America. It's an extreme boat—extremely fast but also extremely narrow and tippy to achieve that speed; extremely light, but extremely thin-skinned and fragile. A traditionally-built guideboat is an extremely difficult piece of boatbuilding, and it has always been extremely expensive.

It is also the first small inland boat to have been thoroughly studied. Kenneth Durant retired from his career in international journalism in the 1950s and spent the rest of his life studying the boats he had rowed as a child at his family's camp on Forked Lake. He discounted the romantic myth that the Abenaki guide Mitchell Sabattis "invented" the guideboat and demonstrated that it had evolved within the space of a generation or two among the early European-American settlers of the Adirondacks. These backwoodsmen needed a boat to get around because the extensive waterways were relatively navigable and the terrain was not; it was mountainous and covered with deadfall, windfall, swamps, and streams. The boat had to be easy to row because the settlers would be covering long distances. It had to be lightweight so it could be carried around beaver dams and waterfalls and from watershed to watershed. It had to be built of materials found nearby because of those very conditions that inspired it—transportation was poor and manufactured goods and materials brought in from outside were expensive.

By the 1840s, this regional boat was well known to the small but growing group of upper middle class men who had the leisure and means to escape the cities and seek mental rest and physical sport in the North Woods. It was increasingly referred to as a "guideboat" because it was the essential tool of the hunting and fishing guides hired by these "city men." Its most distinctive characteristic was that it could be easily carried by one man, a feat that seemed "as impossible as carrying a man o'war," according to an observer in 1859.

By the 1890s, according to Durant, "the standard working boat of the professional guide...averaged 15 to 16 feet overall, with an inside beam between 36 and 39 inches. Its weight, complete with all accessories, averaged 70 to 75 pounds." These accessories included three seats, one pair of oars, a paddle, and a yoke for carrying. The frames, or ribs, were cut from naturally-curving spruce roots and the skin, planked in a modified type of lapstrake (a widely-used technique in which each plank up from the bottom laps over the one below it, rather as in a clapboard house), was smooth inside and out.

The heyday of the guideboat was brief. The antebellum tourist travelled nearly everywhere in one, but his son or granddaughter had a range of boats from which to choose, just as he or she sought rest and relaxation in activities other than hunting and fishing. The new generation of Adirondack tourists took small steamboats between hotels and rented St. Lawrence skiffs or lapstrake rowboats for "botonizing" or picnicking once they got there. Their children, exploring Adirondack waters as the twentieth century began, most likely used factory-built cedar canoes with a waterproof outer skin of canvas. Adirondack guides found less and less work as the travellers used guidebooks, maps, and well-marked routes. The guide and his boat disappeared from general use.

By the 1950s, when the Adirondack Museum was founded, the guideboat was seemingly just an icon. Aluminum had supplanted wood and canvas as the preferred small boat material, and most of the wooden guideboats that had survived a search for kindling or being left overturned in the woods languished under camp porches or in the rafters of barns. They could be had for a song—or for the trouble of taking them away. The Museum, recognizing the boat as the single most important artifact of the region, began to do just that, and has since acquired sixty-nine guideboats. They form the cornerstone of its boat collection, the second-largest in the country.

In the course of his work on guideboat history, Durant corresponded with John Gardner, a boatbuilder who was very interested in traditional small craft and who was publishing descriptions and lines in Maine Coast Fisherman. Gardner agreed to come study the boat

from the boatbuilder's point of view. Between 1959 and 1963, he spent his summer vacations in the museum's storage shed examining *Virginia*, a guideboat built by the Boonville builders Floyd and Lewis Grant in 1905. He measured the thickness of each plank, counted the copper tacks and brass screws, and generally turned his boatbuilder's eye to the ways in which Adirondack builders had met the challenges they faced. The plans Gardner produced eventually were published as an appendix to Durant's monumental work on the history and traditional construction of the region's boat, published in 1980.

Gardner strongly believed in the value of boatbuilding as a way of expressing creativity and independence. He also believed in putting people back in good boats—boats that were designed and built for the particular requirements of the rower and his water, not mass-produced boats that were supposedly good for everybody and everywhere. He spent a good part of his career exploring traditional small craft types and publishing histories, descriptions, and lines for them, work that eventually was collected in three books on building classic small craft. Gardner never included an Adirondack guideboat in his publications, however, partly because it was such a specialized boat, and partly because material for the sawn frames was hard to find and the feather-edged planking was too difficult for the average independent builder. "In spite of all this," Gardner observed, "some purists do not look kindly on the use of glued laminations or glued-lap planking in guide-boat construction. There is no reasonable justification for this rejection from a functional and utilitarian standpoint."

Some purists continue to decry the use of epoxy in guideboat construction. Many other guideboat-fanciers (including several commercial builders and John Michne and Michael Olivette) see in the use of modern materials and technologies a further development in the evolution of the Adirondack guideboat. An Adirondack guideboat built with laminated ribs and strip planking is not only functional and utilitarian, as Gardner indicated it would be, but it also has the classic lines of the traditional boat and it continues to reflect the lives of the people who build and use it. With the help of Michne and Olivette, you can be one of them.

Hallie E. Bond, Curator
Adirondack Museum
May 5, 2005

CHAPTER 1

FROM HUMBLE BEGINNINGS

The Adirondack Mountain region of New York comprises most of the northern part of the state, lying wholly within an area bounded by the western shore of Lake Champlain on the east, the St. Lawrence River and Lake Ontario to the north and west, and the Mohawk River valley to the south. Within this area lies the Adirondack Park. It is not a national park, but an intricate collage of public and private land, mountains, rivers, and lakes.

The New York State Legislature created the original Park in 1892 when it established a 2.8 million-acre preserve in the heart of the Adirondack Mountains, delineating it on its maps with a blue line. "Blue Line" became the term for the Park boundaries and remains so today, still used on most maps of the region.

Since its inception, the size of the Park has increased several times. Presently, the area within the Blue Line represents approximately 6 million acres—about one-fifth of New York State's 30.2 million acres. Put into perspective, this 9,375 square mile section of New York is roughly equal in size to the state of Vermont and is larger than the entire state of New Hampshire. The Adirondack Park is three times the size of Yellowstone, the largest national park outside of Alaska, and is 120 miles long north to south, and 80 miles wide east to west. Within its boundaries are some 30,000 miles of rivers and streams, nourished by 2,300 lakes and ponds. Although there are about 2,000 promontories in the Park, only about 200 are prominent enough to be considered mountains (Figure 1.1). The highest, Mt. Marcy, in the High Peaks region, rises to 5,344 feet.

Figure 1.1

One of many panoramic views in the Adirondacks.

The Adirondack Park was—and most of it still is—a wilderness, although intensive logging during the nineteenth and early twentieth centuries has resulted in most of the forest today being at least second growth. Some of the few pockets of virgin forest remaining are protected by the state constitution, which stipulates that Forest Preserve lands within the Park shall remain forever wild.

The economy of the region is mostly based on the land itself, with the forest and tourist industries predominating. Paper companies own large tracts from which logs are harvested for pulp, and the native Adirondack white ash is legendary in the manufacture of baseball bats. Loggers harvest birch and maple, along with eastern white pine and red spruce.

Efforts over the years to attract winter tourism culminated in 1932, when Lake Placid hosted the Winter Olympic Games in the heart of the High Peaks

1

region. Whiteface Mountain at Lake Placid is renowned for its world-class ski slopes and Lake Placid again hosted the Winter Olympics in 1980.

The mining industry once flourished, with open pit iron mines supplying the many forges nearby. Gore Mountain, which hosts a popular state-run ski center, is also the site of a garnet mine that still produces much of the garnet abrasive used in making sandpaper. There are no large cities within the Park, only towns, villages, and hamlets, some thriving, some barely surviving, and a few abandoned. The climate can be harsh; winter temperatures routinely fall lower than anywhere else in the state.

Wildlife abounds, perhaps less now than in earlier times, but it is still an attractive lure for those seeking to commune with nature. There are no longer wolves, cougar, or elk in the Park, but the moose is coming back thanks to itinerant individuals from Vermont. A small herd of breeding stock has become established, and based on a recent estimate, numbers more than 100 animals.

Whitetail deer and black bear are common, with deer boldly begging for a handout from tourists along some of the more popular haunts. Before the days of landfill management, it was great fun to take the kids to a town dump in the evening to watch the bears forage for their evening meal. The beaver has come back, their numbers approaching nuisance levels in pockets of prime habitat.

The native Adirondack brook trout (Figure 1.2) and lake trout have similarly been reintroduced in many of the Park's lakes after being nearly wiped out because of the chemical pesticide DDT. Thus we learned the legacy of Rachel Carson's *Silent Spring*, spreading copious amounts of pesticide to control the Adirondack's most prolific and despised resident, the voracious black fly. Acid rain has also had a deleterious effect on the Park, rendering some lakes devoid of aquatic life, and affecting the growth and natural reproduction of some tree species.

Figure 1.2
A nice catch! (Courtesy of Wayne Failing.)

There are resorts for tourists, and summer residents with vacation homes. Towns situated on the shores of pristine lakes boast population explosions from Memorial Day to Labor Day, which fatten the coffers of the area's economy and help sustain it during the leaner winter months. Only about 130,000 residents live year-round inside the Blue Line.

Hundreds of public and private campsites throughout the Park provide facilities for those who would prefer to fish, canoe, hike, climb mountain trails, or otherwise enjoy the Adirondacks on a more intimate level. One of the more popular activities is hiking the mountains. A coveted designation for serious hikers is that of an Adirondack 46er; one who has hiked to the summits of all 46 of the Adirondack High Peaks. A marked trail system maintained by the State provides a measure of safety and information for hikers, from beginner to expert (Figure 1.3).

Figure 1.3
Winter in the Adirondack High Peaks.

Let us now step back from this snapshot of today's Adirondacks to a time in the first half of the nineteenth century. Since roads were nearly impassible in winter, became mud and wagon wheel ruts in spring, and were little more than dusty trails in summer, people used the waterways as their best means of travel. Brook trout abounded, and beaver, mink, and otter were plentiful. Scratching out a living from the land required a pioneering spirit. Fur trapping was an alternative seasonal pursuit for those who took leave of the hard and often dangerous logging work in the woods. In the short growing season, crops could be grudgingly coaxed from fields carved from the forest and "de-rocked" to a depth at least minimally sufficient for tilling.

In the second half of the century, word of the natural bounty of the Adirondacks and its potential for sport and recreation spread, as the entrepreneurs and industrial tycoons of New York, Philadelphia, and Boston began to discover the region. Names like Durant, Morgan, and Whitney were soon heard in the Adirondacks. It did not take many summers for their comfortable camps to be built and staffed, roads to be improved, and access to the woods facilitated. They gave their "Great Camps" names like Pine Knot, The Cedars, and Sagamore. Large resort hotels sprang up at eye-catching speed, catering to vacationers of more modest means.

The city outdoorsman, or "sport," as he was called, often required assistance to catch a stringer of trout or bag a trophy deer, and some of the male residents of the region, experienced in the ways of the woods, provided that assistance. Thus was born the legendary Adirondack guide. He would single-handedly take the sport afield or to favorite fishing spots, provide his meals, and ensure his comfort and welfare.

Some guides were independent, hired by the day; others were on the staff of private camps. Still others worked as "guides-in-residence" for the many hotels and boarding houses that became so prevalent. In fact, a certain class system existed for guides; those who worked for the hotels typically were considered to be of lower quality and were paid about two dollars a day. Many of the independent guides, whose reputations earned them greater respect, could earn three or four dollars a day.

To be successful, the guide needed a boat. A suitable boat had to be light yet sturdy, and able to carry the guide, his sport, their duffel, and their game (Figure 1.4). It needed stability in open water with a full load, and had to float whisper quiet while stalking game from the water. More importantly, perhaps, the guide also needed to carry the boat himself over portages (or "carries" as they are referred to in the Adirondacks), and around rapids.

3

Figure 1.4
A fully loaded guideboat. (Courtesy of Adirondack Museum.)

A portable craft did exist in the Adirondacks before the advent of the guides, a workboat the equivalent of today's pick-up truck, which would do everything the guide needed. It was especially useful because with so few roads, the best means of travel was from one waterway to another with short carries in between. It was inevitable that guides would use such a craft and that it would evolve into what became known as the guideboat.[1]

History does not record the origin of the guides' boat, but it can be inferred from writings and photographs that the European wherry and the bateau made significant contributions to the design. Early boats from around the mid-1800s, 16' long by approximately 36" wide, were lapstraked, but later H. Dwight Grant, and those who worked for him, used the "Grant lap," or the bevel lap, resulting in a smoothly planked hull, thus reducing noise. The wine glass transom, a square stern, gave way to double-ended versions, most probably in the interest of improved maneuverability.

Propulsion was by rowing, with two sets of oarlocks provided. The choice of rowing station was dictated by the amount and placement of the total load the boat was to carry. Bow, stern, and middle seats were standard, and rowing was possible from either the bow or middle seat. With a single rower, the oars were placed at the center position; when a passenger occupied the stern seat, the rower maintained trim by shifting his rowing position to the bow seat. Note that even though two sets of oarlocks were available, two people rarely rowed at the same time. The additional speed that might be gained was usually of little significance, and the precise coordination required would make rowing too difficult.

The middle seat was easily removed, as it could be kept in place by being simply lashed to risers. This created a relatively large open hold that carried the game and equipment, and when the boat was carried, created space for a carved removable shoulder yoke mounted amidships. A single paddle was included, useful for maneuvering the craft in tight quarters.

These boats, with their unique Adirondack design, varied little. There were nuances in the construction of different builders, but overall, the purpose of the vessels was readily recognizable. From about the middle of the nineteenth century to well into the twentieth, several thousand were built, many by the guides themselves during the winter. Most were sold to other guides or to camp owners.

Construction of a guideboat began in the woods, where spruce was abundant and intensely logged. The boat builder prized the stumps, which were useless to the logger but invaluable in the making of the stems and ribs. He laboriously dug them out of the ground, and then cut them vertically into slabs, including the roots. After drying for two years or more, stems and ribs for boats were cut from the slabs, also called crooks. The grain of the wood followed a natural curve from the root to the trunk. The rib halves cut from the slabs followed the grain, preserving the curve as much as possible. This technique did not require steam bending, yet produced a rib of outstanding strength for its weight with little tendency to warp. The rib halves were cut in matching pairs so that when fastened together at the foot, a pair had virtually the same grain pattern on each half, and therefore the same strength.

The ribs in the center portion of the boat were all the same shape, but varied in number and spacing to adjust for final boat length. The ribs for the bow and stern sections were identically matched fore and aft, thus producing a true double-ended boat. This economy of design required only a dozen or so different rib patterns for the entire boat. A typical 16' boat may have contained as many as sixty-six individual half ribs, all produced from only thirteen different rib templates.

Builders screwed the ribs to a bottom board, which some consider analogous to a keel. It is probably more appropriate to look at it as a very narrow flat bottom, comparable to the much wider bottom of a dory or bateau, both of which had their rib feet fastened to it. In these boats, a distance proportionate to the width of the bottom separated the feet of opposing ribs. The very narrow bottom board of the guideboat does not permit this type of mounting, resulting in the overlap of opposing rib feet. The contribution to overall strength is obvious, the ribs forming a continuous member from gunwale to gunwale, with a double thickness at the overlaps across the bottom. This reinforcement made it possible to use a thinner bottom board, reducing overall weight.

The bottom board was usually made of pine, and the thickness varied from ½" to ¾", depending on the builder. The width of the bottom board amidships ranged from approximately 7" to 9", depending on the length of the boat, tapering to the ends in a fair curve to a width that would allow flush mounting of the stem foot. The edges were beveled to match the curve on the bottom of the ribs, allowing the garboard plank to be fastened both to the ribs and to the bottom board.

Once the basic framework of bottom board, ribs, and stems was assembled, planking could begin. Quarter sawn pine was the common choice, in thicknesses of from ³⁄₁₆" to ¼" and approximately 3" to 4" wide. Shorter lengths were scarfed together to make up the full length required, with the scarf joints positioned at a rib and the outer knife-edge of the scarf pointing aft. The edges of the planks were precisely tapered oppositely so that the bottom edge of one plank overlapped the top edge of the next, the whole assembly producing a smooth continuous skin. When bedded and fastened, the lapped joint was essentially waterproof.

Some builders further refined the planker's art by first scraping or planing a curve in and along the length of individual planks such that the plank fit on the rib without bending. "Getting out the siding" was a tedious exercise in precision fitting, expertly accomplished by few builders. Some builders preferred not to fit the curve of the ribs, but simply screwed the thin flat planking directly to the ribs, bending it to the curve of the ribs in the process.

Fastening the planks to the framework required more than a thousand screws. Each plank was fastened to each rib with three or four screws, including one through the lap joint. Literally thousands of tiny copper tacks were driven through and clinched the length of the lap joint between the ribs, alternating from the inside to outside of the boat.

Decks were installed fore and aft, and risers were screwed to the ribs in position for the seats. In early examples, the seats were merely fitted planks, but were soon replaced with much lighter open frame caned seats. Matching caned backrests were often included for the comfort of passengers, and some later boats had bottom slats across the ribs.

The boats were either painted with dark colors or varnished, as the customer desired. Two-tone color schemes were common, with dark browns, greens, and blues predominating. Guides generally preferred their own boats painted (Figures 1.5 and 1.6), while those sold for recreation were usually varnished.

As the population and popularity of the Adirondack region increased, the kind of boats people used changed. Advances in building design and technology brought craft such as the lightweight canvas covered wood canoe with its lower costs and relative ease of production—no need for spruce stumps. Access to lakes and ponds that formerly required the guide and his carry-boat became but a pleasant drive in an automobile. Longer passages that took the guide the better part of the day to row were reduced to a matter of minutes by the outboard motor, and the guide himself became the resort rowing instructor and storyteller. Many of the unique carry-boats that evolved from humble beginnings to become regional classics found their way to the rafters of camp boathouses, or were left abandoned in the woods that bore them, all but forgotten.

Perhaps because of the period in which the guideboat was developed or because of the rugged country and the equally rugged people who built them, tables of offsets or naval architectural drawings for guideboats were virtually non-existent. Builders kept just the patterns or

5

templates for the ribs, bottom board, stems, and the garboard plank, from which they could construct a boat. It was only through the work of a dedicated researcher that we know more about the Adirondack guideboat, its construction, and about some of the men who built it.

Figure 1.5
Built for Boonville guide William Commerford in 1904, this 72 lb. boat has a 14½' bottom board. It is painted dark blue and forest green with black trim. This was the third boat built in Grant's shop that year. The family who had owned it for over 90 years recently sold the boat, after some light restoration, for $14,000.

Figure 1.6
The last of seventeen guideboats built in the Grant shop in 1903. At 59 lbs., it has an 11' bottom board and was built for Boonville guide Richard Crego. Dubbed "Raiders" by Grant, shorter boats like these were often used to pack into remote ponds for sneaking up on wary trout. Painted inside and out with the same shade of green, and with varnished trim, the boat was professionally restored and now resides in Cazenovia, New York.

Kenneth Durant spent his summers as a young lad at The Cedars, the camp his father, F. C. Durant, owned on the shore of Forked Lake. There he learned the lay and the lore of the Adirondacks, and when considered old enough, was given his very own guideboat. He loved his guideboat and his interest in them continued throughout a successful career as a journalist.

Upon retirement, Durant and his wife, Helen, undertook exhaustive research, conducting interviews with the few remaining builders. They relied heavily on the recollections of Lewis Grant, who provided a wealth of detailed information about boats built by his father, H. Dwight Grant, of Boonville, New York. The Grant shop was still intact, with artifacts and records from the boat building work of Lewis, his brother Floyd, and his father (Figures 1.7a and b). John Gardner, long associated with Mystic Seaport Museum in Connecticut and a small boat historian, designer, and builder, provided the Durants' additional research.

Figure 1.7a
Grant's house and shop on Post Street in Boonville, New York as it appears today.

Figure 1.7b
Although now used as a garage, the shop's exterior is relatively unchanged from its days as a boat building shop. The Grants built 378 boats in this shop over a fifty-two-year period from 1882 to 1934.

Gardner measured a typical Grant guideboat, the *Virginia*, which is presently in the extensive guideboat collection of the Adirondack Museum in Blue Mountain Lake, New York (Figures 1.8 and 1.9). Lewis and Floyd Grant built the boat in 1905 in their Boonville shop. It was the third of thirteen boats built by the Grants that year. The buyer was Robert M. Jeffress of Richmond, Virginia who owned a camp at Big Moose, New York, and named the boat after his alma mater, the University of Virginia. In 1980, the Adirondack Museum published the Durants' work and the detailed drawings, lines, and offsets of the *Virginia* taken by John Gardner in the definitive book, *The Adirondack Guide-Boat*. The book is still in print.

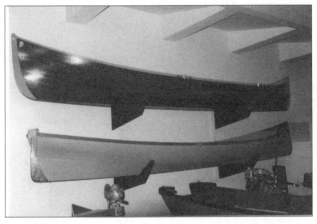

Figure 1.8

The *Virginia* (top), on display at the Adirondack Museum in Blue Mountain Lake, New York.

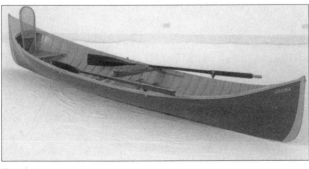

Figure 1.9

The *Virginia*, built in 1905. (Photo courtesy of Erik Borg, Adirondack Museum Collection.)

In a chapter written for the Durant book, Gardner discusses the possibilities of building a guideboat using modern materials such as thin, edge-milled cedar strips and epoxy. He further speculates that had these modern materials been available at the time, builders most certainly would have taken advantage of them. Gardner also experimented with making ribs from laminated spruce, and both he and Durant proclaimed them at least equal or even superior to natural sawn spruce crook ribs. Combining the laminated ribs with cedar strips could produce a boat equal to a traditionally [2] built boat in lines, looks, and performance, with the added advantage of minimal upkeep.

It is popular today to build small paddling craft such as canoes and kayaks with narrow strips of cedar or other suitable lightweight wood edge glued over a temporary mold, and sheathed in fiberglass and epoxy. There are a number of books on the subject and readily available materials and supplies. These boats are ribless, depending solely on the fiberglass-wood-fiberglass composite for their strength.

Ribless guideboats are also built this way, maintaining the visual lines of traditionally built boats. One can buy commercially built boats of wood and fiberglass, along with versions built of high impact plastics, all of which resemble guideboats. Prices for commercially built guideboats can range from roughly $1,500 for a ribless fiberglass version, to $16,000 or more for a 16' wooden boat built in the traditional manner. Strip-built reproductions like those described in this book can typically be purchased for $10,000 or more. Kits and plans are also available for cedar-stripped boats built without ribs and sheathed in fiberglass.

Moreover, accomplished amateur builders have faithfully reproduced the *Virginia* directly from the data in the Durant book, including the cutting of a spruce stump. Compared to the guideboats built in Dwight Grant's shop between 1880 and 1882 that sold for $20 to $70, these accurate reproductions are priceless. Of course, a late nineteenth or early twentieth century Adirondack guideboat in reasonably good condition is considered a museum piece. Guideboats in restorable condition are always in demand, and bring premium prices.

As popular as the cedar-strip building method is, the literature is limited mainly to canoes and kayaks. There is no book or manual describing the "how-to" for a woodworker of modest accomplishments to instruct him or her in building a reproduction guideboat. Adaptations of the canoe/kayak strip building methods have been applied to guideboats, but it is the ribs that, when fitted with strips of pine or cedar, uniquely define and proclaim: "*This* is an Adirondack guideboat."

In this book we present a complete and detailed description of the building of a fully ribbed reproduction of the Grants' *Virginia* using laminated spruce ribs, cedar strips, and lightweight fiberglass to cover the outside of the hull. This is in keeping with John Gardner when he suggested the use of these materials to build a modern version of the traditional guideboat. We explain the building of the seats, decks, trim, and accessories to original design specifications with clear and precise descriptions accompanied by photographs and illustrations. While the rowlocks and oars are now commercially available as faithful reproductions, other hardware is not. We describe the working of the brass for the stem bands and caps, and the making and fitting of brass bottom shoes. To spare the reader the necessity of learning the strip building method from specific canoe or kayak literature, we give full instruction for the preparation and use of high quality cedar building strips from basic lumber.

Building a small boat requires experience with a selection of common power and hand woodworking tools. This project is not for the beginner, but a moderately experienced and confident amateur woodworker desiring to step into the fascinating world of small boat building will find that stripping the *Virginia* is both challenging and rewarding.

1 Our spelling of the word "guideboat" is consistent with the style manual of the Adirondack Museum, the recognized authority on guideboats. We are aware of two other spelling variants in past and present literature: "guide boat" and "guide-boat." The latter is the form used by Kenneth Durant and John Gardner.

2 "Traditionally" refers to boats built in the traditional manner, ie. sawn spruce ribs and lapped pine planking fastened with screws and clinched tacks, built at any time, and including modern boats.

The evolution of the Adirondack guideboat continued, even after its popularity faded. A few makers persisted beyond the middle of the twentieth century, building new boats and repairing those that had survived the ravages of time in a condition that augured well for restoration. With the advent of modern adhesives, coatings, and materials, it was inevitable that the classic guideboat would continue to change even though its original purpose was long ago relegated to history. A new generation of Adirondack aficionados discovered the pleasure of rowing a light but sturdy boat, causing the popularity of the craft to rise once again.

In the 1960s, significant advances in the technology and technique for building small wooden boats brought boatbuilding into the average woodworker's shop. People started building canoes, kayaks, and small rowboats by gluing thin strips of wood together on their edges over a suitable temporary framework. They covered the hull with a cloth woven from extremely fine glass fibers, held to the wood by a catalyzed polyester resin. The fiberglass and polyester combination, which had migrated from the auto body shop to the wood boat shop, has since been refined, largely replaced by epoxy over a superior fiberglass designed for boat building.

Could it be possible to build a creditable guideboat using these methods and materials? John Gardner, in the "Modern Materials and Tools" chapter in the Durant book, has largely answered this question. Not only does Gardner suggest how one could build such a boat, he encourages it. Citing experimental work done by a few amateur builders in the 1960s, he offers empirical evidence of the superior strength of ribs built from laminated spruce. The boat would be planked with several edge-glued strips much narrower than the eight pine planks characteristic of a Grant boat, and epoxy would render the boat waterproof, unlike traditionally built boats.

Following Gardner's suggestions and accepting his challenge, we have strip-built four versions of the Grants' *Virginia,* using Gardner's lines and data as published in the Durant book. We built our first boat of western red cedar, without ribs (Figure 2.1). Since there was no internal ribbing, we also had to cover the inside of the hull with fiberglass and epoxy, resulting in a boat of excessive weight but perfectly usable nevertheless. Because of the ribless construction, the center seat was not removable and there was no provision for a carrying yoke. There are builders currently making similar boats, all resembling the classic guideboat form.

Figure 2.1

Cory David launches a ribless strip-built guideboat.

Our three other boats based on the Grant design were strip built over ribs. We did not follow the Grants' methods precisely and could not, since the use of laminated ribs and fiberglassed cedar strips required concessions to both the construction method and convenience.

We began the construction of our boats with the bottom board. The methods we used to cut it to shape and mark the rib locations were similar to those of the original boat shops. We used power tools where convenient, such as to thickness plane a ¾" pine plank to ½". Next, we marked for the rib locations, and traced a quarter pattern to mark the curved and tapered shape. We cut the shape with a power jigsaw, and then marked the limits of the rolling bevel along the edges. We did the actual shaping of the bevel with hand planes, there being no power tool capable of precisely making the compound cut. At this point, the bottom board was identical to one that could have been produced 150 years earlier.

The ribs for one of our boats were laminated from Adirondack spruce obtained from within the Blue Line; spruce for the two other boats was found in 2-by construction lumber at a local dealer. In both cases, we carefully selected the lumber to get planks as straight and knot-free as possible and with a minimum amount of checking, a common problem with spruce.

We either steamed or hot soaked the ⅛" thick rib laminations and immediately bent them around a form representing the inside curve of a rib. There were thirteen such forms required, as well as an additional one for the stems. We glued the dried laminations together with epoxy around the form, producing a blank from which four separate identical ribs were cut. According to Gardner, this type of laminated rib is superior in strength to one cut from a spruce crook. Following a cleaning and light sanding, we screwed the ribs to the bottom board. Here again, the structure thus far was identical to a traditionally built boat but for the laminated versus cut ribs.

Construction of our stems was totally different from the construction of those cut from spruce crooks. In the traditional one-piece stem, a rabbet is cut following the curve of the stem, into which the ends of the planking are screwed. Good craftsmanship dictates that these planks must be carefully fitted around the curve of the boat, and at the same time the plank ends must fit into the rabbets at each end. Doing this with narrow strips is an exercise the average woodworker ought best leave to history; there is an easier way.

We separated the stem into inner and outer pieces, which permitted the more precise fitting of the strips, while still maintaining a close fitting joint of the outer stem to the strip ends. We laminated the inner stem, defined by the rabbet line, from spruce similar to the ribs. The rest of the stem, forming the outer portion, can be either laminated or cut from a different wood at the whim of the builder.

During stripping, we ran the ends of the strips beyond the inner stem and cut them flush with the stem's leading edge. We later glued the outer stem and screwed it on from inside the inner stem, forming a tight joint with each strip end. There is the added advantage here of being able to choose a different wood, such as cherry, maple, or ash, for the outer stem. The final result is a stem shaped in all visible respects like the traditional, made in a way that is much less difficult.

At this point, the traditional builders mounted the bottom board, with stems and ribs attached, to a stock plank held with its narrow edge up. They had cut the plank with a concavity along its top edge representing the rocker or curve of the bottom board. The bottom board was forced into the concavity and screwed to the stock plank, the whole assembly held upright for planking.

Strip building a small boat, whether it is a canoe, kayak, or guideboat, is usually done with the framework or forms inverted. To strip the *Virginia*, we cut the stock plank with the rocker curve convex, with notches cut to receive the ribs where they attached to the bottom board. We then mounted the stock plank on supports and laid the boat framework over it, upside down. Screws inserted temporarily near the ends of the bottom board and driven into the stock plank forced the bottom board to the rocker curve.

Before the outer skin of the boat is attached, whether it is the eight pine planks of the traditionally built craft or the cedar strips of our modern reproductions, a temporary batten is fastened to the rib ends outboard (above) where the sheer line would ultimately be formed. The battens, fastened on each side of the boat from stem to stem along all of the ribs, serve to strengthen the assembly and hold the ribs in alignment, and generally define the overall shape of the hull. Any deviations from a fair curve are immediately visible and corrected.

Note that the ribs are rectangular in cross section, while the batten curves around the square edges. The ribs, from about rib number 7 to each stem, must be shaped to the angle of the curve at each point. This beveling allows the planking or strips to make a firm flush joint with the outboard edge of the ribs. Here again, this shaping of the ribs is common to both the traditional and modern boats.

With the assembly thus far supported in the upright position, the traditional builders next applied a garboard—the first plank along the bottom board. The garboard plank had a slight flare in its width near the ends to compensate for differences in the planked length of the ribs from the bottom board to the sheer (Figure 2.2). They then cut the remaining planks to approximately the same width for the rest of the boat.

In a modern stripped guideboat hull, all of the strips are the same width. Replacing the flare of the garboard planks of the traditional boats with strips may be handled in two ways. Short tapered correction strips are added when stripping from the bottom board to the sheer, or the flare is simply ignored while stripping from the sheer to the bottom board. In this

second approach, the flare is compensated for automatically by the short strips required to close the hull along the bottom board. It must be noted that either method is acceptable and will produce an excellent hull. The only visual differences are in the pattern of the strips and are of no consequence.

Figure 2.2
Joshoa Swan, hand planing a garboard plank for a guideboat at the Adirondack Museum in Blue Mountain Lake, New York.

John Gardner spoke highly of modern adhesives, including epoxy, indicating that the builders of a previous generation would have readily embraced these products had they been available. In the modern versions of the guideboat, epoxy is used both as glue and as a sealant. For certain gluing operations, epoxy is thickened by the addition of a thixotropic agent such as colloidal silica and may be colored with extremely fine wood dust known as wood flour. Unthickened epoxy is used to bond a light covering of fiberglass cloth to the outside of the hull, producing a durable waterproofing unknown in traditionally built boats.

Once we constructed our reproduction hull, as briefly described above, we added the decks, trim, seats, and other accessories with little or no deviation from the traditional design. The seats are caned, in either natural cane or in plastic cane, some variations of which bear a remarkable resemblance to the natural product. Oars, paddle, and yoke differ from the older traditionally built boats only with respect to the use of power tools to produce them. Some reproduction brass hardware is commercially available, such as the

11

rowlock plates and rowlocks, faithfully cast and machined according to the dimensions in the Gardner drawings.

The finish on old traditional boats may have been paint or varnish, depending upon the service the boat was intended for. New boats are similar in that either varnished or painted boats, or combinations, are common.

Our discussion outlines the differences between the traditional Adirondack guideboats built in the late nineteenth and early twentieth centuries and their modern equivalents. Today's guideboats have the same lines, look, feel, and performance of the older boats, and differ only in the use of more advanced materials and construction methods. Gone are the requirements to dig out a spruce stump, clinch a few thousand copper tacks, and produce a boat primarily using hand tools. Modern methods and materials open the way for a modestly equipped woodworker to build a faithful reproduction of a guideboat rivaling, or even surpassing, the quality of the old traditionally built boats, and which would surely please both Dwight and Lewis Grant.

We have no doubt that by carefully following the procedures outlined in this book you too will be able to build a beautiful and faithful reproduction of the *Virginia,* the value of which will be many times greater than the cost of your materials. More important perhaps, is the pride you will have in your accomplishment, knowing you have reproduced a remarkable piece of Adirondack history. Be forewarned, though! Building these boats can be addictive, and chances are you will want to build more than one.

One final word before we get to work: The greatest pleasure in building an Adirondack guideboat, at least for us and for other builders we have talked with, is the time spent actually *building* the boat. Working with hand tools, spending time in a shop filled with the aroma of spruce and cedar, and watching a functional work of art materialize before your eyes is an experience to be cherished, enjoyed, and above all, not rushed. If at times you get frustrated during the

building process, step back for a short while. Go do something else (sharpening your plane blades and chisels is always a good idea), then come back to the project with a clear mind. Take your time and enjoy the process. Doing so will lessen the number of mistakes you make and will result in a much better and more beautiful boat!

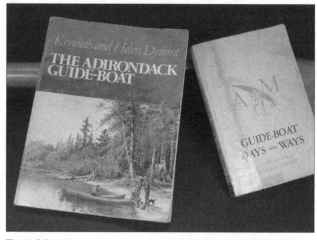

Figure 2.3

Two of Kenneth Durant's books, published by the Adirondack Museum. The book on the left, first published in 1980, is still widely available and contains John Gardner's drawings of the *Virginia.* The book on the right, published in 1963, is currently out of print but can be found at libraries. Both books are "required" reading for guideboat enthusiasts!

CHAPTER 3

TOOLS, SCREWS, AND GLUES

The first boat was probably a fallen log, made without tools. Then fire was used to hollow out the log, creating a vessel one could sit in, rather than sit upon. The nineteenth century guideboat builders had the luxury of steel-edged cutting tools, and machines powered by water, steam, or muscle, and occasionally, electricity.

POWER TOOLS

In the modern woodworking shop with its array of electric tools, from the battery-powered screwdriver to an assortment of power saws, we can build from wood with more precision and ease than was known during the guideboat era. We are fortunate to be able to quickly rip a plank into strips or plane a true edge with little more effort than flipping a switch.

We do not mean to imply, however, that a shop full of power tools is required to build a modern guideboat. After all, the nineteenth century builders got along nicely with handsaws, simple screwdrivers, chisels, assorted planes, and a few dedicated tools specific to boat building. Until late in the heyday of the guideboat, when electricity became widespread in the Adirondacks, the only "power" tool to be seen was a foot-operated treadle sewing machine modified to perform as a jigsaw. But a contemporary woodworking shop includes at least a few basic power tools, and they can certainly be used for boat building.

We consider the table saw the workhorse and centerpiece of the shop (Figure 3.1). It is used to reduce the 2-by spruce planks to the billets from which rib-laminating stock is cut. You can quickly assemble the building jig or strongback from table-sawn stock and the ripping of siding strips from planks is almost trivial.

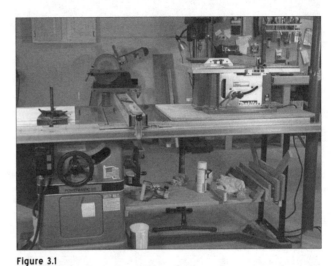

Figure 3.1
Cabinet and portable table saws.

Although some builders of strip-built boats may use a band saw for ripping strips, it is less precise and not as efficient as the table saw. We will address the use of both for strip making in Chapter 8. For cutting the rib foot transition curve from the laminated blanks and the simple curves of the outside stems, the band saw is the saw of choice (Figure 3.2).

A high quality portable jig, or saber, saw is a satisfactory, if not nearly as efficient, substitute for the band saw. Older models may be somewhat underpowered for cutting the rib bending forms from 2-by stock, however.

If the builder contemplates making his own strips from planks (as opposed to buying ready-made strips), a thickness planer is essential (Figure 3.3). Planing the rough planks to a uniform and consistent thickness before cutting strips is important if you will be scarfing short strips together later. Planing the rough-cut strips to a precise thickness in preparation for edge milling, and planing the ½" thick pine bottom board from standard lumberyard 1-by stock are also easily and precisely done.

Figure 3.2
Band saws. The larger, more powerful saw on the left is more suitable for resawing, and thus lends itself well to cutting rib laminates.

Figure 3.3
Portable thickness planer. Larger, more expensive models are also available, but a small unit like the one pictured is adequate.

Cleanup of the laminated rib and inner stem blanks is a simple task with the planer. You can plane the individual laminations, which are rough-cut slightly oversize with the table or band saw, to the final thickness. This assures parallel surfaces and fewer gluing problems. Thickness planing also helps in the preparation of stock for decking, seat frame material, seat risers, etc.

The jointer is a power tool not usually found in the casual woodworking shop, but for those fortunate enough to have access to one it can perform some tasks better than the planer (Figure 3.4). When cleaning up

the excess glue squeeze-out on the sides of rib laminations, it will produce a clean surface square to the curved surface of the blank.

Figure 3.4
6" long bed jointer.

You will use the drill press as a stationary drilling machine and, if you do not have an oscillating spindle sander, as a power source for small sanding drums (Figure 3.5). You can easily sand the rough-cut inside curves of rib templates and rib blanks to final shape with a drum sander chucked in the drill press. If you do not have access to a dedicated mortising tool (Figure 3.6), you will appreciate the drill press when drilling mortises during construction of the seat frames and, later, accurately drilling the few hundred cane holes in the seat frames.

But as useful as the drill press is for stationary work, the shop's real workhorse drill is a battery-powered variable speed drill/screw gun. You will use the portable drill, fitted with the appropriate size drill bit and countersink, for virtually all of the over two thousand screw holes in the boat. If the drill of choice is battery powered, we recommend you keep a second battery on trickle charge.

A related tool is the battery-powered screwdriver. After a day of driving screws, plug it into its charger for an overnight charge to make sure it is ready for the next day's work. Unlike the battery powered drill/screw gun, the screwdriver does not usually come with an exchangeable second battery.

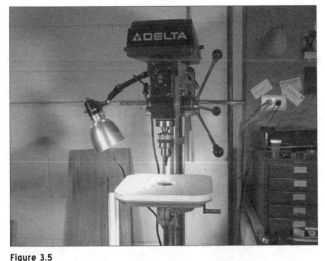

Figure 3.5
14" stationary drill press.

Figure 3.6
Dedicated mortising machine.

include a belt sander (Figure 3.7). A 9" or 12" disk, fitted with 80-grit sandpaper, is ideally suited for the precision sanding and shaping of the roughed out band sawn outer curves of rib templates, outer stems, and rib and inner stem bending forms. When full-length strips are not available (or chosen not to be used), the disk sander will cut precise scarf joints with speed and ease. The crepe rubber disk-cleaning accessory is essential, and some sort of dust collection, either dedicated or portable, is practical for both safety and dust control. As with any sanding operation performed without adequate dust control, a well fitting dust mask is a minimum requirement.

Figure 3.7
Stationary disk/belt sander.

15

Using a screw gun for driving screws as well as drilling requires many annoying bit changes, and the higher torque of the screw gun may set the small planking screws too deeply. It is much more efficient to use the drill with a combination pilot bit for making the screw holes followed by the electric screwdriver to drive the screws. A 3.6-volt screwdriver has sufficient torque for even the larger boat screws, and is less likely to slip and damage the wood than the heavier and more cumbersome screw gun. The driving bit must be sharp and a perfect fit in the screw slot to minimize slippage.

Another tool that you will use in much of strip building's preliminary work is the disk sander, available in both stationary or bench mounted models that often

An acceptable substitute for the bench-mounted disk sander is the portable belt sander. When solidly bench-mounted on its side so that the sanding surface is vertical and moving either horizontally or vertically, the belt sander can quickly and precisely sand outside curves as well as the disk sander. It remains for the builder to make a suitable feed table and support rack for it. A 3" wide belt is common, but a 4" unit will have sufficient power to easily handle the sanding and shaping of the rib bending forms.

Dust collection with a belt sander, like the random orbit machines described below, is marginal at best. A cloth bag usually comes with the sander, into which the internal motor cooling fan blows the sanding dust. There is an additional practical use for the dust bag, however. You can easily make fine wood sanding dust, also known as wood flour, with the belt sander. First empty, thoroughly clean, and reassemble the dust collection bag. Support the sander with the sanding side up, and aggressively sand scraps of stripping wood and collect the dust.

This nearly cost-free operation can quickly provide sufficient wood flour for use with thickened epoxy filler for an entire boat in a matter of a few minutes (Figure 3.8). A distinct advantage is being able to make different shades of color depending on the wood used. This high quality sanding dust is superior to that found inside the collection tank of the shop vacuum, even when you empty and clean the tank prior to sanding a hull. Vacuum cleaner sanding dust can contain bits of dried glue and other foreign material that could compromise the quality of the wood flour. It is also a mixture of all the colors of the woods that were sanded, making it difficult to match the color of the wood you need it for.

Figure 3.8
Wood flour produced by sanding.

A portable power sander is indispensable when building a stripped boat. You will first use it after you strip the hull, quickly reducing the rough ridges between strips to smooth and fair surfaces. Hardened glue squeeze-out is also no match for the power sander, and we recommend the variable speed versions for smoothing epoxy in preparation for a finish, be it paint or varnish.

The sander that performs all of the preceding tasks well is a variable speed random orbit sander with a 5" diameter pad (Figure 3.9). The sanding disks for these machines are readily available (see the list of sources in Appendix 5), and may be a hook and loop design or have a pressure-sensitive adhesive (PSA) backing. The hook and loop seems to be more popular, since it is easier to change the disk, either to replace a worn disk or change grit. Trying to preserve the adhesive on the PSA disk for reuse after you remove it is a problem unknown to the hook and loopers.

Figure 3.9
Random orbit sanders.

These moderately aggressive sanders are not without their drawbacks, however, not the least of which is the sanding dust. All of the more popular machines are designed with an array of holes in the orbital pad that, when the disc is properly installed, align with similar holes in the sanding disk. When you operate the sander, the built in cooling fan draws air through the holes, ostensibly carrying the sanding dust along with it. A small, attached filter bag or canister then collects the dust.

The reality is that these systems are usually inefficient, allowing a significant amount of dust to become airborne. Aside from the fact that dust then covers everything in the shop, there is concern within the boat building community as to the toxicity of airborne wood and epoxy dust and its adverse affects on health. An excellent solution is to attach the shop vacuum to the sander in place of the filter bag or canister.

Most sanders are capable of this, requiring only the hose and possibly an adapter or fitting to connect it to the sander vacuum port.

Sanding with a random orbit sander generates heat. If the sanding disk is worn or if too much pressure is used to force more rapid stock removal, especially when sanding epoxy, the heat generated contributes to the wear and ultimate failure of the hook and loop attachment system. The life of a sanding pad is long but not infinite, and the pad will fail in time.

Companies that specialize in sandpaper and sanding supplies often offer replacement hook surfaces. They also sell these replacement hook surfaces to convert the PSA pad to the hook and loop system. The more expensive alternative is to replace the machine's entire sanding pad. Fortunately, frequent changing of the sanding disk and moderate pressure while sanding extends the life of the system well beyond the sanding of a single boat.

A random orbit sander fitted to a shop vacuum can be annoyingly noisy, not only because of the simultaneous operation of both machines, but also the vibration and reverberation induced in the hull. So much so, that hearing protection becomes essential. The trade-off here is that you no longer need the dust mask, since the dust collection with this combination is so efficient.

The 5" random orbit sander, ideal for sanding the outside of a hull, is much less useful for sanding the inside of a ribbed guideboat hull. Without ribs (not a consideration here), sanding the inside of a canoe or ribless guideboat is routine. Given the 5⅛" rib spacing in the *Virginia,* however, the 5" random-orbit sander will not fit between the ribs. (This gives one cause to wonder if some of the modern ribbed guideboats were designed with their wider rib spacing just to accommodate the sander.) One can resort to a finishing sander, but with its limited aggressiveness better suited to finishing operations, it becomes an exercise in patience (Figure 3.10). We have found that the Fein detail sander, fitted with the dust-collecting accessory, performed the job satisfactorily, if not that rapidly.

Figure 3.10
Finishing sander.

Figure 3.11
The Metabo 3" random orbit sander, fitted with a vacuum hose for dust collection. Disks on the left were shop-made; the ones on the right were OEM.

Just before we had finished the construction of our boats, yet another sander entered the ever-changing power tool market and it proved to be ideal for sanding between the ribs. This sander is made by Metabo (Figure 3.11) and is a random orbit tool with a mere 3" diameter sanding pad. Sanding disks in assorted grits were available from the same manufacturer, but the economy offered by bulk purchasing disks from aftermarket suppliers had not yet been established. Cutting one's disks from rolls of 80- and 120- grit bulk hook and loop backed stearated paper was an effective, but time consuming, substitute. With the accessory dust collection hose and fittings and the firm but pliant accessory extension sanding pad, the machine did an excellent job during the final sanding inside the boat.

17

Over time, excessive use of the drill press for spindle or drum sanding can produce a certain amount of runout, causing the drill press spindle to wobble or vibrate as it rotates. This, of course, has a detrimental effect on the accuracy of the machine when you use it for drilling and may lead to premature motor burnout.

For this reason, a dedicated oscillating spindle sander is more appropriate for extended spindle sanding. Builders are using these machines more and more because they are well suited for sanding inside curves such as rib templates and bending forms. When a vertical fence is used, the sander can be used to thickness sand the ribs after slicing them from the blanks (Figure 3.12).

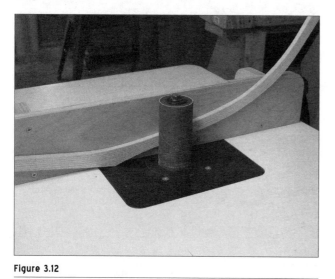

Figure 3.12
A portable oscillating spindle sander mounted in a router table used for thicknessing a rib.

The shop vacuum is not only a dust collector when sanding, but also a general cleanliness tool. Removing sanding residue, scraper debris, and shavings from the hull, cleaning the shop prior to varnishing or painting, cleaning tools at the end of the day, and vacuuming the floor all contribute to a tidy shop and reduce the tracking of dust to areas where it would not be welcome. We recommend a large capacity unit, being more powerful than the smaller one- to five-gallon sizes. The larger units also have the added advantage of being capable of wet pickup, which, while not immediately applicable to boat building, is useful outside the shop.

If you opt to buy strips with the bead and cove edges already milled, you can dispense with the shop router. But if you are going to cut strips from planks and mill the edges, the router is indispensable. Regardless of whether you will cut the mortises in seat frames, round the gunwale edges over slightly, or any other boat-building job the router could perform, there are simpler tools that can be used. But fitted with relatively inexpensive bits and mounted in a good-quality flat and sturdy table, the router can easily cut high-quality bead and cove edges on strips comparable to those commercially available. The savings are significant (as much as $500 or more on a 16' guideboat).

HAND TOOLS

The beginner's woodworking shop is defined by a collection of a few screwdrivers, a hammer, and a handsaw or two. Add a square, then a plane, perhaps a chisel, some sandpaper, a can of paint, and plans for building a birdhouse. But, except for the birdhouse plans, the nineteenth century boat shop boasted a similar but larger array of hand tools, the most important of which were the hands of the boat builder. It was those deft hands that produced the guideboat, occasionally borrowing the use of a power band or table saw at the local millwork shop to augment a treasured collection of hand tools. While we have the advantage of power tools, hand tools are indispensable, and at times preferable, for our work.

Handsaws come in just about every conceivable size, shape, and function. It seems that with the arrival of each new tool catalog, a newly designed handsaw or two is featured. Besides the classic rip, crosscut, hack, and coping saws, we have dovetail saws, pull saws, plug-cutting saws, spiral tooth saws, and other saws *ad nauseam.*

Of this vast collection of handsaws, only one or two are useful in building a guideboat (Figure 3.13). The Japanese pull saw, of which there are several variants, is very useful for trimming excess strip lengths once they are mounted on the hull, and in other trimming and fitting situations. The saw cuts on the pull stroke, providing a greater measure of control than is possible with the western design saw that cuts on the push stroke. Because of the pull-cutting design, the blade is much thinner and the framework lighter, adding to the saw's comfort and control. The kerf is also thinner than that of a "conventional" saw. These saws are not resharpened; rather, the blade is simply replaced.

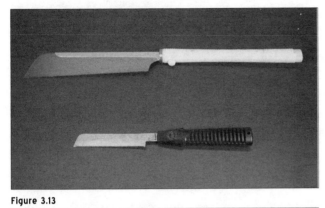

Figure 3.13
Japanese pull-saw (top) and flexible flush-cutting saw (bottom).

Another handy type of Japanese saw is a short flexible flush-cutting saw. The teeth have no set on one edge, allowing the saw to cut flush with the surrounding wood. It is useful for rough trimming the strip ends at the stems, and trimming dowels used to plug screw holes.

The ubiquitous and humble flat blade screwdriver is used for a virtually infinite number of tasks besides driving screws. The screwdrivers used to pry open a can of (birdhouse?) paint or scrape some nondescript "goo" from the innards of a bicycle wheel should be put safely away from the boat-building tools. Driving a slotted screw into wood requires that the tip of the screwdriver be square with sharp corners, and accurately sized to fit the slot of the screw to be driven. Gunsmiths routinely grind screwdrivers to fit a particular screw slot, significantly reducing the probability that the tool will slip and mar the surrounding surface. A ratty or dirty screwdriver, slipping off a shiny brass deck or gunwale screw, can leave a scratch or gouge that will surely elicit an invective or two inappropriate for mixed company.

One of our favorite screwdrivers is an inexpensive ratcheting model (Figure 3.14). Not only can you fit it

with an assortment of driver bits and, if you need to, custom grind it to fit a particularly small slotted screw (e.g., the #3 slotted brass screws used to secure siding strips to ribs), it is also ergonomically friendlier than the traditional fixed driver. You are also not required to lift the driver off the screw head and reposition it each time you need to turn the screw. If you decide to drive all your screws by hand, this is the way to do it!

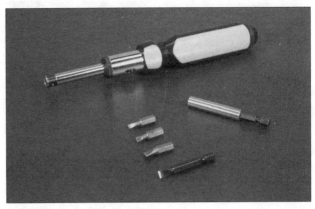

Figure 3.14
Ratchet driver with assorted bits.

Since a boat is defined by curves, the use of a square in building it would seem unnecessary. However, to accurately lay out the building form, loft the rib shapes, set up power cutting tools, etc., a selection of squares is essential. The adjustable or combination square is a good utility square, useful for marking cut lines on raw stock. The try square, being fixed, is easily manufactured to exacting tolerances. You should keep a good quality try square for precision work, such as setting up the blade and miter gage on the table saw. A framing square is a fairly large fixed square with a lot of markings and numbers stamped on it, most of which are not used in boat building (except maybe for an ark, only one of which is known to have been built). Because of its large size, it is quite useful for lofting the full size drawings of the ribs.

Another tool mostly taken for granted is a ruler. Obviously, you will be making measurements for any boat-building project. The steel tape is the most common, but the usual ¾" wide retractable steel rule seems a little clumsy for smaller jobs. A smaller ½" wide steel tape is a lot handier. For general use on tool set up,

19

checking board thickness, and other small jobs, the 6" steel ruler is ideal, and the 2' or 3' steel ruler has no equal for making accurate drawings (Figure 3.15).

Figure 3.15

An assortment of squares and rules.

A level is essential for setting up the framework on the building form. After you attach the ribs to the bottom board and mount it on the stock plank, leveling it across its width in several places eliminates any twist that could lead to distortion of the hull. Carefully located shims between the bottom board and stock plank can usually take care of any leveling problems. With a level bottom board assuring no twist, accurate symmetrical layout of the sheer strip is easily done.

A spoke shave and a few hand planes round out the necessary straight-edged cutting tools (Figure 3.16). The spoke shave is capable of removing a lot of stock with but a few strokes. It must be razor sharp, and requires a lot of practice to get comfortable and proficient with. The most common mistake is trying to cut too deeply in a single pass, which can cause chatter or tear-out.

Woodworkers often speak of the block plane as "my favorite tool." With its low angle of attack, a well-sharpened and adjusted block plane is capable of cutting a shaving so thin you can literally read a newspaper through it. The shape of the block plane is naturally ergonomic, fitting the hand so that control is almost automatic. It is useful not only for shaping the rolling bevel on the edges of the bottom board, but in a variety of joint fitting situations too numerous to mention.

Figure 3.16

An assortment of spoke shaves and planes. These tools are essential for the boat builder and are a pleasure to use when razor-sharp.

Scrapers come in a variety of types, sizes, and shapes, all suited for different but related tasks. A common paint scraper can be ground or filed with a convex curved edge and sharpened, useful for scraping partially cured glue squeeze-out from between strips. The convex curved blade works well on the inside surfaces and the concave outside areas near the bottom board. Many paint scrapers have more than one scraping edge, so one can be ground convex while the other can retain a straight edge.

A more sophisticated version is available with several interchangeable blades of differing shapes. For lack of another name, woodworkers usually refer to it by its commercial name, the Pro-Prep scraper (Figure 3.17). It consists of a straight handle, with the blade mounted across the end at an angle. The blade is a quality piece of steel, ground to shape with a beveled scraping edge. After it is correctly sharpened and burnished, it will cut thin shavings of wood rather than scraping the wood fibers to dust, and cured epoxy will come off in curls with precision and ease. Dried glue is no match for the Pro-Prep, and cleaning the concave inside of a hull can be completed in short order.

Other scrapers with interchangeable blades include the Sandvik scrapers with their solid carbide blades. They do an excellent job on epoxy runs, and you can use them for shaping the round over on the ¼" square brass stock used for the stem bands. Sharpening is possible with a diamond stone, though we did not need to sharpen our scraper during the entire time spent constructing our boats.

Figure 3.17
Assorted scrapers. Top left: Pro-Prep with replaceable curved blade; top center: Sandvik carbide scrapers; top right: paint scrapers. Bottom: cabinet scrapers.

Cabinet scrapers, sometimes called the woodworker's best kept secret, are simply thin rectangular pieces of steel. The cutting edges are burnished with a nearly microscopic "hook" that does the cutting. Sharpening and using a cabinet scraper is a skill that, once learned, will be indispensable in some of the finer fitting jobs on the boat. Smoothing the mortised seat frame joints after gluing, leveling runs in partially cured epoxy, and scraping the residual epoxy stains remaining after filling defects in the stripping are some of the tasks easily performed with a sharp cabinet scraper.

No woodworking shop can call itself such without a selection of clamps (Figure 3.18). One often hears, "you can never have too many clamps," and that rings true in the boat shop as well. Like handsaws, the selection of clamps is enormous, but you can winnow it to a few useful types. A dozen or so 2" spring clamps will be used constantly while stripping the hull, and several 4" C-clamps are required to properly clamp the stack of laminations to the bending form during glue-up.

We recommend several 2" C-clamps if strips are scarfed to length on the bench. Those clunky wooden-jawed cabinet clamps have more clamping power than a comparably sized C-clamp, and may be pressed into service gluing rib laminations. A few bar clamps hold seat frames while the glue cures, and the Quick-Grip clamp, with its single-handed operation, is extremely useful while bending steamed or hot soaked rib laminations around the bending forms.

Figure 3.18
Assorted clamps.

Another handy clamp is the cloth-covered rubber bungee cord with hook ends. With this simple tool, the builder can clamp a newly glued strip to the previously mounted one, and insure a high quality tight joint throughout its entire length. It is perhaps the single most overlooked but important tool in building any type of stripped boat. Screws hold the strips against the ribs, but the bungee cord makes the glued joint look as if it grew that way.

One of the handiest tools around the boat shop is one that is made on the spot—the sanding stick (Figure 3.19). All that is required is a strip of wood measuring ¾" wide by ¼" thick, and about 30" or so long, or other size to fit the application at hand. On both sides of one end, glue 6" or 8" strips of coarse (60-grit) sandpaper. Pressure sensitive adhesive sandpaper is even easier.

We found this simple tool to be indispensable for shaping the rolling bevel on the inner stems as we stripped the boat, as well as accurately shaping the

21

bevels on the outside edges of the ribs. Lewis Grant, in quoted correspondence in the Durant book, describes shaping the rib bevels with a spoke shave before the installation of any planking. It is almost inconceivable that he, or any other builders, had not developed such a simple tool as the sanding stick to shape rib bevels not only accurately, but rapidly as well. We will describe its use in detail in the stripping chapter.

Figure 3.19
Assorted shop-made sanding sticks.

Sandpaper, though disposable, is also an important and probably the most used tool in building a boat. Both simple full size sheets and shapes cut to fit your particular power sander are required. Grit sizes of 80 and 120 are the most useful, but you can sand with the coarser 60-grit cautiously for rough shaping. 220-grit is sometimes good for final sanding if you will be applying varnish directly to wood.

Buying sandpaper at the local hardware store will significantly increase the cost of building the boat, and the selection of types and grit sizes is usually not very extensive. A bulk purchase from a sanding products supplier (see Appendix 5) will be more economical, and the selection of sizes and types is usually more extensive. For general boat work, we recommend stearated (non-loading) aluminum oxide papers.

You can use wet-or-dry silicon carbide sandpaper for wet sanding between coats of paint or varnish. It is readily available in several grit sizes at auto parts and accessory dealers. There is no need for a bulk purchase

of this paper, since it is long lasting and only a relatively few sheets are needed for a boat.

A relatively new tool useful for building a guideboat is the Microplane (Figure 3.20). It consists of a thin strip of stainless steel that has a multitude of tiny three-sided tabs cut into it, with the tabs bent out and sharpened to a cutting edge. It is available in several shapes and sizes, including flat, curved, and round, and a version that is mounted in a drill press. Stock removal is similar to a rasp or file, but a lot cleaner and more efficient, generating tiny shavings rather than dust.

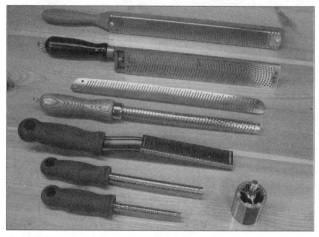

Figure 3.20
Assorted Microplánes. The small round Microplane is designed for use in a drill press.

Use the Microplane for shaping sculpted surfaces, and do the final shaping of the taper on the outer stems with good control using the flat-bladed version. The initial stock removal for shaping the rolling bevel on the inner stems before using the sanding stick is simple with the coarse round tool. The single caution with a Microplane: do not use it on a fiberglassed surface. To do so will ruin it for cutting anything except for maybe grating cheese,[1] and you cannot effectively sharpen it.

After fiberglassing the hull, you will need to trim away partially cured excess epoxy and fiberglass. When the wet-out coat of epoxy has initially cured, there will be some overhang of fiberglass along the sheer (Figure 3.21). This cloth contains some partially cured epoxy, which is still soft and leathery after the initial cure. You must trim this excess, and the general-purpose utility knife does a good job here. The blades are disposable, but be sure to wrap the used blade in masking tape before disposal to prevent injury.

Figure 3.21
The excess fiberglass and epoxy must be trimmed with a sharp utility knife.

After the epoxy fill coats on the hull are cured and it has been given a preliminary sanding, the hull is removed from the stock plank and supported right side up. There will be cured epoxy on the sheer, from just a slight coating to hard cured drips. You must use a small tool to remove the epoxy here because there are rib-ends every five inches or so. A handy tool for the job is the 4-in-hand rasp. This simple tool has four cutting surfaces—a fine and a coarse, in both flat and curved. The coarse surface takes care of most of the cured epoxy, and the fine surface gets down to the wood edge with good control. A cabinet scraper gets the last of it, and a quick sanding finishes the job.

SCREWS

Reproducing the *Virginia* requires as many as 2,000 or more screws, depending on the approach you take to securing the strips to the ribs. We have experimented with two different methods. In the first, we fastened each strip to each rib with a screw. In the second, we use fewer screws by employing an "every other rib, every other strip" method (Figure 3.22).

Both result in an equally strong hull, but the alternating method more closely approximates the screw patterns found on the *Virginia*.

Figure 3.22
Alternating screw method for fastening strips to ribs.

As with traditionally built boats, the screws are all brass for reproduction accuracy and aesthetics (though some builders, including Dwight Grant, did use iron screws except on varnished boats, where he used brass). You can sometimes purchase brass screws as single items in local hardware stores, but the selection is limited and the costs are high. Catalog suppliers generally have excellent selections of sizes, and buying in bulk reduces costs. To help you get an easy understanding of the screws necessary to complete this boat, we have provided a comprehensive table of screw sizes and quantities in Appendix 2.

One would think that there is nothing special about a simple brass screw. While building one of our boats, we bought the #3 x ½" strip mounting screws in two different orders. Even though both orders fit the catalog description of *#3 x ½"* and were from the same supplier, we received two distinctly different screws.

After noticing a difference in driving and holding properties, we critically examined representative screws from each lot. One had 7 full helix threads that were sharp and deep, showed signs of being machine

23

cut, and measured a full ½" long. The other had only 4½ full helix threads of poor quality, not as deep as the first, appeared to be rolled into the blanks, and were very nearly a full ¹⁄₁₆" shorter than ½" screws. The better quality screws were also oxidized to a dark color that contrasted with the bright brass of the cut threads. The poorer screws were all the same color brass. There was no evidence of difference in quality due to the distinctly different coloration, but it does suggest a possible difference in alloy composition.

When driven into holes predrilled with a properly sized combination tapered bit and countersink, the better screws were able to pull into the wood so that the heads were slightly below the surface of the strips. With the same driving torque, the poorer screws refused to pull any deeper than just into the countersink, and in most cases, appeared to strip the wood if we attempted to drive them snuggly home. Later sanding of the hull resulted in these screw heads remaining slightly, but perceptibly, above the sanded surface. If you are going to paint the hull over the fiberglass and epoxy rather than varnish it, you will not be able to fill in the raised screw heads. They will telegraph through the finish where you can both see and feel them.

In all fairness, there were no similar problems noted with other screw sizes from the same supplier. The lesson you learn here is to at least request samples from your supplier prior to committing to an order for 2,000 screws.

GLUE

Creating a finely crafted boat from a pile of lumber requires a number of complex operations, the least understood of which seems to be the use of glue. Virtually any of the common woodworking glues will create a joint that is stronger than the wood itself—provided the joint is correctly made before the glue is applied. A proper joint must fit together smoothly and be snug, but without binding, and without the use of clamps to force the closure of the joint. Once the joint has the proper amount of glue between the

mating surfaces, the clamps holding the joint serve to maintain alignment until the glue sets. If you use the clamps to force the closure of the joint, you will force glue from the joint resulting in it becoming starved and weak, possibly leading to failure.

When gluing strips together, the bead and cove edges provide the perfect mating surfaces. Glue is applied, and the new strip clamped to hold the joint. It may seem an inconsistency to say that you are not using the clamping to force the joint. Not so. Often, due to the bends and twists required in the strips, the clamps force the strip to shape—they should NOT force the closure of the joint.

Regardless of the glue chosen, it has to penetrate the pores of the wood in order to produce a bond "stronger than the wood itself." There must be just the right amount of glue between each surface of the joint. Too much, and the joint is weak. Too little, and the joint is starved and weak.

Some builders make the mistake of cutting their bead edges shallow with a flat on top, ostensibly to act as a reservoir for the excess glue between it and the properly cut cove. Excess glue creates a weak joint, and is more susceptible to creep, where the glue can soften and allow the joint to distort. Boats exposed to hot summer sunlight often absorb enough heat to soften some types of glue. A well-built boat will have tight joints between strips, nearly invisible glue lines, and look and feel like the hull grew that way.

WHAT GLUE TO USE?

The glue of choice for gluing strips is a polyvinyl acetate (PVA) formulation, also called yellow or carpenter's glue. This glue is readily available, inexpensive, easy to use, and easy to clean up. It does not harden in the bottle, and does the job quite nicely.

Titebond (a brand that includes Titebond Original, Titebond II Premium, and the recently added "waterproof" Titebond III Ultimate) and Elmer's are some of the commonly available brands. They set up rather quickly and have open working times on the order of five to ten minutes, which is ample for gluing strips together. The type II PVAs are water resistant and are recommended by the manufacturer for outside applications above the water line. One would think that this would be the glue to use for boat building. It is perfectly acceptable, but not for its water resistant properties. The entire boat is covered with fiberglass and epoxy on the outside and finished with paint or varnish on the inside, thereby sealing the wood from water.

There are a few caveats when using PVA glues for strips. First, the temperature of the shop, glue, and wood must be greater than 50° F. Below that temperature, the PVA glues do not cure properly, they lose their strength, and the joints are subject to failure. If the squeeze-out appears to be a powdery white or chalky residue, the temperature is too low. Using a wet cloth or sponge to remove wet squeeze-out can also cause problems. The glues are water soluble, and therefore diluted somewhat while being wiped. The diluted glue soaks into the pores of the wood, later to become a stain that you can see under a bright finish.

Epoxy glue is used extensively in boat building for laminating ribs and stems, gluing seat frames, gunwales, deck work, etc., but is not recommended for gluing strips together. It is expensive, tricky to use, messy, and not needed for strip gluing. It does not take too well to certain hardwoods used for boat work, such as ash and oak.

In order for the epoxy we use for fiberglassing to be effective as an adhesive for hardwood boat parts, some mixed but unthickened epoxy is applied to the pieces to be joined and allowed to soak in. The remaining mixture is thickened with colloidal silica, wood flour, or other thixotropic additive and applied to the joint after wiping off the excess soak coating. If no preliminary soak is performed, there is a potential for the resin in the thickened mixture to soak into the wood, leaving a starved joint behind. Joint failure is a distinct possibility.

Epoxy is the only glue to use for gluing a wood part to a previously fiberglassed area, like gluing the outwales to a fiberglassed hull. Also use it for gluing the outer stems onto a newly stripped hull, since the deep soak into the end grain of cedar provides for an excellent bond.

Epoxy is great for the mortise and tenon joints on seat frames, nicely filling any gaps that may be present in the joints. We recommend preliminary wetting, of course. It was also our glue of choice for making the rib and inner stem laminations. Some professional builders use a type II PVA glue for laminating ribs with acceptable results.

One occasionally sees reference to using polyurethane glue. It can be used anywhere a type II PVA is used, and it has the advantage of expanding (foaming) to fill gaps. But if you have to depend on filling gaps with foam when gluing strips together, your craftsmanship is in serious need of attention. The expanded foam produced when the glue cures is no substitute for a tight joint.

Polyurethane glue can also be expensive, and cleanup before curing requires solvents. You can scrape or sand off cured glue, but once cured on your hands, you wear it off. The shelf life can be shortened once you have opened it because of elevated humidity in the air, but it does require moisture to cure properly, usually provided by high humidity or a very light water misting of the joint. Safety is another concern. We recommend at least gloves for intermittent use, and protective equipment for long-term use as significant health problems can occur when used over time.

A few other glues used for general boat building are resorcinol and urea formaldehyde, although not usually for strip boats. They are powders, mixed with water or a liquid catalyzing agent. These glues also contain formaldehyde, a known health hazard. Other unfriendly components may also be present, like furfural alcohol and phenol. These glues have largely been replaced by epoxy for boat building.

1 Really! The Microplane was originally designed as a kitchen tool for peeling and grating, and is available in kitchen supply stores.

CHAPTER 4

FIRST, WE NEED A PLAN

There were no plans for guideboats left behind by the masters: no tables of offsets, no line drawings—maybe a crude sketch or two of unknown origin—nothing definitive but the boats themselves. Even Noah, the biblical boat builder, was given some measurements, and the Native American canoe builders used a story stick when it was necessary or convenient. Fortunately, a number of guideboats survived a gradual descent into obscurity, and those boats provided the models for the plans we are using today.

PATTERNS AND DRAWINGS

The early builders did not depend on drawings or measurements; they used a set of patterns. The casual observer of these pieces of thin boards with curved edges might dismiss them today as curious antiques. Once informed of their purpose, however, it would immediately become clear to the potential guideboat builder that here were the plans! With a set of patterns for the ribs, stems, and bottom board, a builder could construct a boat. However, these patterns are not generally available to the modern builder.

We can build the *Virginia* because we are fortunate to have a solid link to the past: John Gardner's detailed drawings and measurements of the original 1905 boat, reproduced in the Durant book. With these data and drawings, included in Appendix 1, we will work backwards to make patterns and use the patterns to build our *Virginia*.

The boat is symmetrical along two axes. Imagine cutting the boat in half, first across the gunwales and then lengthwise. The two pieces from each cut are mirror images of each other. The front half is the same as the rear half, and the left side is the same as the right. Also, the left front is identical to the right rear, and the right front is identical to the left rear.

These imaginary geometrical gymnastics suggest that we only need patterns for one quarter of the boat. For example, each complete rib is made from two identical pieces, one piece for each side. These same two pieces also form the identical matching rib set for the other end of the boat. Rather than requiring four patterns, you can make the four identical ribs from a single blank derived from a single pattern.

The *Virginia* requires thirteen different rib patterns. From this assortment, we will need four ribs each of numbers 1 through 12, and eighteen each of rib number 0. The multiple ribs 0 are used in the center section of the boat and are defined as 0 for the center rib, and 0^1 through 0^4 for the ribs on each side adjacent to rib 0.

The bottom board pattern is similar—a quarter pattern will be used to draw the complete shape, one quarter at a time, on the blank stock. Accurate and careful work drawing the four quadrants insures perfect symmetry in the full bottom board. There are only two stems, but they are identical, requiring only a single pattern.

Interestingly enough, should a builder desire a boat shorter or longer than 16', he or she need only modify the number of 0 ribs, rib spacing, and the length of the bottom board. Grant's tally boards showing key dimensions for bottom board length, rib number, and spacing, etc. for nearly all of the boats he built are in Appendix A of the Durant book.

The traditional rib patterns we have seen were cut from quarter-sawn pine, around a quarter of an inch thick. Wood of this size and type was common in the early boat shops, since builders made boat planking from it. To use it today would be expensive, since the average lumber dealer does not stock clear quarter-sawn pine, requiring a special order. A good alternative is quarter inch plywood, which is readily available and inexpensive. Douglas fir is acceptable, but southern yellow pine has a smoother and harder surface, which makes drawing easier. Baltic birch plywood is probably the best, but many lumberyards do not stock it.

Whatever you choose, it should have an A or at least a B quality surface. While a full 4' x 8' sheet is not required for all of the patterns, the off cuts and leftovers are useful for making support gussets for the building form. You can also use it to make other patterns, such as an oar shape, deck beams, yoke supports, etc., especially if you plan to build more than one boat.

Boats are described on plans or drawings as a set of curves. Since it is impossible to dimension a curve with measurements from point A to point B in the manner of a table leg or birdhouse, we must devise another method. Instead of referring to a measurement from A to B on a curve, we define a point on a curve as a measurement from each of two set and constant points of reference. From those points of reference, the point on the curve can only be at one single precise location. Now, from those same points of reference, change the measurements, and another point on the curve results. By plotting a series of points from given measurements, the curve can be drawn by connecting the points. Of course, a straight line connecting each point to its neighbor will not form a smooth curve. But if we draw a smooth curve connecting most or all of the points, the curve is said to be *fair*. A *table of offsets* gives the measurements and *lofting* is the process of plotting the points and drawing the curve.

This preliminary step is important for building any type of boat, since it produces drawings of full-size fair curves from which patterns may be made or parts constructed. It is also important because it allows the builder to check the measurements in the table of offsets by refining and smoothing a fair curve. Errors do creep into a table of offsets, usually through transcription. You can easily correct these errors by fairing.

LOFTING THE RIBS

John Gardner's Plate IV in Appendix 1 shows the table of offsets for all of the ribs required to build the *Virginia*. At first glance, it appears overwhelming with all of the numbers and cryptic abbreviations. Once understood, however, it is really quite simple. The sketch in the upper right on Plate III provides the key. This sketch shows vertical and horizontal measured lines, an arc having a 15" radius, and a series of lines from the arc to the edges of the sketch seeming to radiate from a common origin at the top right corner. Along the bottom and left sides are the points of intersection of the radiating lines, lettered A through U, with corresponding marks lettered A' through U' on the arc.

Before describing the lofting of the ribs, a few preparatory details are in order. There are thirteen rib drawings to be made, but accurately laying out thirteen identical axes with the radiating lines would take nearly as much time as actually doing the lofting. Laying out a single blank set of axes and having a sufficient number of photocopies made provides a clean sheet of paper for each rib drawing. A copy center that handles large drawings can usually provide a few blank sheets of large drawing paper, and can then copy the original drawing of the blank axes the requisite number of times. The standard size paper used in our shop was 24" x 36", which we also used for the stem drawing.

Note at this point that the rib patterns we will make differ significantly from the traditional rib patterns. These consisted of a curve cut on the edge of a rather wide board, with one end of the curve intersecting the edge of the board at a very precise angle. The curve represented the *outside* of the rib, and the angle at the edge was the bottom of the rib foot, the surface that the builder would mount on the bottom board. When the builder placed the pattern on a spruce crook and aligned it with a favorable curve of the grain, he traced the outer curve shape along with the intersecting straight line for the rib foot. The inner curve was then drawn ("molded") ¾" inboard, and was the cut line for the actual inside of the rib. The builder also drew the inboard transitioning curve above the rib foot from similar patterns.

In building a boat with laminated ribs, we require the *inside* curve shape along with the rib foot shape. The laminations will be bent around a mold or form representing the inside curve, and the outside curve will be simply the outside of the ¾" thick stack of laminations. We will also glue sufficient laminating material to the outside curve in the area of the rib foot, to be cut later to final shape. In order to accurately make the bending forms and draw and cut the final shapes of the ribs, a pattern for each of the thirteen full-size complete ribs is required.

The tools you need for the rib lofting are a sharp pointed pencil (a mechanical pencil with soft thin lead is ideal), a three-foot and a six-inch steel ruler, a framing square, and an eraser. Some sort of flexible edge is needed to draw the fair curves, such as a very thin wood or plastic batten used on edge or a flexible drawing spline that will hold its curve when set. (We found the rubber coated lead wire drawing accessory commonly available in art supply stores to be unacceptable.) The wood batten, with three or four heavy weights to hold its position, worked well. With a well-lit drawing surface and the tools at hand, we can now begin to construct a reproduction of the *Virginia*.

Fasten a fresh sheet of paper to the drawing table with a short piece of masking tape at each corner, oriented in landscape (long edge horizontal). Draw a horizontal base line a few inches from the bottom, and make two marks on it 24½" apart. Align the framing square

at each mark on the bottom line and draw two vertical lines 20" high.

Connect the tops of the two vertical lines with another line, forming a rectangle. Check the rectangle for square by measuring between the diagonals (upper left corner to lower right, and lower left to upper right). The measurements should be identical. If not, make any necessary corrections.

Beginning at the right corner of the base line, make marks every 2" from right to left. There should be a ½" space left over on the left end. Label the marks A through L, beginning at the right end. Now make marks 2" apart on the left vertical line beginning at the base line, and label these M through U.

The full radial lines from the 15" radius arc to the edges of the drawing are not required; in fact, they tend to clutter the drawing. Gardner probably included them for illustrative purposes. We do need the points on the arc, however. Place the end of the measuring edge of the three-foot ruler precisely at the upper right corner, such that the edge also passes exactly through mark A on the bottom axis. Make a mark at exactly 15" from the upper right corner. Swing the ruler to point B on the bottom axis, and make another mark at 15".

Repeat for all of the marks on both the horizontal and left vertical axis. All of these 15" marks should be in the form of a smooth arc. Mark each point just drawn as A' through U', beginning at the rightmost point, and moving from right to left. The completed drawing of the blank rib drawing axes should look like Figure 4.1.

Check the drawing for errors. Accuracy here is critical, since the shape of the finished boat depends on the ribs, which you cannot make correctly from an inaccurate drawing.

With the drawing completed and checked for accuracy, have at least thirteen copies made. A few extra is not a bad idea, in case you make an irrecoverable error (too many points plotted wrong, spilled coffee—accidents happen!). Now we will move on to the actual lofting.

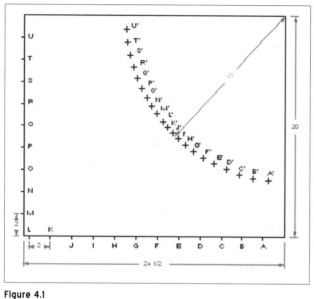

Figure 4.1

Blank rib drawing axes. (Drawing by Dick Millet.)

A CURIOUS ASIDE

We guess that John Gardner was left handed. We found it awkward to draw the axes with the origin of the radii at the upper right. In fact, we built one of our boats from rib drawings that were reversed mirror images of the Gardner drawing on Plate III, *MOLDING LAYOUT—GUIDEBOAT FRAMES:* we placed the origin of the radial lines at the upper left, and reversed the labels A through U. It just felt more comfortable for a right-handed draftsman to do it this way.

Secure a blank axes sheet to the drawing table, and look at Plate IV. The first column is headed *DISTANCE ON LINE.* The next several columns are headed *AA', BB', CC',* etc., to *UU'.* The data begins on the next line. The first column on the second line is *FR.0 OUTSIDE,* with the next four columns containing simply *B.L.* The best way to explain this is, "A point on the outside of frame 0, on a line from point A to point A', is on the base line."

The next three points are identical, all being located on the base line, *B.L.* The first value in the column

headed *EE'* is *6-18,* which is naval architectural shorthand for 6 and ¹⁸⁄₃₂ inches. Lay the three-foot ruler with the end on point E' on the arc and passing exactly through point E on the base line. Make a mark at $6\frac{18}{32}$" from the arc. Do not move the ruler yet. Look at the very next line in the *EE'* column, which is the *FR. 0 INSIDE* data. The value is *5-24,* or 5 and ²⁴⁄₃₂ inches from point E' on the arc. Make a mark at that point. Now move the ruler to point F' on the arc, and passing through point F on the base line. Make a mark for the outside of the rib at $6\frac{27}{32}$", and another for the inside at $6\frac{3}{32}$". The remaining points on the inside curve are given as *UNIFORM ¾" MOLDING,* which simply means that all of the rest of the points are drawn ¾" inboard from the outside curve along the respective radial lines.

Recall that we started lofting the inner and outer curves at point EE', the points A through D all being on the base line. The inside transition curve must yet be plotted. Plot these points the same way, using the data for *FR.0 INSIDE* at *AA'* through *DD'.* The drawing thus far should look like Figure 4.2.

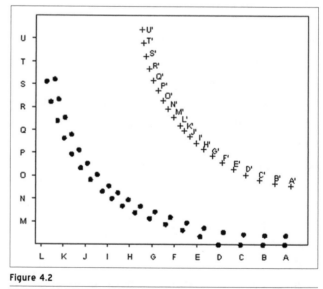

Figure 4.2

Rib 0 points plotted, ready for drawing curves. (Drawing by Dick Millet.)

The next step is to connect the points in a fair curve. You will need a batten and some weights to hold it in position (Figure 4.3). You can easily make a suitable batten by slicing about ¹⁄₁₆" or less from the edge of a ¾" straight-grained hardwood board, about 3' long.

30

You may have to experiment with the actual thickness to get one that is not too stiff, yet stiff enough so that it will not distort when you move the drawing pencil against it. The weights should be compact and heavy enough so that the force of the bent batten will not move them.

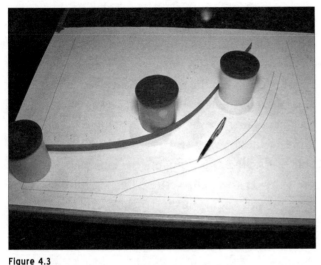

Figure 4.3
Batten and weights used for drawing fair curves.

We used three or four plastic ready-made cake frosting containers filled with sand or coins. These containers had straight vertical sides, which held the batten vertical. Sloped-sided containers may cause the batten to distort, making it difficult, if not impossible, to hold a fair curve.

With the batten on edge, align it with the points on the curve using the weights to hold it in position. Do not try to draw the entire curve in one placement of the batten—do it in two or three sections, with each section overlapping to preserve a fair curve. A smooth curve should result with each point on, or very nearly on, the curve (Figure 4.4).

If forcing a particular point to lay on the curve results in the curve becoming unfair, ignore it. If more than a few points cause unfairness, check your work. We found that there were very few points in Gardner's data that had to be corrected or ignored. The completed drawing should look like the one in Plate III, without the radial lines.

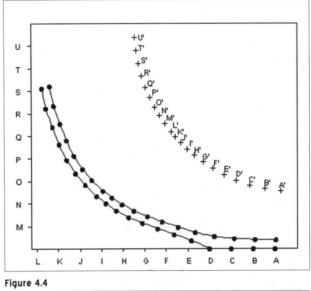

Figure 4.4
Completed rib drawing. (Drawing by Dick Millet.)

Be sure to extend the inner and outer curves to the last upper points, and a few inches beyond. You will not use this extension in the actual boat, but you must construct the ribs initially with at least a 3" or 4" extension beyond the sheer to allow for the mounting of a preliminary alignment batten. Similarly, make the rib foot length equally generous so that later you can trim it to a fair length, a length that you will not know until you make the bottom board quarter pattern.

The seat riser mounting marks are made on the drawings for ribs 5 and 8 (bow seat), 0^3 and 0^4 (middle seat), and 8 and 11 (stern seat). Be sure to identify the marks as to seat location and identification—note that rib 8 requires two marks. With the framing square aligned on the base line, adjust its position so that the appropriate height intersects the inner rib curve. The hull sketch at the bottom of Plate XII gives the heights for mounting the seats. You will copy these marks on to the respective rib patterns and then later transfer them to the ribs for mounting the seat risers.

Marks for the height of the sheer from the inside of the bottom board can also be made from the data in Plate II, marked *SHEER*, in the *HEIGHTS ABOVE BASE LINE* row. These are approximate values only, but are helpful later in determining placement of the actual sheer strip.

31

LOFTING THE STEM

Grant guideboat stems were complex. They were cut from favorably grained spruce crooks, had a rolling rabbet cut into each side to accept the plank ends, and were tapered from the rabbet to the cutwater (the foremost part of the craft, projecting forward of the bow). Some modern builders make one-piece stems similarly when they use traditional planking.

There are variations possible in the wood and construction of our stems. The stems may be built up from laminations and shaped, or built with a solid or laminated cap piece glued along the outer edge. We built one of our boats with a laminated spruce outer stem; the other with solid hardwood.

Traditional style complex stems are not required for a strip-built boat, eliminating the need for cutting the rolling rabbet and the tedious fitting of strips between the rabbets on each end. We retain the traditional stem form, but build it in two pieces. We build up the inner stem from laminated spruce, while the outer portion is either solid wood or laminated similar to the inner stem. With the solid wood outer stem we can choose wood of aesthetically pleasing color and figure, accenting the overall classic lines of the boat. We replace the rolling rabbet with a much simpler rolling bevel to which we fasten the strips. Once we trim the strips flush with the leading edge of the inner stem, we glue the outer stem to it, completing the construction.

Gardner's Plate VI contains all of the data you need to loft the stems for the *Virginia*. The approach is similar to lofting the ribs, as you can see in the drawing on the right side of the page. Begin by taping a blank sheet of large paper to the table oriented in portrait (the long edge vertical). Draw the base line, and make two marks 14½" apart. With the framing square, draw vertical lines at each mark 28" high, and connect the tops to form a rectangle. Once again, check for square by measuring the diagonals. The vertical line on the left side represents frame station, or rib, 12. Draw another horizontal line 10" above the base line. Measure 9¼" to the right of the frame 12 line, and draw anoth-

er vertical line from the top to the 10" line above the base line. Mark point "X" at the intersection of the 10" line and the left vertical line. There should now be a narrow rectangle on the right and inside of the top rectangle, above the 10" line. Starting at the 10" line, make marks every 2" above the 10" line and draw horizontal lines within the 5" wide rectangle.

The small table at the bottom of the page gives the locations of marks A through G on the base line. Point A is 2¹⁄₁₆" to the right of the frame 12 line. Point B is 4" from the frame 12 line, and the remainder of the marks increase by 2" from point B to point G. Note in the drawing that point G is not quite at the end of the line. To complete the labels, make marks every 2" on the right vertical line, beginning at the bottom, and ending at the 10" line. You should now have marks from the bottom to the top, every 2". Beginning on the bottom, label these marks H through T. The drawing should look exactly like the drawing in Plate VI, without the curves. Once again, you do not need the radial lines from point X, you will use the edge of the steel ruler instead. We are now ready to loft the stem.

The table in the upper left on Plate VI contains all of the required data. Since we will be using a two-piece stem, the data for the bearding line is not required. The bearding line is the beginning of the rabbet for traditionally planked hulls. We will separate the stem into an inner portion and an outer portion along the rabbet line, eliminating the need for the bearding line. Do not even bother to loft it.

The data table is in two sections. The top section gives the measurements from point X radially to points A through L, similar to the lofting of the ribs. The bottom section of the table gives the measurements from the inside vertical line to the respective points on the curves. As with the ribs, the table gives the measurements in inches and thirty-seconds. Lofting the stem is not difficult, and no further explanation is necessary. The lofted drawing should look like that in Plate VI, without the bearding line.

The only area of the table that may be confusing is the one marked *INSIDE BOTTOM*. This line defines the angle of the stem with the bottom board, and shows where and how you join the stem to the bottom board. When you eventually cut the stem pattern, the notch for the bottom board in the end of the pattern must be accurately made.

COMPUTER-AIDED DESIGN (CAD)

Lofting the ribs and stem as described above is a fundamental way of converting a table of values to full-size curves from which parts may be made. It is somewhat primitive by contemporary drafting standards, which have virtually eliminated pencil and paper in favor of computer-aided design, or CAD. Numerous software packages are available for doing the lofting using the table of offsets as input data. Not every builder has access to, or is proficient with, these programs. But if the software is available, it can be used to draw not only full-size rib and stem drawings, but in the hands of one who knows the program, can output renderings and sketches surpassing the best work of an experienced draftsman in a fraction of the time. Ribs and stem drawings fully lofted in CAD have been used to build guideboats, one of which is shown in Figure 4.5.

Figure 4.5

CAD rendering of the *Virginia* using Gardner's data. (Drawing by Dick Millet.)

CHAPTER 5
PATTERNS AND FORMS

In this chapter, we will finally get to make some sawdust—not for the boat, but for the patterns and forms. Before planking can begin, we will need the ribs and stems. Since making these parts requires time for the steam or hot soak bending and time for glue to cure, it is important to start rib and stem construction early.

PATTERNS

We have already made full-size drawings of each of the thirteen rib shapes and the stems. We will now trace them onto plywood to make the patterns, and then use the patterns to make the bending forms. In the next chapter, we actually get to make the ribs. To make the patterns, we will need a sheet of ¼" plywood, the rib and stem drawings, some carbon paper, a ballpoint pen for tracing, and a dozen or so pushpins.

Before going any further, this would be a good time to discuss the concept of a reference. A *reference* is a surface (plane), edge (line), or point from which you make measurements. When making a measurement, the reference is the zero point or beginning of the ruler or tape. When you rip a plank on a table saw the reference is the edge against the fence, producing a ripped section whose width is measured from the fence to the blade. For the ribs, the reference edge is the bottom of the rib foot, shown on the rib drawing as the *base line*. In order to produce ribs correctly from the rib drawings, you must accurately duplicate this reference edge on the patterns.

The easiest way to achieve this is to have a perfectly straight and smooth edge on the plywood before doing the tracing. If the factory edge of the plywood is straight and true, you can use it as is. If there is any question, you can rough out a piece of the plywood sheet and cut and joint a straight edge. This is perhaps better than trusting the factory edge, and is what we recommend. Do not try to trace the entire rib including the bottom of the foot and then cut it out. Any error in the reference edge, especially the angular relationship between the bottom of the rib foot and the curve of the rib, may lead to difficulty in stripping or cause an unfair hull.

We did not attempt to glue an oversized cut-out of the rib drawing to a piece of plywood and then cut it out. While builders have used this technique successfully in making the broad forms for strip-built kayaks and canoes, we were concerned with the accurate alignment of the reference edge and possible distortion of the rather narrow drawing while gluing it to the plywood. We also do not recommend cutting a true base line after the fact, as previously discussed. Preservation of the rib drawings is also a consideration, since you will use them later to help shape the rolling bevel on the bottom board.

To align the drawing of the base line with the reference edge of the plywood, both must be simultaneously visible. Since the drawing paper is not transparent, cut a small flap in the paper across the base line on each end outside of the rib foot ends. Fold the flaps out and position the drawing on the plywood so that the base line is aligned with the plywood edge as seen through the holes.

Using the pushpins, secure the paper to the plywood at a few points near the bottom of the drawing

(Figure 5.1). Carefully slide carbon paper between the drawing and the plywood, being careful to place it under the complete drawn curves of the rib. A few sheets will be required. Smooth the paper from the base line outward, securing it to the plywood with additional pushpins. There must be no folds or creases in the paper, and it must lie flat.

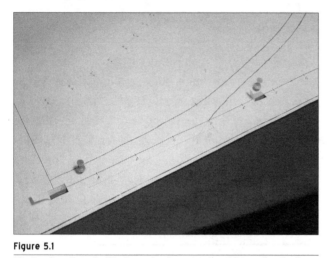

Figure 5.1
Rib drawing aligned with plywood reference edge visible under the flaps.

Carefully trace over the rib drawing with the ballpoint pen, using sufficient pressure to transfer the tracing through the carbon paper and onto the plywood. Move the pen slowly, and hold the paper down so that it does not creep or distort. Make sure the tracing extends beyond the sheer by 3" or 4", and an inch or so beyond the expected end of the rib foot. The actual rib foot length will be determined later after you have made the bottom board quarter pattern.

Cut the pattern out with a jig or band saw wide of the line. A drum sander in the drill press or oscillating spindle sander can be used to sand to the concave lines, and the disk sander takes care of sanding the outer curve. Sanding to the lines is also a fairing operation, since the hand-traced line is likely far from perfectly smooth.

Lay the completed pattern back on the drawing and check for accuracy. Once again, what is critical here is the relationship of the reference bottom of the rib foot and the outside curve beyond it. With the pattern accurately aligned on the drawing, transfer marks for the sheer and seat risers for any applicable ribs to the patterns. The

measurements for positioning the seat risers are on the boat profile drawing on Plate XII of the Gardner drawings in Appendix 1. The sheer heights above the base line are in the offset table on Plate II. These measurements should have been marked on the rib drawings when they were lofted, but can also be done now.

Ribs 11 and 12, referred to as "scribe" ribs because they were scribed to fit the hull after it was completed, have no feet, so there is no practical reference to be had directly from the plywood edge as with the footed ribs. You can safely obtain one after the fact, however. To do this, extend the bottom of the tracing an inch or so below the base line, and trace the base line across this extension using a straight edge to guide the pen. Do not cut the base line when cutting the pattern from the plywood—leave the extended portion. Later, after you cut and fair the pattern, trim the bottom extension just shy of the base line and sand up to it with the disk sander. Any small error here will be of no consequence, since these ribs are not attached to the bottom board. The worst case is a slight gap between the end of the rib and the bottom board.

Make patterns for the inner and outer stems similarly. The leading edge of the inner stem, which is the same as the trailing edge of the outer stem, is the rabbet line (Plate VI). When you cut and shape the patterns for both inner and outer stems, they should fit together smoothly. Figure 5.2 shows a complete set of rib and stem patterns for the *Virginia*.

Figure 5.2
Complete set of plywood rib and illustration board stem patterns.

CONSTRUCTING THE BOTTOM BOARD QUARTER PATTERN

In order to cut the bottom board to its exact elliptical shape, you will first need to construct a quarter pattern. A quarter pattern is exactly what it sounds like. Given that each half of the bottom board is identical, all that you need is a pattern for one-quarter of the bottom board (which, coincidentally, is much easier to handle!).

You can easily cut this from thin plywood ripped to exactly 4½" and cut to a length of 7'4¾" (the extra length will be explained shortly). Gardner's Plate VIII provides the measurements for making the quarter pattern for a 14'6" bottom board. It should be noted here that there is a discrepancy between Gardner's drawing of the quarter pattern and the actual width of the bottom board of the *Virginia* at amidships. Gardner's drawing shows a width of 4½" at the widest end of the pattern. This measurement would produce a bottom board width of 9" amidships as opposed to the actual 8¾" on the *Virginia*. An additional discrepancy is evident in the measurement shown for *LAP FASTENING* in Plate IX. Here the bottom board width amidships is 8⅝". No explanation exists that we are aware of for these discrepancies. Our solution to the problem was to follow Gardner's drawings and utilize the 9" amidships measurement (4½" on the quarter pattern).

Measuring from the left end of the piece that will become your pattern, make a mark with a sharp pencil or a pen on the bottom edge at 1', 2', 3', 4', 5', 6', and 7'. Additionally, place a mark at 7'3", and another at 7'4¾". Do the same at the top edge, again measuring from the left end. Using a square, connect the marks for the top edge measurements with those on the bottom edge. Be sure to clearly indicate the 7'3" line as the center of the bottom board (we like to use a fine-point red pen for this).

Working from the bottom edge of the plywood, measure up exactly ¼" at the extreme left end of the piece and make a mark. At the 1' location, measure up 1⅝" and make a mark. At 2', place a mark 2⅝" up from the bottom edge. At 3', measure up 3⅜"; at 4',

measure up 3⅞"; at 5', 4¼"; at 6', 4⁷⁄₁₆". The remaining measurements are all 4½" up from the bottom edge.

Run a long flexible batten (approximately 8' in length) from right to left along the top edge of the plywood, taking extra care to align the edge of the batten at the marks you made at each interval. Align the batten at the right most mark (4½") and work down in a smooth curve to the ¼" mark on the left end of the plywood. Before drawing the curved line, check by eye for a fair curve. If the curve needs adjustment, now is the time to do it. However, do not change the location of the batten at the ¼" mark on the left or at the 4¼" mark on the right. These measurements are critical and need to remain intact.

Once you are satisfied with the fairness of the curve, carefully trace along the batten with a sharp pencil or a pen. Next, cut the pattern using a jigsaw, coping saw, or band saw, but make sure to leave the pencil line. Trim up the curved edge with a low angle block plane or sanding block. Your quarter pattern is done!

DETERMINING RIB FOOT LENGTHS

The length of each rib foot is a little shorter than the full width across the bottom board. The amount by which the feet are shorter varies, so that when sighting down the inside of the boat, the trim line forms a pleasant curve. To determine the lengths of the feet for the rib patterns and ultimately the actual ribs, refer to Plate III. There are three dimensions shown near the top center of the page, which are the distances from the edge of the bottom board inboard to the end of the trimmed rib feet at frames 0, 4, and 10. The length of the rib foot at any rib is twice the width of the quarter pattern at that rib location less the trim distance.

To determine these lengths easily, start by drawing lines across the bottom board quarter pattern at each rib location. You should first erase the layout lines used to define the shape of the quarter pattern, since they are not necessarily on a frame line and could be confusing. With the rib station lines drawn, mark the dimensions given in Plate III for the three frames shown. Spring a batten through the points, and mark the batten location at each of the remaining rib lines.

The width of the quarter pattern added to the distance from the reference edge of the pattern to the trim line mark is the length of the rib foot at that frame or rib. There is no need to measure these dimensions in actual inches if a story stick is used. Using a piece of stripping or similar batten as a story stick, place the end of the stick at the outside edge of the pattern at a rib location, and make a mark where the stick crosses the inside (center) edge as seen in Figure 5.3a. Move the stick so that this full width mark is shifted to the trim line, and make a second mark on the stick at the far edge, Figure 5.3b. The distance from the end of the batten to the second mark is the length of the rib foot.

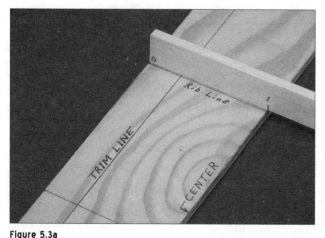

Figure 5.3a

Width of quarter pattern...

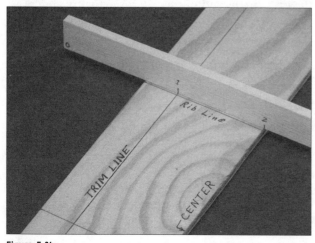

Figure 5.3b

...added to trim width.

Lay the reference end of the story stick on the bottom of the rib pattern at point D (intersection of base line with the outside curve), make a mark on the pattern at the length just determined, and trim the pattern square with the bottom edge, sanding to the cut line. You can use the finished rib pattern later for aligning the rib blank on a cutting sled to accurately form the bottoms of the actual ribs.

FORMS

Bending forms were unknown to the master builders. They simply cut the ribs and stems from spruce crooks. They may have used a bending form for the coaming or deck circle, and Dwight Grant, unique among all builders, used them for the seat back rest, but that is still several chapters away.

The design requirements for the bending forms are simple, but important. They must be rigid, sturdy, and have an accurate surface representing the inner curves of the ribs and stems, and that surface must be square to the form mounting plate. The reference surface must be tall enough to support the stack of laminations during gluing and clamping, and the width of the form must be able to accept whatever clamps will be required, in addition to the thickness of the lamination stack and clamp pads. Given these requirements, suitable forms may be cut from ordinary 2-by construction lumber and mounted on plywood plates. Wide pieces are preferred, such as 2 by 10 or 2 by 12. You may use narrower stock, butting two pieces together to get the requisite width and curve as shown in Figure 5.4. A good source of form material is scrap from a construction site.

Clean up a piece of form material a few inches longer than required for the entire rib, and make sure it is not cupped. Lay a rib pattern on it so that you can fully draw the inner curve. The curve can be quite close to the edge—the outer curve is not needed since it will be formed on the rib blank by the laminations. Sketch another curve about 2" inside the inner curve. This line need not be precise, since it is simply the cut line for the form width and has no bearing on the shape of the laminated blank. If it is about 2" from the reference surface, and allowing for an additional ¾" for the molded blank, there is still enough room to permit using 4" C-clamps with pads for clamping most of the glue-up. The ends of the forms can be a little thinner, but the clamping area should be parallel to the reference surface to prevent slipping and to assure good clamping pressure. An alternative is to cut the form about 3" wide, and then cut flats into the inside edge for clamping points. This limits the variation in clamp positioning except when you use larger capacity clamps.

Figure 5.4
Rib forms 0 (top), and 12 (bottom).

Cut the forms out with a band saw. Make sure the sanding disk is square with its table, and sand the reference surface to the line, fair and true. Cut any flats required on the inside, and mark the rib number. Lay the rib pattern against the form and make sure the form is an accurate representation of the inside of the rib. Mount the completed form on a piece of plywood[1] sized so that the entire stack of laminations, including the extra short pieces required in the foot area, will fit on the mounting plate. Five or six sheetrock screws into the form through the bottom of the mounting plate are sufficient.

Estimate the dimensions of the plate by laying the pattern against the form and making sure there is sufficient room for building the laminated blank. When the form is mounted, lay the pattern against the form making sure to place it accurately. Trace the outline

of the entire rib on the plate, so that the number, length, and position of the additional rib foot laminations may be estimated.

The process described above applies to bending forms for ribs 0 through 10. Since ribs 11 and 12 have no feet and are simply molded ¾" wide their entire length, a simpler form may be used. A length of 2 by 4 is convenient. Lay the rib pattern for one of the molded ribs on the 2 by 4 and trace its outline. Cut the outline out with the band saw and discard the center portion. Smooth the insides of the cut surfaces to the line and mount one of the pieces on a plywood base as with the other forms, positioning it so that when in use, both pieces fit comfortably on the base.

Mark and identify the location of the bottom of the rib and the sheer line, transferring these marks from the pattern. When laminating, be sure to extend the stack about 3" or 4" beyond the sheer. Since you will later cut off this extension after stripping the hull, it need not be curved and may simply extend beyond the form for clamping. The bottom end of the laminated blank will be trimmed to the proper angle and need not be extended any more than an inch or so. Build the other molded rib form the same way. Note that a single cut through the center of the 2 by 4 may work, since the rib blank is ¾" thick its entire length. The two pieces of the form will not be aligned when the laminations are clamped together, however, and any transferred marks must be carefully checked for accurate placement.

1 If the plywood is warped, two straightening cleats may be screwed on the edges.

39

CHAPTER 6
MAKING THE RIBS

There are sixty-six ribs in the *Virginia.* Having to laminate that number individually would discourage the average first-time builder from ever building a second boat, or possibly even the first. The old traditional builders cut their ribs from a double thick blank, and then split the cutout into two matching ribs of similar strength and grain. In building ribs from laminations, we can go them two better—our ribs are made in fours, there being four ribs cut from a single laminated blank. We will need one blank for each rib set numbered 1 through 12, and five identical blanks for all of the 0 ribs. There will be two 0 ribs left over using this scheme.

One or two glue-ups per day is a comfortable pace, depending on the number of clamps you have. While several strong clamps are required for gluing, you only need a few for the initial bending. Spring-back after the initial bending makes a lot of accurate clamping at this point unnecessary.

THE WOOD
Almost without exception, Adirondack red spruce was the wood of choice[1] for ribs in the traditional guideboat. It was plentiful in northern New York, grew to large diameters, and thereby produced stump flitches suitable for ribs and stems. It is among the strongest of woods for its weight yet light and easily worked. With spruce intensely logged during the heyday of the guideboat, suitable stumps were plentiful and could be had for the asking (and the digging!). With such an abundance of spruce stumps, there was no need to laminate ribs.

But with the demise of the guideboat, loggers were becoming more efficient, cutting the trees closer to the ground. Stumps suitable for boat building were in short supply, about enough to satisfy the needs of the few remaining traditional guideboat builders.

Most contemporary builders rely on commercial lumberyards for wood. Spruce is still available, although large suppliers of common construction lumber now use the term "spruce" generically. Adirondack sawmills can supply spruce, and some builders fortunate to live within or near the Blue Line can sometimes find red spruce at reasonable prices.

We advise the woodworker contemplating building a guideboat to begin accumulating suitable spruce planks well ahead of the start of the project. Clear knot-free lumber is not on a separate stack or pallet at the lumberyard—you must search it out from the ordinary knotty construction grade lumber. One may get lucky on any particular visit to the lumber dealer and find all the clear stock needed. One can also make several visits before finding the perfect plank.

If all of the planks were perfect, the minimum amount needed for the ribs would be two 2 by 6 planks 8' long, with one additional for the stems, the short pieces for building up the thickness for the rib feet, and some insurance. But a spruce plank that is totally free of knots is a rarity. The more knots one is willing to accept, the more suitable planks there will be.

We have found that a few knots here and there are unavoidable, and that we needed three or four planks of various widths (2 by 8, 2 by 10) to get enough clear stock for all of the rib and stem laminations. Also take care to avoid planks cut from near the center of the tree. Such wood may contain the center pith, which is not usable, and the small diameter annular rings have a grain structure that is not conducive to easy bending. The ideal plank, therefore, is straight and free of knots, cut with a nearly flat grain from large diameter logs.

CUTTING THE LAMINATIONS

Before doing any cutting, let us look at some design considerations for the laminations. Rib 0 measures about 28" from the end of the rib foot around to the sheer. If we add 1" for trimming the rib foot end to its final length and 3" for the temporary extension beyond the sheer, we get 32" for the length of the laminations. An 8' plank can therefore provide three lengths of stock for ripping into lamination strips.

The next dimension to calculate is the width. The four ribs are cut from the laminated blanks across the width, so the width of the lamination must include four rib thicknesses, three saw kerfs, and some extra for sanding and clean up of the glued stack. The design thickness of the ribs is $5/16$", which sums to $1\frac{1}{4}$" for the four ribs. If a blade with a $1/16$" kerf is used on the table saw, we would need $1\frac{7}{16}$" of total width. If we cut the stock billets so that laminations are the thickness of the original 2-by plank of nominally $1\frac{1}{2}$", we are left with a mere $1/16$" for distribution in clean up and sanding each rib face.

We could use a band saw to slice the ribs from the blank and thereby waste less wood for the kerfs, but the inherent roughness of the band-sawn surfaces requires more clean up than ribs cut with a good thin kerf table saw blade. The safe solution is to cut the billet $1\frac{3}{4}$" wide from the 2-by plank, then rotate it 90° for ripping the laminations (Figure 6.1). You can then safely clean up the laminated blank, and cut the four ribs comfortably from it. The nominally flat grain in this cutting orientation is also more conducive to easy bending. The approach thus becomes:

1. Cut the plank into 32" long pieces.

2. Rip each piece into $1\frac{3}{4}$" wide billets.

3. Rotate the billets so that the wide side is against the fence, and rip the laminations.

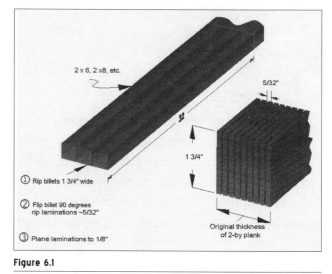

Figure 6.1

Cutting laminations from construction lumber. (Drawing by Dick Millet.)

We must now address the thickness of the laminations. John Gardner suggested using $1/16$" thick laminations glued with epoxy, and did not mention steam bending. Certainly, such thin laminations should bend easily by merely clamping them to the form, but the number of laminations and the necessary accompanying epoxy and kerf waste seem excessive. Since the curved portions of the ribs above the feet are $3/4$" wide, it is convenient to use six $1/8$" thick laminations to produce the requisite thickness.

Obtaining consistent $1/8$" thick laminations directly off the saw is not impossible, but is certainly unlikely. 2-by construction lumber is not furniture quality, and is rarely straight, flat, and without cupping, crown, or twist. It is highly likely that when ripping such stock, variations in lamination thickness will occur. Roughing out billets slightly oversize in width leaves sufficient material for jointing, which should be done to square the edges against the fence and on the table.

Then rip the lamination strips, again slightly oversize, to a thickness of $5/32$" after which you plane $1/64$" off each side. The first pass merely cleans off the saw marks, and then the strip is turned over and taken down to the final ⅛" thickness in a single pass. The resulting laminations are of consistent thickness, with parallel surfaces that will not creep when glued and clamped. A single lamination that does not have parallel gluing surfaces (wedge-shaped cross-section) can slip and rise out of the clamped stack, requiring additional stock removal during clean up and possibly resulting in a thin blank that may produce only three good ribs rather than the required four.

Not all lamination strips will be totally free of defects, such as knots. These defects can be cut away, and the shorter pieces that result can be used for building up the rib foot area in the lamination stack.

BENDING CONSIDERATIONS

The application of heat to wood will soften it so that it can be bent with a lower risk of failure than bending it without heat. This is a blanket statement, subject to all sorts of variables. Some woods bend readily; others do not. Thin wood bends more easily than thick. Flat grain is generally easier to bend than vertical grain. For our purposes, bending spruce is relatively easy, and given a reasonably straight grain, bending the ⅛" thick laminations around the rib forms quickly becomes routine. The laminations for all of the footed ribs should be heated; the scribed ribs 11 and 12 may be glued directly, and need not be heated.

The Grants sometimes used moist heat in building bent parts for their boats. They wrapped the wales in burlap and wetted them down with hot water, and bent deck circles in a steam box. For our boats, we used both steam boxes and hot water soaking for the rib and stem laminations, and later for the deck circles.

The steam boxes are roughly 4' long and square, built from 1 by 6 pine, closed at one end, with a hinged cover on the other end (Figure 6.2). Insert ¼" dowels every 6" or 8" through the sides about ½" off the bottom. The dowels support the stack of laminations off the bottom so that steam can freely circulate around all sides. Use a camp stove to boil water in a covered container, with the steam fed to the box via a rubber hose. Use a dial

thermometer, available at hardware stores or "borrowed" from the gas grill, to monitor the temperature inside the box. Drill a ½" diameter hole at the back end underside of the steam box for draining the condensate.

Figure 6.2
Typical steam box.

Our hot soaking tray had been built for other applications, but served well for the rib bending work. It was a covered copper tray, 4' long, 6" wide, and 3" deep, heated by a two-unit electric hot plate. We simply immersed the laminations in water in the tray, and heated the water to boiling for ten to twenty minutes.

The choice of steaming or hot soaking involves some trade-offs. The equipment for steaming is relatively easy to build or acquire. A tray long enough to hot soak the full-length laminations may be more difficult to obtain. You may use a shorter tray, like a roasting pan, to hot soak the foot ends of the laminations, ignoring the sheer ends. The severity of bending for several inches below the sheer is minimal, and the laminations could easily be bent and glued without heating.

Laminations removed from the hot soak remain hot long enough to comfortably get them bent and on the form. Successful steaming, on the other hand, requires retrieving the stack from the steam box and bending on the form in as short a time as possible—no more than about 45 seconds—since the thin steamed wood cools rapidly. Thicker laminations would stay hot longer, but would be more difficult to bend.

Another trade-off between hot soaking and steaming is the time required for the bent stack to dry before gluing can be done. Steamed laminations can be dry enough to glue within 24 hours, while hot soaked pieces require four or five days before gluing can be safely attempted.

The trade-offs continue with the effectiveness of the bends. The hot soaked laminations retain their shape a little better than the steamed. This seems to have no effect on the final glue-up, however, since you can glue and clamp laminations to the forms without difficulty using either method.

See the additional laminations for the rib foot areas in Figures 6.3a and b. Guideboat ribs have also been built without these extra laminations by first laminating the blanks ¾" thick over the entire length, ignoring the rib foot. Solid pieces of spruce were then fitted and glued to the cured blank in the foot area, and the final rib shape cut with the band saw. This composite rib seemed entirely satisfactory on the one boat that we examined. Once again there is a trade-off in the time spent cutting, fitting, and gluing the additional piece, compared to gluing extra laminations at glue-up time.

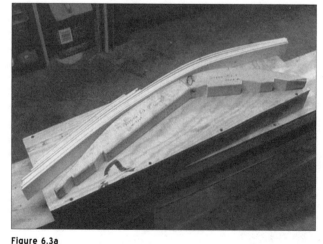

Figure 6.3a
Steamed laminations.

Another method for making laminated ribs is less demanding in terms of the precision of the glue-up. With this method, laminations are built up thicker than the design ¾" thickness, with the additional foot laminations also included. The glue that is used is a

Type II polyvinyl acetate formulation, with a small amount of spring-back in the glued blank. The final rib shape is band sawn, there being enough extra wood to compensate for the spring-back. In a similar approach, fewer forms are used.[2] The reasoning is that two or three adjacent ribs are so similar in shape that they could all be cut from the same oversize blank.

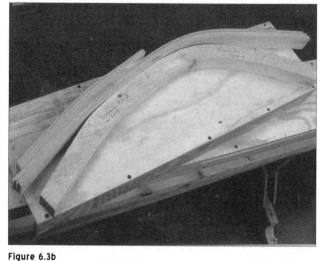

Figure 6.3b
Hot-soaked laminations.

Cutting the rib shapes from oversize laminated blanks requires the additional smoothing of the sawn surfaces to a fair shape, a feat that is not the easiest job in the boat shop. Laminating the proper number of strips to their final thickness on individual forms results in ribs requiring no further shaping other than in the transition area between the foot and the outside curve of the rib. In addition, the glue lines exactly parallel the curve of the rib, rather than being cut through when sawn to shape. This last point is purely aesthetic, and if the inside of the boat is painted, is of no consequence.

DOING THE BENDING

You may heat all of the laminations required for a single blank at one time regardless of the method chosen. For hot soaking, place the laminations in the water bath, and then heat to boiling. After 10 to 20 minutes of hot soaking at or near boiling, remove them with tongs, keeping the stack of full-length strips loosely together while still in the water. The full-length strips are then quickly placed on the form and clamped at two or three places with rapid action clamps such as Quick Clamps.[3]

The extra foot laminations can then be removed similarly and clamped in position. It is very helpful to have the forms close to the heating tray, with tongs, clamps, and gloves (the strips are hot!) ready. When all of the laminations are in place, additional clamps may be set to fine-tune the bending, although bending to a close approximate shape at this time is sufficient.

For steam bending, the stack is assembled on the bench with spacers between the laminations, and rubber bands are used to hold the stack together (Figure 6.4). Round toothpicks with square centers make excellent spacers.

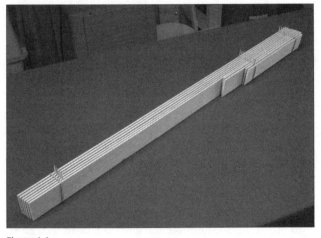

Figure 6.4
Stack assembled, ready for placing in the steam box. Hold the extensions of the toothpick separators together with a few turns of masking tape.

Place the assembled stack in the steam box, oriented such that when removed for bending, it will slide right over to the nearby form in the proper orientation without having to turn it. Monitor the temperature, and when it reaches 200° F, timing can begin. Continue steaming for about 20 minutes at that temperature. Any further steaming will have little if any effect on the bending, but less than that length of time may not sufficiently soften the wood.

Speed and efficiency of motion are essential to bend the steamed laminations successfully. In addition to the fast-acting clamps and gloves, a single-edge razor

blade is extremely useful for cutting the rubber bands rather than taking the time to remove them. The procedure then becomes:

1. Set the clamps to the approximate opening and have them well within reach.

2. Open the door on the steam box and slide the stack out, cutting the rubber bands as you remove the stack, and remove the toothpicks. Keep the laminations together to minimize heat loss.

3. Immediately place the stack on the form, and set the clamps.

4. Place a few additional clamps, especially at the ends of the form.

The grain orientation in the laminations could have an effect on the final rib. It is safe to say that the grain will not be perfectly flat, but somewhat curved or at an angle when viewed at the end of the lamination. When you cut and plane the laminations, you should keep them in order as they come off the saw.

When the stack is set up for soaking or steaming, every other lamination should be rotated 180° within the stack and turned end for end. This distributes the grain directions in an alternating fashion, similar to the way plywood is made. This reorientation of the grain helps to neutralize any internal stresses, and the rib will lie flat when cut. We have seen ribs that had significant twist after cutting from the finished blank, which may have been avoided if the grain was alternately arranged in the stack. Also, the additional strength imparted to the rib by arranging the laminations in a cross-grain fashion is a plus.

45

BENDING WITH DRY HEAT

Long after we completed the two boats that are the subject of this book, we began construction on another Grant design guideboat. Rather than using steam or a hot soak to soften the spruce laminations for bending, we tried a method in which a heat gun is used. The heat gun was capable of blowing air at temperatures that could scorch the wood if we did not keep the gun moving and held a safe distance away. This type of heat gun is readily available in hardware stores for use in stripping paint, softening floor tiles, and numerous other tasks around the home.

The first step in this process was to hold a lamination strip at each end (with gloves on, of course!), about an inch away from the hot air discharge, and apply a gentle bending force to the strip. Very soon, the lamination relaxed against the bending force and could be bent quite easily. Placing the bent strip on the bending form to check its shape revealed where we needed to next apply heat, and this process was continued until the strip fit the form.

The final result was laminations bent much more precisely to the shape of the bending form than was possible with either steam or hot soak bending (Figure 6.5). With this process, bending all of the laminations, including the rib foot fill pieces, for a single rib blank took less time than it would take to heat up the steamer or hot water. A significant added benefit was that we were able to glue the laminations as soon as they cooled—no drying out time required.

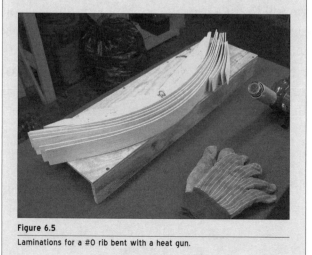

Figure 6.5

Laminations for a #0 rib bent with a heat gun.

Dry heat bending worked very well, and a complete set of laminations for ribs 0 through 9 was formed in short order. For rib 10, the severity of the bend at the rib foot transition prevented complete bending with the heat gun, but we think it was probably due more to variations in the grain than the severity of the bend. For this rib only, we did a hot soak for the rib foot area.

Some laminations bent more easily than others, for no readily apparent reason. For the more difficult strips, longer application of heat and careful bending force produced a good bend.

GLUING THE BLANKS

The day after bending, remove the clamps from the laminations. There will be some spring-back, but the fact that the laminations were able to conform to the shape of the form without cracking indicates that forcing them around the form once again will not be a problem. If the inner surfaces feel cool or damp, leave them standing but separated for air circulation for at least another day. The cool or damp feeling indicates insufficient drying, so do not attempt to glue yet. Once the laminations are dry, you can begin the gluing process.

You must thoroughly coat the forms with a wax of some sort, or cover them with two or three layers of masking tape in the area where glue will be used. This is vitally important on the form support plate from the bottom of the form outward a sufficient distance to cover the entire stack including the rib foot laminations. Coat the bending surface of the form as well as the top to prevent any squeezed out glue from bonding.

Failure to adequately cover the form with wax or tape can cause extensive damage to the blank and form when trying to release the cured blank. A commercial paste wax may be used; shredded paraffin or beeswax dissolved in a very small amount of mineral spirits to make a paste is also acceptable. Note that beeswax makes a smoother paste than paraffin, but paraffin will work. If you are going to use wood cushion blocks to protect the wood during gluing, you should also wax or tape them. Cover both sides as well as the ends so that there will be no question later.

We glue our rib blanks together with epoxy, as suggested by Gardner. About an ounce and a half of mixed epoxy is required for each blank. The actual amount will vary according to the length of the laminations and the thickness with which it is spread. Experience will dictate the proper amount. Appendix 3 details the mixing, handling, and safe use of epoxy.

We found a curious effect when clamping the glued stack using 4" C-clamps. With the stack against the form, should the C-clamp be placed so that the screw presses against the stack, or against the inside of the form? Intuitively, there should be no difference, but indeed, there seemed to be. When the cured stack was cut into individual ribs, there were times when gaps appeared between some of the laminations. This occurred when blanks were glued together with the C-clamp screws pressing on the *back* of the form. When the position of the clamps was reversed so that the screw pressed directly against the stack, no gaps appeared (Figure 6.6). Whether this effect was due primarily to improper clamping or to the orientation of the clamps is unknown.

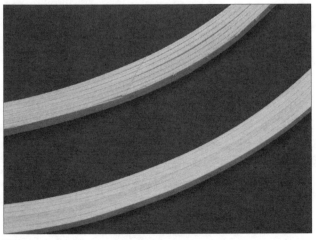

Figure 6.6

The rib at the top of the photo was glued with the C-clamp screw pressing the back of the form. The one at the bottom had the clamp screw pressing the laminations to the form.

The procedure for gluing is:

1. Mix 1½ oz. of epoxy, and thicken it with colloidal silica.[4] Sufficient silica has been added when the mix will not run off the end of the mixing stick. Approach this point carefully when adding silica so that the mixture is not overly thick. You may use some fast hardener along with the slow to hasten curing, but we do not recommend rapid curing. With MAS epoxy, the hardeners used are 75% slow and 25% fast.

2. Place the innermost lamination against the form. Spread thickened epoxy over the entire inner surface of the next lamination, using the mixing stick as if you were buttering toast. The coating should have a just visible thickness, but not to excess, and should not appear dry. Place the glued surface against the first lamination, making sure the ends are aligned.

3. Continue building the stack in this fashion, including the short rib foot laminations.

4. If any lamination ends do not line up, slide them into alignment by pushing at the ends.

5. Place a C-clamp near the sheer end and tighten it firmly, but not enough to squeeze out a lot of the epoxy and starve the joint. You should use a small block of waxed wood to cushion the screw end of the C-clamp. Add more clamps, moving sequentially to the foot end. Make sure no laminations rise above the stack. If any do, be sure to press them back down before tightening the clamps. If the stack extends beyond the end of the form, place a few small clamps on the extension to keep the ends of the laminations tight.

6. Verify that all of the clamps are sufficiently tight, and that the stack is flat on the bottom plate. The stack should be in contact with the form along its entire length. Do not tighten the clamps to the point where all of the glue is squeezed out, but visually examine the top of the stack to make sure there are no gaps (Figure 6.7).

7. Allow the stack to cure overnight. Test the squeeze-out the next day by pressing a fingernail into the surface. If it is easily dented, leave the clamps in place. When the glue is hardened so that the fingernail test shows a nearly complete cure, you may remove the clamps.

8. Now remove the blank (Figure 6.8). A putty knife may be required to help free the stack from the bottom plate.

Figure 6.7
Several clamps are required to insure the stack is perfectly pressed against the form.

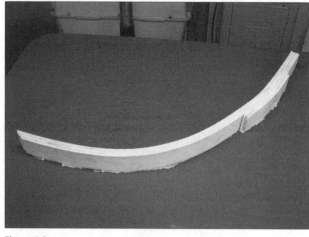

Figure 6.8
Glued rib blank after removal from form. You must remove the squeeze-out along the bottom front.

CLEANUP AND SHAPING

The glued blank does not look much like a stack of ribs at this point, as it requires the removal of a lot of squeezed out epoxy. The top of the blank has the most, it is very rough and lumpy, and the bottom should have the least and be quite smooth. There should not be any on the sides.

It is particularly important that the outside curve be free of any cured epoxy, since it will be the reference surface for the next step. Fortunately, that is the only epoxy that you must clean off with hand tools. Paint scrapers are effective here for roughing out the clean up, and the job can be finished with a cabinet scraper and block sanding. Sanding should only be done if the epoxy is hard. If it is not fully cured, it may clog the sandpaper. The stepped areas where the short rib foot laminations end do not need any cleaning other than to insure that the outer surface is also free of epoxy, and is smooth. There should be no epoxy blocking a smooth transition between the main outer curve of the rib and the outside surface of the foot laminations.

At this point, there is only one reference surface. The outside curve is free of epoxy, smooth, and will require no further clean up or shaping until mounted on the bottom board and the stripping begins. By holding that surface against the fence of a jointer, you can quickly clean up the bottom surface and make it square with the outer surface. The bottom does have some epoxy on it, but it is relatively flat and easily jointed. Be careful to remove the epoxy only down to a smooth clean wood surface. After completing this step, you now have two reference surfaces—the outer curve and the bottom (Figure 6.9). There is still a mess on the top of the blank, which you can take down parallel to the bottom surface with a thickness planer.

Before slicing the ribs from the blank, you must shape the rib foot. The bottoms of the ribs are reference surfaces, and will eventually be screwed to the bottom board. On the lofted drawings of the ribs, this edge is the base line. You must accurately maintain the angular relationship of this edge to the curve of the rib in order to produce a fair hull. The task at hand, then, is to reproduce the base line by cutting it from the rib blank.

You must make the cut square with the side of the blank, or the four ribs sliced from the blank will not be identical and the ribs will not mount square to the bottom board. This suggests using a table or band saw to make the cut. With a band saw, however, further cleanup will be required since a rip fence cannot be used, requiring a freehand cut. You may not be able to maintain the angular base/curve relationship, and the ribs, when mounted, could be out of fair.

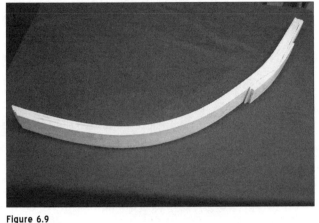

Figure 6.9
Rib blank cleaned and squared with the surface of the outer curve.

A table saw and a panel-cutting sled can be used to simply and accurately cut the rib foot bottom reference edge. But how do you place the irregularly shaped rib blank on the sled in the correct alignment and make the required cut? To do this, we need the rib pattern with the correct length of the rib foot already trimmed, and the bending form. On the pattern, make two somewhat arbitrary marks several inches apart on the inside of the curve. Somewhere around the transition of the foot to the curve, and near the sheer would be fine. Now lay the pattern on the bending form, and transfer the marks to the form, extending them to the top of the form. This step preserves the location of the marks so that you can accurately transfer them to the blank.

Lay the blank back on the bending form, and transfer the marks to the blank. You now have the marks on the blank in exactly the same location on the curve as on the pattern. Lay the pattern on top of the blank, align the marks, and trace the full shape of the rib on the blank. Trim the rib foot end off the blank as you did for the pattern. The pattern already has the base or bottom of the rib foot on it, so it follows that you may now cut the base on the blank using the marks as references.

Lay the pattern on the cutting sled with the trimmed rib foot end against the sled's fence, and the bottom of the foot exactly flush with the cutting edge of the sled. Hold it firmly, and transfer the marks to the sled. Now lay the blank, with the rib foot end trimmed, against the fence, and align the marks on it with the marks on the sled. Clamp it firmly to the sled and make the cut (Figure 6.10).

Figure 6.10
Cutting the rib foot bottom. Be careful with the position of the clamp nearest the blade.

The only thing left at this point is to cut the transition curve on the outboard side of the blank. If you have not already done it, trace the pattern onto the blank and make the cut with the band saw. Clean up the cut with the sanding drum or oscillating spindle sander, and trim the sheer end as long as possible (Figure 6.11).

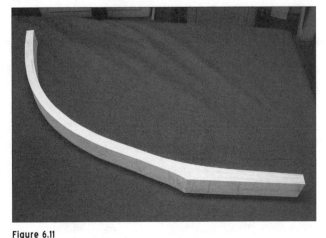

Figure 6.11
Cleaned and shaped blank, ready for slicing. You may trim the sheer end just enough to clean it up.

49

SLICING THE RIBS

The blank now looks like a guideboat rib, albeit quite wide. You have cleaned up the curves and foot and the top and bottom of the blank are parallel and square with the sides. All that is left is to slice off the four ribs. You can use either a band saw or table saw. For cutting with a band saw, a resawing blade and a fence are necessary and you must compensate for any blade drift before cutting begins. Verify the compensating fence angle using a piece of scrap before committing to the actual rib cutting. The band-sawn surface will be rougher than a table-sawn surface, so leave some additional width over and above the design rib thickness for smoothing.

With the table saw properly set up, it is a simple matter to run the blank through to cut the four ribs. After each pass, the cut surface remaining on the blank can be jointed or planed very lightly, only enough to remove the saw marks. This leaves a smooth flat surface for running against the fence for the next cut.

Slicing the ribs from the blank on the table saw demands strict attention to the job at hand, since you cannot use a blade guard. A sacrificial push stick is mandatory. We found that a piece of 1 by 2 about 10" long with a "bird mouth" notch cut into one end worked well. You may round the other end for comfort. You can maintain downward pressure with this simple tool, as well as forward feed pressure. The saw blade will cut into the push stick as the end of the work passes over the blade, but that is an essential contribution to safety.

The blade should be of the narrow kerf variety. We recommend a 7¼" blade with a 1⁄16" kerf. A "thin kerf" 10" blade has a kerf that is too wide. Also, a zero clearance insert should be prepared beforehand to fit the blade to be used. Because you must raise the blade to a height that will cut the thick portion of the rib foot, a significant portion of the blade is exposed. *Be careful!* There should be no distractions during the cut, and you must clear the table of anything but the blank and the push stick—standard table saw safety procedure.

Set the fence for a fat 5⁄16" cut, and adjust a wide feather board if used. It should be positioned at the infeed side of the blade, and must be repositioned before each cut. Lay the outside curve of the blank flat on the table with the side of the blank pushed against the fence.

Begin the cut by slowly feeding the blank into the blade, making sure to keep it against the fence and feeding it straight. Keeping the blank from twisting is important here to prevent binding and a possible thin spot in the finished rib. A higher accessory fence could be used, but we have not tried it.

You must roll the blank as it is being fed so that it can be cut all the way through. As you approach the end of the cut, use the push stick to complete the feed. Be sure to keep the side of the push stick flat against the fence, and maintain downward as well as forward pressure. The push stick will pass over the blade as the cut is completed. Repeat the sequence for the remaining ribs (Figures 6.12a and b).

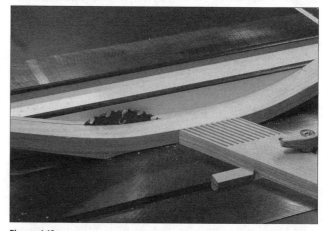

Figure 6.12a

Slicing the ribs on a table saw.

Figure 6.12b

The four ribs, as cut from the blank.

AN ALTERNATE METHOD FOR SHAPING RIBS

You can also shape rib blanks and stems very accurately using a router in a router table. If you have cut your patterns precisely, you can use them, along with a flush trim bit, to produce ribs and stems that match your patterns exactly (Figures 6.13a and b).

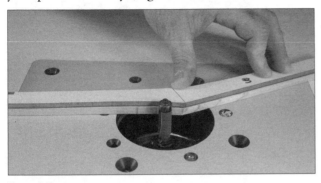

Figure 6.13a
Using the router to shape a rib.

Figure 6.13b
Note the pattern on top of the stock and the flush trim bit with the pilot bearing mounted above the cutter. Although a single rib is being shaped in the photo, thicker stock can be used to shape multiple ribs. This method also works nicely for shaping stems.

Begin by attaching the pattern to the shaped and squared rib or stem blank with double-stick tape. Place pieces of tape all along the underside of the pattern and make sure you securely fasten the pattern to the wood. If there is more than about $3/16$" of material around the pattern, remove it with the band saw. This minimizes the amount of wood you need to remove using the router and also results in a smoother cut.

Insert a flush trim-cutting bit in your router (use a bit with a $1/2$" diameter shank if possible for a smoother cut). Flush trim bits have the pilot bearing located *above* the cutter when mounted in a router table. This position allows you to work with the template on top of the wood, gives you a clear view of what you are

routing, and helps you to work more safely and accurately. In addition, when choosing a bit, carefully consider the thickness of the template as well as the thickness of the stock you wish to cut. Flush trim bits are available with cutting lengths ranging from $1/2$" to 2". You should use a bit long enough for the combined thickness of the pattern and stock to be cut. We find it easiest to cut the original rib blank into two pieces first, flush cut both halves, and then slice each half in two, yielding the four final rib pieces. Each stem section (inner and outer) can be routed separately.

To make the cut, turn the router on and *slowly* push the work piece into the bit. Move from right to left as you make the cut. Do NOT attempt to cut the ends of the rib (the 90° angle at the foot and at the sheer) with this method. This is not only unsafe, but doing so will inevitably result in tear-out, rendering the rib blank useless.

FINISHING UP

Before setting the nearly finished ribs aside to await mounting on the bottom board, a few final operations are necessary. First, identify each rib by marking its number on the bottom of the rib foot. This is the only surface that will not be affected by the operations to come.

Sanding the flat sides of each rib is next. Unless a thicknessing drum sander or oscillating spindle sander is available (see Figure 3.12), a random orbit sander or a hand-sanding block with 120-grit paper will suffice. We do not recommend thickness planing, since the planer knives will be cutting cross-grain due to the curve of the rib, and the planed surface would require further sanding anyway. You can sand all four ribs simultaneously provided you can hold them stationary. Sand each side of each rib, taking it down to the design thickness of $5/16$".

The next operation is rounding over the inside edges. This can be done using anything that works—sanding, a fine rasp, a sharp scraper—the objective being to round over the sharp edges. A table-mounted router with a $1/8$" radius round-over bit works well, followed by 120-grit sanding to remove the center ridge left by the routing operation.

51

Before doing the smoothing, be aware of how the ribs will be mounted. Take two ribs and hold the feet together as they will be mounted on the bottom board. Assume you are facing toward the bow of the boat. The port (left) rib should have its foot ahead of the starboard (right) rib, in keeping with the Grant design. The inside edges in the area where the feet overlap should not be rounded, merely lightly sanded to cut the sharp edge. You should round the area above the overlap to the end of the rib on both inboard edges. Do not do anything to the outboard edges.

Since the rib feet are already trimmed to the correct length, a bevel may be sanded on the vertical outside corner. Do any touch up sanding on the ribs now; doing it after the ribs are mounted is not impossible, but is not any fun either. The ribs are now complete. For convenient storage, wrap a rubber band around each end of the stack of four ribs, and set them aside.

1 Modern traditional builders may also use larch (also called tamarack) for sawn ribs.

2 Ford, Howard. "Building the Adirondack Guideboat," *WoodenBoat,* no. 18 (September/October 1977): p.55.

3 The clamps used for bending, and later for gluing, should have cushioned faces to prevent the marring of the soft wood. Small wood blocks may also be inserted between the clamp surface and the wood to be bent.

4 If using a structural adhesive epoxy such as T-88 made by System Three, no thickening is needed. Otherwise, the epoxy mix should be thickened with colloidal silica as described.

CHAPTER 7
CREATING THE SKELETON

In this chapter, we focus on the frame of the guide-boat: the skeleton upon which the stripping is applied, and the phase of construction that determines the guideboat's graceful lines, maneuverability, and durability. This chapter will describe how to build the bottom board, the backbone of a guideboat, and how to fasten the ribs to it.

The guideboat's graceful lines and elegant curves are a pleasure to the eye, but there is also a functional beauty in the way it moves through the water. A guideboat tracks straight, is remarkably swift, even when burdened with a heavy load, and is quiet, particularly when handled by a skilled rower.

As the guideboat's design evolved, it was refined to achieve these properties, especially its light weight. Its lines, curves, bottom board design, light weight, and smooth skin all work together to make the boat a pleasure to row. One reason for the boat's swiftness is a simple design feature of the bottom board, which, if overlooked, can seriously impede the performance of the boat. We will talk about this next.

THE CONCEPT OF ROCKER
On paper, the guideboat looks to be a completely flat-bottomed craft. However, if placed on a flat surface such as a dock, garage floor, or driveway, it becomes apparent that each end of the bottom board rises off the surface. The bottom board in fact is flat for a short distance amidships, but then begins a gradual rise toward the ends, where the rise is an inch or so above the otherwise flat plane (Figure 7.1). This is a critically important feature in guideboat design, as it reduces the hull's resistance as it moves through the water. In

effect, as the boat moves, it literally cuts through the water faster and quieter with less drag—at both ends.

Figure 7.1
Bottom board rocker.

"Rocker," this upturn in the bottom board, also helps the boat to pivot more easily. The rower needs only to pull on one oar while pushing on the other to turn the boat. This kind of maneuverability is simply not possible with a flat-bottomed boat, and if you do not incorporate rocker into the construction, the boat will not perform as a guideboat should. Fortunately, this is not difficult to do. It requires the construction of what Grant and other builders referred to as a "stock plank."

BUILDING THE STOCK PLANK
A stock plank is nothing more than a long wooden board on which a convex or concave edge is faired. Its purpose is to force the bottom board, with ribs attached, to take the shape of the stock plank's edge, and to keep that shape as the siding is applied. When siding is applied with the boat in the upright position (bottom board down), as was the case in Grant's boat shop, a concave-edged stock plank is used. When the

boat is sided with the bottom board up, a convex-edge is applied to the stock plank. This was the method used by the builders Theodore and Willard Hanmer of Saranac Lake, New York, and the method we have adopted for building our boats.

John Gardner provides the measurements for a 13' stock plank in Plate VIII. Although this is the appropriate length for the *Virginia* with its 14'6" bottom board, the measurements given are for cutting a concave edge. As our stock plank requires a convex edge, a different set of measurements is needed. You will note that Gardner's drawing indicates a 5" wide stock plank. The width of the plank is not terribly important, though it should be approximately 5" for stability and durability.

Your first decision in constructing the stock plank is the type of board to use. The simplest and least expensive alternative is to obtain a common 14-foot 2 by 6 board available from lumberyards or home improvement centers. The actual dimension of these boards is 1½" x 5½". If you choose this option, sort through the boards to find one that is flat and free of twists, and with as few knots and surface defects as possible. Keep in mind that every board will have a natural crown on one edge. The opposite edge will be concave. Try to find one with as slight a crown and concave edge as possible.

A second option for the stock plank is to purchase a higher-grade board at a lumberyard, cabinet shop, or custom mill. Yet a third option might be to laminate a board using plywood. For example, you could laminate two pieces of standard ¾" plywood together to get a 1½" thick board. Whichever way you go, the goal is to end up with a relatively flat, twist-free board no less than 13' in length. We prefer the first two options because it is sometimes necessary to hand plane the final convex edge of the board to remove any bumps or depressions left by sawing, and to achieve a fair curve.

The board you choose for the stock plank will need a straight reference line near one edge from which all measurements are made. To do this, first locate the crowned edge of the board, and mark it as such. Next, snap a tight chalk line the length of the board, making sure that line falls completely on the plank. Next, cut the board to exactly 13', and then draw a centerline at 6' 6". This centerline serves as a point of reference for aligning the stock plank to the bottom board later. Working from one end of the board to the other, make a mark every 12" along the chalked reference line. With your square, draw a 2" line down from each point along the reference line. For reference, label these lines 1', 2', 3', etc., all the way up to 12' (0' and 13' can be used to reference the ends).

Using the measurements in Table 7.1, work from one end of the board to the other, and measure down from the chalked reference line of the board as indicated.

TABLE 7.1
STOCK PLANK MEASUREMENTS*

AT THIS LINE	0'	1'	2'	3'	4'	5'	6'
	13'	12'	11'	10'	9'	8'	7'
MEASURE DOWN	1"	¾"	⁷⁄₁₆"	¼"	⅛"	¹⁄₁₆"	0"

* Note that the measurements for 7' through 13' are the same as those for 0' through 6'.

Attach a flexible batten to the board, making sure to line it up with the marks you just made. Tack the batten in place using brads or small finish nails, or hold it in place with small clamps or weights. Now trace along the batten from one end of the board to the other. Remove the batten.

Now you are ready to cut the curve. Use a jigsaw for this cut and make sure that you leave the pencil line. Once you make the cut, use a hand plane to smooth out the convex edge. Check by eye for a fair curve. Do not worry if you plane past the pencil line; the idea here is to get a fair curve on your board. With a combination square, draw a centerline along the entire curved edge of the stock plank. This line serves to align the stock plank and bottom board accurately when you fasten them together.

Now you are ready to cut the notches on the stock plank so it can fit over the ribs on your bottom board. You may do this now by measurement and layout, or you can wait until you mount the ribs on the bottom board and use the actual mounted rib positions for layout.

To do it now, locate the center of the stock plank and draw a line down from the rockered edge marking the *center* of a notch for the rib 0 position. Draw similar notch centerlines every 5⅛" out to each end. Be sure to check your layout now; once the notches are cut, it is too late. Using a piece of scrap about ⅞" wide and 1¼" long as a notch template, center it over the notch centerlines and trace the notch outlines. Saw the sides of the notches and knock out the waste plug with a mallet and chisel. Finally, if you are going to mount your stock plank to construction stanchions, drill three holes on the side of the stock plank about ½" in diameter.

As an example, consider the dimensions shown in Figure 7.2. These holes should be positioned about 1¾" up from the bottom edge of the stock plank. The two outer holes are 19¼" in from the ends; the middle hole is 80⅝" from the 0' end. The purpose of these holes is for fastening the stock plank to the construction jigs, which we will make next.

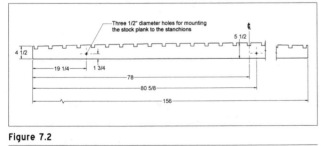

Figure 7.2
Stock plank dimensions. (Drawn by Rob Axelson.)

BUILDING THE CONSTRUCTION JIGS

There are probably as many ways to support the stock plank and bottom board during the stripping or planking process as there are guideboat builders.

Grant's method was to support the entire assemblage using an elaborate floor and ceiling fixture that allowed the hull to be planked while at different heights. Because boats in his shop were planked right side up, it was necessary to be able to adjust the height of the hull as the planking progressed.

Our method of supporting the hull during stripping is more closely aligned with that used by Theodore and Willard Hanmer in their Saranac Lake boat shop. Their setup is part of a permanent exhibit at the Adirondack Museum in Blue Mountain Lake, New York.

Although there are many variations of this design, we show the two that we have used in Figures 7.3a and b. Regardless of the design, three stanchions are required for stability. They are simple to build, and can be constructed of standard 2-by and 1-by pine lumber. The stanchions shown in Figure 7.3a are adjustable in height and use oak 2 by 3s to tie the jigs together and to provide more weight and stability, while those in Figure 7.3b are of a fixed height and are fastened to a strongback used to make cedar strip canoes. Both designs use a different method for attaching the stock plank and bottom board. You can use these stanchions to work the final dimensions of the bottom board, to fasten ribs to the bottom board, and to fasten the stock plank and bottom board/rib assembly for stripping.

Figure 7.3a
Example of a construction jig or stanchion.

Figure 7.3b

The stanchion shown above is built on a strongback commonly used for strip building canoes and kayaks.

During the stripping process, you will be alternating from one side of the boat to the other after the third or fourth strip, so you can modify the jigs to provide a convenient place to store the strips during the process. Figures 7.4a and b illustrate one of the stanchion designs in more detail. The center post is adjustable and is simply held in place with a ½" dowel inserted in predrilled holes.

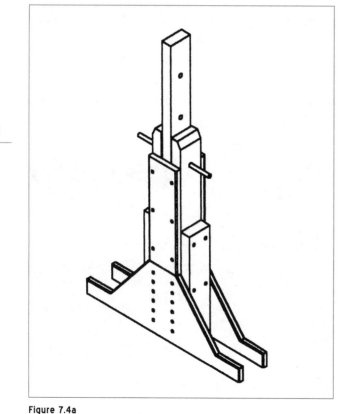

Figure 7.4a

Angled view of stanchion. (Drawn by Rob Axelson.)

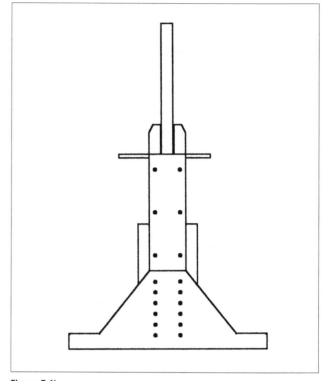

Figure 7.4b

Side view of stanchion. (Drawn by Rob Axelson.)

BUILDING THE BOTTOM BOARD

The bottom board is one of the most essential components of the guideboat. More than any other facet of its construction, the bottom board gives the Adirondack guideboat its distinctive shape. Its length and width, along with an elliptical taper and a rolling bevel on its edge, combine to make this one piece of pine the true backbone of the guideboat. In addition to its importance, the bottom board is one of the most pleasing elements to work on, particularly if you like to work with hand planes and spokeshaves.

Begin with a clear 1 by 10-pine board, approximately 16' long. The board should be as clear and as flat as possible, relatively straight-grained, and free of defects and knots. A few small, tight knots are acceptable, but you run the risk of having one or more of them lie exactly where a screw needs to be placed. Time spent obtaining as good a piece of pine as possible is well worth the effort in the end.

You are not likely to find a board like this at your local home center or lumberyard, unless they carry a very select grade of pine. Check with small independent sawmills if you can, as many of them can custom cut boards for you if they do not already have in stock what you are looking for. If you happen upon more than one good board, consider purchasing at least one more. Furniture quality planks are rare and hard to come by, and we can almost guarantee that once you complete your boat, you *will* want to build another!

We know of at least one contemporary guideboat builder who joined three narrow boards together with glue and biscuits to get the width he needed, not having been able to find a suitable wide board. You should only do this as a last resort, as the bottom board is probably the one structural component of the craft that should not be compromised in any way. Joint failure is a risk you do not want to worry about here.

Once you have a suitable board, plane it to a thickness of ½" before cutting it to its final length of 14'6". It is important not to cut it to length first. The planer may snipe the ends of the board and you would not be able to remove it if you cut the board to length before planing.

Bottom boards not only varied in shape from one builder to another, but in thickness as well. This variation probably continues today. Bottom board thickness ranged anywhere from ½" for builders such as Grant to ¾" or more for builders like Warren Cole of Long Lake, New York and the Hanmers. Some builders were willing to sacrifice weight for the extra durability afforded by a thicker bottom board.

However, a ½"-thick bottom board is quite sufficient. Not only does it cut down on weight, but because the ribs are spaced along its length at relatively close intervals, they provide it protection and reinforcement. A ½" bottom board is more than adequate with respect to durability and structural integrity.

After you have planed the board to its final thickness of ½", sand it smooth, particularly the surface upon which you will mount the ribs. Sanding now serves two purposes: you can more easily mark rib placements on the surface and, once the ribs are mounted,

it will be difficult to do any large-scale sanding later. Next, draw a line at one end of the board with your square, measure exactly 14'6" from the line to the other end, and draw another line square with the edge. You will cut the board to length between the lines later.

The next step is to mark a line down the exact center of both sides of the board. You can use a snap line for this, but the result will more than likely be an unacceptably thick, blurry line. You will be more accurate if you use an adjustable square. Run the square along one edge of the board, from one end to the other, while marking the centerline with a sharp, but soft, dark pencil (Figure 7.5).[1] Turn the board over and do the same to the other side, making sure to run the square along the same edge of the board.

Figure 7.5
Drawing a centerline along the length of the board.

57

Once you have both lines drawn down the entire length of the board and on both sides, mark the exact centerline of the board, at 7'3", across its width, again on both sides. Make sure these centerlines meet at both edges. Now you are ready to transfer the pattern to the pine board (Figure 7.6).

Line up the quarter pattern at one end of the board and align its long straight edge with the centerline running along the length of the board. Make sure the centerline of the pattern, indicated by the red ink line at 7'3", lines up exactly with the centerline across the width of the board. Trace the curved edge of the pattern to the bottom board with a sharp pencil. Repeat this process for the remaining three quarters of the bottom board. The extra length of the pattern helps to insure proper alignment on the board before final marking.

Figure 7.6
Transferring the quarter pattern.

Once you have the bottom board pattern laid out, check all your measurements carefully, making sure the elliptical shape is fair and symmetrical. Before doing any cutting, and while you still have straight edges to work from, you will need to lay out rib mounting position lines on the board.

At this point, you have four important reference lines on both sides of the bottom board: the two ends and the exact centerlines across the width and length of the board. Before proceeding, decide on which surface of the bottom board you will mount the ribs and label it as such for future reference.

The 7'3" centerline serves as the location for the center, or 0 pair of ribs. From that centerline, work toward each end of the bottom board, and using a sharp pencil (a fine point mechanical pencil is a good choice here), mark a line every $5\frac{1}{8}$". With your square, draw the lines across the entire width of the board. Again using the square, continue the lines down both edges of the board.

Turn the board over, and connect the edge lines, in effect duplicating the lines on the reverse side. It is very important that these lines connect exactly, as you will use them to determine screw placement when mounting the ribs. As illustrated in Gardner's Plate I, label each of the lines, on both sides of the board, to

correspond to their respective rib pairs: e.g., 0^1, 0^2, 0^3, etc., all the way to 12. At this point, you should also designate one end of the board as "Stern," and the other as "Bow."

Next, you need to mark three locations along the centerline of the bottom board, one between rib locations 0 and 0^1 (either stern-side or bow-side), and the other two between rib locations 7 and 8 (one on the stern-side; the other on the bow-side). At each of these three locations, drill a $\frac{1}{2}$" or $\frac{3}{8}$" hole through the bottom board. Using a Forstner or brad-point bit, drill from the inside (rib) surface of the bottom board and place a piece of scrap wood underneath where the drill bit will exit to avoid tear out. These holes will be used to mount the bottom board to the stock plank and will be plugged before the boat is finished.

Using a handsaw, jigsaw, or circular saw, carefully cut the bottom board to length. Leave the pencil line so you have room to trim the ends square if needed (Figure 7.7). Next, clamp the board securely and carefully cut out the bottom board using a jigsaw with a fine-tooth finish blade. Follow the curve from one end of the board to the other, taking extra care to leave the pencil line.

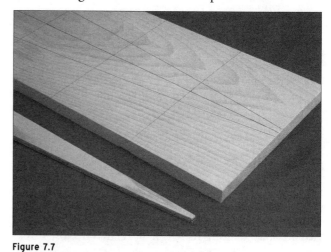

Figure 7.7
Bottom board (with pattern) showing end cut.

Once you have the elliptical shape of the board cut (Figure 7.8), trim the edges with a low angle block plane or spoke shave. Make sure the edges remain square to the surface. Double check the final bottom board dimensions against those on the quarter pattern. Pay particularly close attention to the ends of the bottom board, where the stems will be attached.

Looking head-on at each end, they should measure exactly ½" by ½", a perfect square.

Figure 7.8
Bottom board trimmed to final dimensions.

FORMING THE ROLLING BEVELED EDGES

Each individual rib pattern for the guideboat has a different angle between the heel and the start of the curved side. This angle must be transferred to the bottom board as a bevel along both edges in order for the stripping to fit flush against both the ribs and the bottom board. The rolling bevel occurs because the angle gradually changes from amidships toward bow or stern, where the edge of the bottom board is exactly perpendicular to its surface.

Creating the rolling bevel is much simpler than it appears. To simulate a cross-section of the bottom board at each rib position, draw a series of ½" high by 6" wide (or longer) rectangles on a sheet of paper or scrap wood. Beginning with rib pattern 0, position the pattern so that the bottom edge of its foot sits exactly on the top line of the rectangle, and the heel of the rib (the outermost point on the foot) sits exactly at the vertical line on the left side of the rectangle (or at the right if you are doing this in reverse).

With a sharp pencil, draw a line that continues the angle of the heel down to the bottom line of the rectangle (Figure 7.9). Measure back from this point to the lower left corner of the rectangle. Record this distance, and repeat the process for the remaining rib patterns 1 through 12. Your measurements should approximate

those in Table 7.2. This is a somewhat imprecise method, but as long as you take the measurements the same way for each rib (using a sharp pencil and positioning the ribs accurately) you will be fine. We suggest you take the measurements more than once. If you get the same measurements twice, you are all set! Also, keep in mind that to achieve a fair hull, you will probably have to make minor adjustments to the rolling bevel once you start applying the stripping.

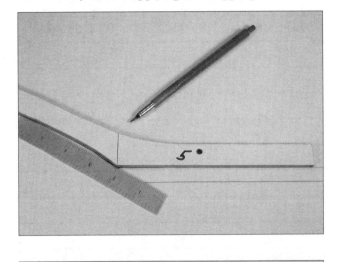

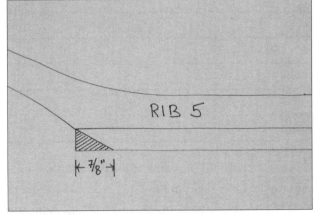

Figure 7.9
Laying out the bottom board bevels (rib 5 shown).

The measurements for the widths of the bevel at each rib position may be alternatively determined on the lofted rib drawings using a similar approach. Extend the rib curve below the baseline of the drawing to intersect a line parallel to the baseline ½" below it. Make the measurements as shown in Figure 7.9.

Now position your bottom board on a flat surface with the underside of the board (the side which will be underwater) facing you. With your measurements in hand, begin transferring them to the bottom board. With the same measuring rule you used to take the measurements, work back from the edge of the bottom board and transfer each measurement to its corresponding rib centerline on both edges of the bottom board.

TABLE 7.2
APPROXIMATE ROLLING
BEVEL MEASUREMENTS

STATION (RIB)	DISTANCE FROM EDGE (INCHES)
All 0 ribs	1⅛"
1	1⅛"
2	1¹⁄₁₆"
3	1"
4	¹⁵⁄₁₆"
5	⅞"
6	¾"
7	⅝"
8	⁹⁄₁₆"
9	⅜"
10	¼"
11	³⁄₁₆"
12	⅛"
End of board	0"

Once you make all of your marks, use a flexible batten to connect the points along each edge, being attentive to the fairness of the curve. Work from the middle of the board (amidships) out toward each end, where the batten should be exactly flush with the edge (no angle). Trace the curves with a sharp pencil. After both bevel lines are drawn, sight down along their length to check for fairness. If everything you have done up to this point has been consistent, both bevel lines should appear fair and symmetrical.

The next step in preparing the bottom board is to create the bevel on both of its edges. The best way to accomplish this is to use a sharp hand plane or spoke shave to remove the bulk of the waste material

between the edge of the board and the pencil line you just drew, finishing with a block plane. Work from the center toward the ends to prevent tear-out. You may find it easier at this point to mount your bottom board on whatever construction jigs you have built in order to get it up to a reasonable working height (Figure 7.10). It is certainly acceptable to work the bevel with the bottom board fastened securely to a flat work surface if that is more convenient.

Begin by using a hand plane to shave away the wood between the inside edge and the pencil line. The wood you should remove is shown in Figure 7.9 as the shaded portion in the bottom photo. Pay close attention to the inside edge, taking care not to dent it, chip it, or change it in any way. It is a good idea not to plane the outside of the bevel to a knife edge, but leave a small flat not planed—no more than about ¹⁄₃₂". Work with the grain, and as you work the bevel down close to its final dimensions, switch to a sharp low-angle block plane or a spoke shave set for a very fine or shallow cut, removing only paper-thin shavings with each pass. Check the flatness of the bevel along the full length of each edge of the bottom board with a straight edge and remove any bumps or depressions. Periodically check by eye for fairness.

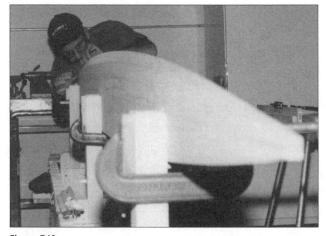

Figure 7.10
Shaping the bevel on the bottom board.

ATTACHING THE RIBS

Congratulations! You have completed the backbone of your boat. Now it is time to attach the ribs. This is a momentous occasion; the point at which the vessel begins to take shape (at least in skeletal form) and the result of a lot of hard work on your part begins to come together.

If you have not already done so, mount your beveled bottom board securely on the construction jigs, but first take some time to remove any markings (except rib positions), center lines, etc., that appear on the inside of the bottom board and on the ribs. Do a final finish sanding on the inside of the bottom board now, before the ribs are mounted; it will save you hours of frustration trying to sand later. Leave a little of the centerline at the ends of the bottom board to aid in aligning the inner stems later.

To mount the bottom board on the stanchions, simply hang or clamp it to the uprights as shown in Figure 7.10. Position the jigs so that you have access to both sides of the bottom board. You will also need to have some spring clamps or Quick-Grip clamps handy, a drill with a ⅛" diameter taper point bit, a countersink for use with #6 screws, a screwdriver (ratcheting or battery-powered screwdrivers work nicely for this operation), and at least seventy 1¼" and seventy 1" x #6 slotted flat-head brass screws. The drill and countersink may be a Fuller bit, which combines both into a single bit, and therefore into a single operation.

Begin with the pair of center, or 0, ribs. Place one rib from the pair on the bottom board with its inside edge positioned exactly on the line you drew on the inside of the bottom board indicating the centerline of the two ribs. The heel of the rib should be positioned exactly at the edge of the bottom board (Figure 7.11). For the center few ribs where the bottom board edge bevel is almost straight, hold a short length of scrap cedar strip on the bevel to act as a positioning stop.

When you are satisfied with its alignment, clamp it securely and screw it in place as described below. Repeat this process for the opposite rib by placing the inside edge of its foot tight against the inside edge of the first rib's foot (Figure 7.12). Place a spring clamp[2] over the paired rib feet to keep them tight against one another. Note that in the original *Virginia,* the rib pairs are positioned such that the port rib is forward of the starboard.

Figure 7.11
Attaching the first rib.

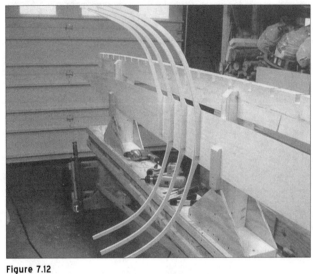

Figure 7.12
Pairs of ribs mounted.

61

As you mount the ribs further away from center, the bottom board edge takes on more of a curve. Position the ribs such that the corner of the heel towards the center of the boat is at the edge of the bottom board, leaving the leading edge overhanging. This overhang is a very small amount initially, but is significant in the higher numbered ribs. You will fair off the overhang later, resulting in a smooth tight joint between the rib and stripping.

SCREW ALIGNMENT AND INSERTION

Fasten each individual rib to the bottom board with two brass screws, one close to the heel of the rib and one close to the toe. Locate the centerline for the 0 ribs on the underside of the bottom board. Remember that this line indicates the exact center of the pair of ribs—

the point at which each rib foot fits against its mate. When fastening the ribs to the bottom board with the brass screws, you need to take extra care to make sure you center the screws in each rib (Figure 7.13). Even a slight variation right or left can cause a screw to tear out of the rib or cause an unsightly bulge.

Figure 7.13
Rib screw pattern on bottom board.

It is best to use the appropriately sized taper point Fuller bit with the countersink cutter installed and drill/countersink in a single operation. If you miss-drill a hole, drill it out to ⅛", plug the hole with a glued dowel, and start over. This allows you to reposition the new hole without drilling into the old hole and maintains the aesthetic line-up of all the screws.

If you constructed your ribs to be ⁵⁄₁₆" wide, the center of each rib foot will be ⁵⁄₃₂" to the right and left of the centerline. Carefully drill a ⅛" pilot hole through the bottom board into the heel of one of the ribs, approximately 1" from the edge of the bevel into the foot of each rib.

Gardner's Plate V serves as a good reference for screw positioning, but exercise caution when using this drawing. Locating the screws with respect to the outer edge of the bottom board will give a visual line of screws that is not parallel to the finished visible curve of the bottom board. This is because of the varying width of the rolling bevel. For this reason, it is advisable to position the screw line with reference to the inner edge of the bevel.

Drill only as far as necessary for a 1¼" screw, and be sure to countersink the hole so the head of the screw sits just below the surface of the bottom board. Place a little soap or wax on the screw and fasten the heel to the bottom board.

If you feel or see a bulge beginning to occur as you drive the screw in, back it out and re-drill the hole to straighten it out or follow the re-drilling and plugging sequence outlined previously. Do not over tighten the screw; doing so increases the risk of snapping off the screw head.

Repeat the process at the toe of the rib, locating the pilot hole approximately 1" back from the edge of the toe, again being careful to center the screw into the rib. Once you fasten the rib, do the same with its mate.

Repeat this process for each pair of ribs through pair 10. Note that as the feet become shorter, the heel and toe screws get closer to one another. Be careful in these instances not to locate screws too close to the edge of a toe, as this increases the likelihood the rib will split.

Ribs 11 and 12 are referred to as scribe or footless ribs. Because they do not have feet like the others, you cannot fasten them to the bottom board in the same manner. We will describe the method for attaching these ribs a little later in this section.

If you have not yet cut the notches in the stock plank, or chose to use the actual mounted ribs to locate the notches, now is the time to cut them. To do this, you will need to place the stock plank on the ribs after they have been fastened to the bottom board. Line up the 6'6" centerline on your stock plank with the exact center of the bottom board—this should be 7'1½", at the center of the rib 0 pair. Make sure you have the convex edge of the stock plank sitting on the ribs.

Now simply mark the position of the ribs onto the stock plank. Remove the stock plank and square up the lines. The ribs are approximately ¾" high where they are fastened at the middle of the bottom board, so your notches can be about 1" deep. Once you have the notches located and drawn, cut them using your jigsaw. You can also cut these notches using a hole-cutting saw or simply cut the sides and knock out the waste with a sharp chisel struck with a mallet.

ATTACHING THE INNER STEMS

With few exceptions, the stems in the traditional guideboats were made from a single piece cut from a spruce crook, with rolling rabbets cut along each side to accept the ends of the pine planks. Our modification to this design is that we use a two-piece stem. The inner stem is laminated similar to the ribs (see Chapter 4), and the outer is a solid piece of hardwood of the builder's choosing, attached after stripping is complete. When the hull is stripped, the inner stem is shaped with a rolling bevel so that the strips will lie flat in total contact with it. The ends of the strips are trimmed flush with the outer leading edge of the stem.

In order for all of the strips to lie flat in a straight line on both sides, we must have some sort of guide or lines to act as stops while performing the shaping. We will shape the stems so that there remains a ¼" wide flat unshaped area running the length of the outside of the stem. This flat area approximates what would have been exposed if we had actually cut an original one-piece stem apart along the rabbet line. It is the bottom of the rabbet that we will be shaping as a rolling bevel.

Before going any further, familiarize yourself with Gardner's Plates VI and VII, which detail the design of the stems of the *Virginia*.

Begin by drawing lines ⅛" on either side of a centerline drawn full length along the outside leading edge of the stem. This defines the ¼" area described above that you will not shape—at no time should you do any cutting or sanding between these lines. We will be removing wood up to these lines, forming a flat, angled area on the sides of the stems to which we will fasten the ends of the strips. It can be seen that the cross section of the stem will be somewhat triangular, with the tip of the triangle cut off to a ¼" flat. Make a center mark on the inboard section of the inner

stem at the foot to aid in aligning the stem with the bottom board centerline. The inner stems should already be notched to fit the bottom board, but if not, you will need to do that now. As noted in Gardner's Plate VI, this notch is 3½" long and ⁷⁄₁₆" deep.

Although not functionally necessary, the square end of the foot should be rounded at this point for a more aesthetically pleasing and refined appearance. This feature is noted in Gardner's drawing of the inner stem in Plate VI. Doing the final softening of the inside edges and sanding the inner portions of the stems can best be accomplished before the stems are mounted to the bottom board.

Once you cut the notch, attach the inner stem to the bottom board by lining up the centerlines on the stem with the centerline on the bottom board. Clamp the stem in place and check for an accurate fit. You may need to work the end of the bottom board and/or the notch to insure a tight, gap-free fit.

When you are satisfied with the fit, drill two ⅛" diameter holes from the underside and along the centerline of the bottom board into the inner stem. Locate the outermost (outboard) hole approximately 1" and the innermost hole approximately 2⅝" from the tip of the bottom board. Countersink both holes. Permanently fasten the inner stem to the bottom board with a #6 x 1¼" slotted brass screw in the outboard hole and a #6 x 1" screw in the inboard hole (Figure 7.14). Repeat this process for the other inner stem.

Before proceeding any further, stand back and take a look at what you have accomplished (Figure 7.15). Go ahead and pat yourself on the back. This is a major step toward the completion of your boat. You also now have an appreciation for why this chapter has the title we gave it!

Earlier in this chapter, we described how to build a stock plank. If you have not built one yet, this is the time to do it. It will be required during the next phase of construction, along with the construction jigs you may have already been using.

Figure 7.14
Stem attached to bottom board. This stem has been faired for planking.

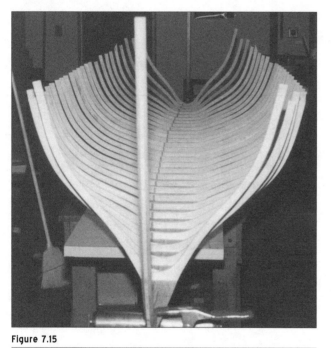

Figure 7.15
Ribs and inner stems attached.

MOUNTING THE BOTTOM BOARD TO THE STOCK PLANK

Fasten the stock plank securely to your construction stanchions with the notched edge facing up. With a helper at the other end, turn the bottom board (with ribs attached) over and carefully set the skeleton on top of the stock plank. Align the notches over their corresponding ribs. Make sure the centerline that you drew along the curved edge of the stock plank shows in the center of the three holes you drilled through the bottom board.

When the alignment is satisfactory, clamp the bottom board securely to the stock plank at each end. Drill a pilot hole into the stock plank at each hole in the bottom board to accept a #8 screw. Cut three wood spacers from a piece of ½" thick scrap stock or plywood, approximately 2" square (or another shape if you prefer—ours are triangular like those used by Grant). Drill a hole through the center of each spacer. Place a spacer over each hole and fasten the bottom board to the stock plank at each location with #8 x 3½" roundhead wood screws and washers. Remove the clamps and check the assembly. The bottom board should contact the stock plank along its entire surface.

You may need to put the clamps back on at the ends to insure that the bottom board does not rise off the surface of the stock plank, thus decreasing the final rocker distance. However, once you attach the alignment battens, this should no longer be a concern and you can remove the clamps.

Before going further, check the mounted bottom board in several places for level across its width and shim if necessary. This will assure a fair hull with no twist, and remove a variable when you install the alignment battens and determine the sheer line.

THE ALIGNMENT BATTENS

The assembly thus far is the skeleton of the hull. The first concern is the fairness of the ribs overall. Do the ribs present a fair support for the surface of the hull? By sighting down the assembly, are any ribs sticking above or below their mates? If you place a strip over the ribs, are there any ribs that are above or below the strip? If there are any misaligned ribs, you must adjust them before stripping can begin.

Misaligned ribs are usually due to the incorrect angle of the rib foot with respect to the curve. If the heel of the rib foot is too high or the toe is low, the rib will be tilted inward. Just the opposite will result with the heel low and the toe high. Fortunately, repairing a misaligned rib is not difficult, but it does take some time. Since you cut the entire rib set of four rib halves from the same blank, it is likely that all four of the ribs require adjustment.

To effect the repair, remove the ribs from the assembly. Fill the screw holes in the bottom of the rib foot by drilling the holes out to ⅛" and gluing pieces of dowel rod into the holes. With the rib foot now solid wood, glue a strip of spruce lamination stock onto the bottom and trim it flush. When the glue has cured, re-cut the rib foot to the correct angle and reinstall it on the bottom board.

With the assembly on the stock plank, the ribs hang downward with no other support. You must clamp or fasten a batten, usually a full-length sacrificial strip, to the rib ends external to the final position of the sheer line. The purpose of the batten is twofold: to hold the rib ends firmly in position, and to provide a bearing edge around which bungees are later wrapped during stripping.

You can easily fasten the batten to the ribs with the same size screws that you will use to fasten the stripping. There is no critical need to fair the ribs here, but doing so makes for a tighter fit of the alignment batten against the ribs. We suggest fairing at the stems so that the batten will act as a reference for later stem shaping.

One question that arises at this point concerns the angle of the ribs with respect to the bottom board. If there were no rocker on the bottom board, all of the ribs would be at right angles to it. But we have a slight amount of rocker, or curve, on the bottom board, and the ribs are no longer parallel. This is easily overcome by spacing the rib ends along the alignment batten with the same spacing at which they are fastened to the bottom board. To do this, we use rib 0 as the starting point.

If not already done, mark the location of the sheer on rib 0. There should be a mark on the rib 0 pattern indicating the position of the sheer that you can transfer to the actual rib 0. The approximate location of

the sheer on the remaining ribs is similarly marked, the locations having been given in Gardner's Plate II.

First screw the middle of the alignment batten securely to the rib 0 end outside of the sheer line by about ½". You can then loosely clamp the ends of the batten to the stems and at a few ribs to hold the approximate position. Note that we are not too concerned with a fair line here just yet, but are simply using a temporary method to align and secure the rib ends.

Now measure the distance between rib 0 and one of the adjacent 0^1 ribs at the bottom board. Use this measurement to position the 0^1 rib along the batten from rib 0, where you will securely fasten it. Hold the position with one hand squeezing the batten to the rib, and drill a pilot screw hole with the other hand. Then drive a screw to complete the fastening.

The next rib to be fastened in the same manner is the opposite rib 0^1. Continue along the batten, measuring the distance between ribs at the bottom board and fastening the rib ends to the batten that same distance apart, alternating fastening ribs fore and aft to prevent warping or distortion. Secure the ribs on the opposite side of the hull the same way. Be sure to leave about ½" gap between the alignment batten and the expected sheer line.

Since the ribs are mounted at precise 5⅛" intervals and are all 5⁄16" thick, one might assume that measuring between ribs at the bottom board is unnecessary. This is theoretically true, but in actual practice, any error in mounting the ribs could lead to the introduction of an error that would continue out to the last rib fastened to the alignment batten. The effect would be skewed ribs, with the severity of the skewing depending on the number and magnitude of the errors. We found that the inter-rib measurements varied by up to about ¹⁄16". We, therefore, advise that you measure each inter-rib distance.

Also, as the bow and stern are approached, the alignment batten slopes further away from the bottom

65

board. Be careful to measure from one rib end directly across to the next, parallel to the bottom board and not along the alignment batten.

You have now made the assembly more rigid. Additional bracing is suggested, and can be done by mounting cross bracing between the battens and fastening them to the support stanchions. Shim blocks may be required between the brace and the stanchion (Figure 7.16).

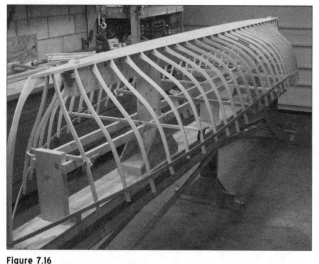

Figure 7.16
Mounted skeleton, showing alignment battens and additional bracing.

SCRIBE RIBS

In most standard length Grant guideboats, the end two pairs of ribs (ribs 11 and 12) had no feet and were simply scribed to ¾". These were not installed until after the hull had been planked, and required a rolling bevel to fair the mounting surfaces—a difficult task to perform with an acceptable degree of accuracy. With our hulls inverted and the stock plank *inside* the boat as opposed to a concave stock plank outside the boat, it is possible to install the scribe ribs prior to any stripping. This allows for the fairing of these ribs along with the others as you strip the hull.

Once the footed ribs are mounted and the alignment batten installed, the scribed ribs can be held in place using ⅛" dowels driven through the bottom board and into the ends of ribs 11 and 12. Clamp the ribs temporarily to the alignment batten and drill the holes with a ⅛" diameter brad point bit, being sure to hold the rib

tightly in place and the drill bit square with the bottom board. Lightly sand a chamfer on the end of a piece of dowel rod, apply some glue, and insert the dowel through the bottom board and into the hole in the end of the rib. A little bit of glue may also be used on the bottom of the rib to help secure it to the bottom board. Trim the end of the dowel flush with the bottom board.

With ribs 11 and 12 mounted as described above, make certain that their bottom ends are contacting the bottom board, and screw their outer ends to the alignment batten at their final position. The bottom shoe strips, installed when the boat is nearly complete, will cover the dowel ends.

1 Soft pine is easily dented by the pressure of a sharp pencil, leaving a line that is extremely difficult to sand off. A very light touch is recommended, and the resulting line can usually be erased later with an ordinary rubber eraser or by wiping with mineral spirits, followed by sanding.

2 Inexpensive spring clamps may have the cushioned tips worn to the point where the sharp metal ends have cut through the cushioning, which will mar the wood. A quick fix is to remove the existing cushioning, and slip a short piece of plastic or rubber tubing over the metal ends.

CHAPTER 8
THE STRIPS

Perhaps the most significant difference between a traditional guideboat and our modern stripped reproduction is the use of many narrow strips to cover the ribbed hull rather than the seven or eight comparatively wide planks on the traditional boat. John Gardner, writing about using modern methods and materials in the Durant book, suggests using narrow strips, waterproof glue, and epoxy to build a guideboat.

At the time of his writing, the building of small paddling and rowing craft from edge-glued narrow wood strips was in its infancy. Strip widths were variable among builders, and edge treatment of the strips to improve the joints was rarely seen. A few boats were built with simple edge-glued joints with the edges beveled with a block plane, but most had no edge treatment at all, depending instead on a lot of filler to close the inevitable gaps. Gardner mentions a double bevel on one edge fitting into a mating "V" notch cut into the other.

Some of today's strip builders still use the rolling edge bevel; a few others simply bevel both edges to the same angle. By far the most popular edge treatment used by modern small boat strip builders is a half round bead cut on one edge that fits into a cove cut into the other. Such strips, when properly fitted, glued, and later faired, produce a hull that is smooth, solid, and gives the impression that the tree grew it that way. In a guideboat, the strips lay flat against the ribs and the strip surfaces align evenly, requiring only a minimum of scraping and sanding to fair the joints between strips. Of course, in order to produce such a near perfect hull, we must begin with near perfect strips, and these are the strips we will make for the *Virginia*.

THE WOOD

Availability, and then cost, often dictate the choice of wood species for constructing a strip-built boat. The two are often related: the desired wood may be available outside of the builder's area, but at a significant increase in the cost. Conversely, many builders find good selections of suitable woods at their local lumber dealer, and at reasonable prices.

Availability and cost factors have contributed to boats being stripped with a variety of woods, ranging from high quality cedars, pines, and redwood, to discarded or recycled wood of uncertain parentage. While a flat sawn plank of virtually any wood can be ripped into planking strips, a few species stand out as favorites among modern builders. These are western red cedar, followed by redwood and white cedar. Quarter sawn eastern white pine is the choice of builders of traditionally planked guideboat hulls, but one rarely sees pine used in strip building. This is probably because wherever pine is commonly available, the lighter weight red cedar usually is also, and at comparable pricing. Redwood is difficult to find on the East Coast, and when available, is more expensive than the more common red cedar.

Several other factors favor the use of red cedar for guideboat construction. We have already mentioned its ready availability. You can purchase it in lengths of up to 16' to 20', it is nearly knot free and straight grained, and is harvested from old growth stands. The old growth trees are slow growing, producing a tight grain structure. There is a wide variation in the color of the wood, ranging from a light cream to almost black. The most common color is various shades of reddish brown.

When coated with epoxy and varnished, it has a very pleasing appearance that invites an admiring touch.

MAKING STRIPS VERSUS BUYING THEM

Builders who prefer not to make their own strips can find ready sources of edge-milled red cedar (see Appendix 5 for sources), as well as white cedar and redwood. Buying these strips shortens the building process by a few days, but at a significant increase in the cost of the finished boat. For example, good quality western red cedar strips are currently priced at approximately 50¢ to 60¢ per lineal foot, depending on the supplier and the strip length you choose. You will need about sixty to seventy strips for your boat, which includes a couple to be used as alignment battens. Assuming you choose full-length, 18' strips, it may cost you over $700, excluding any sales tax and shipping fees (or travel expenses if you pick them up yourself) just to strip your boat. If you contemplate building only a single boat, buying ready-made strips could be an attractive alternative to milling your own despite the additional cost.

The "standard" strip size used for canoe and kayak building and sold by suppliers is ¾" wide and ¼" thick, with interlocking bead and cove edges. Some suppliers will mill special sizes, usually at a higher cost. Keep in mind that strip quality can vary considerably from one supplier to another. Most reputable suppliers will be happy to send you samples of their strips, which may include different wood species, sizes, quality, etc.

Making strips is, of course, more economical than buying the ready-made product, at roughly a quarter of the cost of ready-made strips. But there are trade-offs. More equipment is necessary to make them, and a lot of noise and dust are produced as by-products. The equipment needed is a table-mounted router with bits to cut the bead and cove edges, and a thickness planer. A table or band saw is assumed. Dust control is imperative, and hearing and breathing protection is strongly recommended. Most of these items are already found in a modestly equipped woodworker's shop, with the exception of the router bits. You

can recover the cost of a good set of bits in the savings realized from just one boat.

STRIP LENGTH

Typical strip-built boats, i.e., canoes, kayaks, and guideboats, range between 12' and 18' long. Due to the curvature of the sides of the hull, the strips need to be around 1' longer than the length of the finished hull. This is only an approximation, since the beam of the craft will affect strip length requirements. A longer strip is needed for a 16' guideboat with its 38" beam than for a kayak of the same length with a 24" beam. We found that strips 18' long were required for the 16' long *Virginia*.

While you can obtain western red cedar in lengths up to 20', milling such long planks provides more excitement than you really need for building a boat. Getting planks that are 18' or 20' long from the lumberyard to the shop is also challenging. Towing long planks carefully secured to a trailer is one option. Another popular technique is to lash half of an extension ladder to the roof rack of a car and tie the planks to the ladder. A few feet may hang off the ends, but that is of little concern with the long support provided by the ladder. If you choose to buy ready-made strips, you have reduced the problem to just transporting them into the shop from the curb where the trucker dropped them.

Assuming the perfect plank has been safely brought into the shop, it still must be planed, cut, routed, and stored. That means extended infeed and outfeed tables for the saw and router, and shop space twice or more as long as the board, at least temporarily. You can sometimes find auxiliary shop space by opening a normally closed door to provide for a long infeed table. Another shop extension has been rumored to include an open laundry room window. Do whatever it takes to find the needed space.

On one of our boats, the longest cedar we could find was 16' long, which, as we mentioned before, is too short when the bends required are considered. We selected an assortment of 8', 10', and 12' planks instead. We cut the strips and then scarfed them to 18' lengths before we milled the edges.[1] Some strips had one scarf joint; others had two.

When we mounted these strips on the hull, we placed the joints under a rib, so none of them were visible on the inside of the boat. This is similar to traditional construction in which builders placed scarfed planking joints directly under the ribs. We painted this particular boat on the outside, which covered the joints on the outside of the hull. We varnished our other boat, but built it from natural full-length strips, eliminating the need for scarfing. The point is that you do not need natural full-length strips to make a boat. Shorter strips may even be preferred at times, being easier to handle, less prone to having cove edges damaged by handling, and possibly less expensive than the extra long planks. The color and quality selection is also better, with more of the shorter planks available at the lumberyard than those big long honkers.

STRIP WIDTH
Since strips are cut from a flat plank, the thickness of the plank determines the width of the strip. Without going into the nomenclature used by the lumber industry for sizing board thickness, the common plank thicknesses range from an actual ¾" to around 1½". The red cedar used for home construction trim and decking is usually around ⅞", rough on one side. Construction lumber, e.g., spruce, is 1½" thick, and so-called "five-quarters" is about 1⅛" thick. Common pine can be ¾", 1⅛", or 1½".

Since the common strip width is ¾", a plank of at least that thickness is required. With ⅞" cedar, the boards should be thickness planed to ¾" before cutting strips. You could just as easily cut them into strips at the ⅞" plank thickness and use them to build a boat, but there are two reasons for not doing so. First, you should never assume consistent plank thickness. Two identical-looking planks from the same pile in the same lumberyard may be different enough in thickness to cause problems later. This is especially true if you must join shorter strips in a scarf joint. Different thickness planks will produce strips of different widths, and scarfing such dissimilar strips together risks gaps in the finished hull, which will require filling.

Second, the curve in the ribs defines the curvature of the hull. Mounting relatively wide strips against a curved rib will leave an inner surface consisting of several flats attempting to define a curve. It is similar to trying to draw a circle using only a series of connecting straight lines. The more numerous and shorter the straight lines are, the nearer to a true circle the figure becomes. If you use narrower strips to plank a hull, the curve becomes fairer.

You will normally plane and sand the ridges from the outside of the hull regardless of strip width, but the narrower the strips, the less wood you have to remove to fair the surface. On the inside of a stripped guideboat hull, the ribs prevent anything but a cleanup sanding, and make it nearly impossible to do any extensive fairing to shape the hull. In our boats, cutting strips from planks all planed to a consistent ¾" thickness proved acceptable on all points.

Plane the planks to ¾" by alternately removing a little from each side until you obtain the desired thickness. Planing both sides cleans up any dings in the board, and exposes surfaces that have equal moisture content and are the same color. The equal moisture content also discourages cupping. Trying to cut strips from a cupped board will likely produce strips with a lot of saw marks, and can be downright dangerous if the board binds while being ripped.

STRIP THICKNESS
With the planks all planed to ¾", we now have to know how thick we want the strips before ripping the planks. Although the planking thickness on Grant boats was ³⁄₁₆" for the pine planks above the ¼" thick garboard plank, a cedar stripped hull of that thickness would be of questionable strength without fiberglass inside and outside. The reduction in weight resulting from using ³⁄₁₆" strips rather than the common ¼"

69

strips is negligible, since the weight of the strips is but a fraction of the weight of the entire craft.

Some experienced builders, professionals among them, do build light weight canoes and kayaks from cedar strips as thin as ⅛", but such thin strips have no place in a guideboat. The stresses imparted by pulling on the hull-mounted oars are different from those produced by paddling a canoe or kayak, where the seat of the paddler's pants is the only attachment to the hull.

The ¼" thick strips are easier to make accurately, and are easier to work with. For the builder who chooses to buy strips, the ¼" are readily available. Special orders for thinner strips could raise the price considerably. We have built all of our boats with the ¼" strips with no consideration given to thinner stock, and we will give it no further consideration here.

As we said earlier, western red cedar followed by redwood and white cedar are the best-suited woods for strip building, and we want them to be ¾" wide and ¼" thick. The width is easy to get, while the finished thickness takes a little more effort. Since we will be using a bead and cove edge treatment, and since the router bits commonly available for milling these edges are sized to 0.250", it is imperative that the router-ready strip thickness be 0.250" ± a few thousandths. This also assumes a consistent thickness the entire length of the strip.

If you fail to adhere to this seemingly rigid thickness tolerance, problems can result later that would impact hull aesthetics and require significant time and effort to correct, if corrections would even be possible. For example, assume a long plank is run through a saw set to cut nominal ¼" thick strips, and the edges of those strips are immediately routed. Unless the plank has a perfectly straight reference edge against a long fence and the wood shop has a very long infeed and outfeed table and possibly a stock feeder, it is nearly impossible to single handedly cut the entire strip without changing one's feed hand position. Inevitably, slight wavering will result. This means some rather nasty saw marks, and a

varying strip thickness. Routing the edges so that the bead and cove are perfectly centered across the thickness of the strip is impossible. When you try to mount that strip on the ribs mated to the previous strip, there will likely be thinner areas where you cannot get the strip to lie tight against a rib. An unsightly gap will be left between the rib and the strip. Filling these gaps takes a lot of time, work, and patience, and leaves behind telltale evidence of questionable craftsmanship. It is so much more pleasurable to take justifiable pride in good work than to take time to fix avoidable mistakes.

CUTTING THE STRIPS

The solution is to rough cut the strips slightly oversize and plane them to the final thickness. Either a band saw or table saw may be used. With the table saw, it is possible to gang cut two or even three strips at a time, if you have a saw powerful enough. If two 7¼" diameter thin (1/16") kerf blades are substituted for the normal ⅛" kerf single 10" blade, two strips may be cut with the total kerf waste of a single strip cut with the larger blade. Since two of the smaller blades produce the same waste as the larger single blade, the power requirements are comparable. Three blades may be a stretch in a saw with less power, such as a tabletop model. See the side bar in this chapter for more on gang cutting.

Cut the strips about 9/32" wide (thick) off the plank, then run them through a planer to remove about 1/64" from one side. Then take the other side down to 0.250" ± a frog's hair. Use a three- or four-foot long strip to adjust the planer—using a full-length strip requires that the entire strip be run through, perhaps several times, and doing so is time consuming. A planer with an adjustable thickness stop is a real help here, but careful adjustment and measurement can accomplish the same result if you do not have a stop. A dial vernier caliper is also quite useful when approaching the planer setting for the final 0.250" thickness.

This may all seem like a lot of work, and professional builders might scoff at the extra time required since time is money. And there is the "too much waste" argument. However, the amount of extra time and waste is a pittance when considering the quality of both the strips and the boat. Certainly, you can build a boat with strips cut right off the saw. You can easily fair out inconsistencies in strip thickness in a hull built without ribs, but in the classic ribbed guideboat, variations in strip thickness lead to the problems previously described.

A well-tuned saw, a sharp thin kerf blade or blades, long and rigid infeed and outfeed tables, and the capability to feed the plank tight against the fence for the entire length of the cut with no wavering may produce acceptable sawn strips. Not impossible, but not likely, either.

Many canoe and kayak builders prefer to use a band saw to cut strips, reasoning that since they will sand the strips extensively after they mount them on the hull, the wavy and/or rough surfaces on band-sawn strips will be sanded off anyway. True enough. But the reason for making the nice smooth uniform thickness is that it is easier to accurately mill centered bead and cove edges on the strips, which leads to a cleaner hull. The idea that there is less kerf waste when cutting with a band saw is a non-issue, since planing off the saw marks generates waste comparable to that generated after cutting with a table saw. Band-sawn strips, when cut oversize and planed as described above, are perfectly acceptable, however.

ROUTING THE EDGES

If an accurately centered half round bead is cut on the edge of a precise ¼" thick strip, that edge will fit perfectly into a recessed edge cut with a matching ¼" cove bit. When you mount these strips to the ribs, the ridge along the outside of the glue joint will be quite small, requiring a minimum of scraping or sanding to bring fair. This accurate fit ensures a good glue joint with no gaps or voids. No gaps mean fewer fills. Fewer fills mean less work filling, scraping, and sanding.

The bead and cove router bits, sometimes called "canoe bits" by suppliers, are widely available, usually by mail or Internet order (See Appendix 5). They are virtually all made with ⅛" radii, or ¼" diameters. Builders sometimes make boat hulls with strips thicker or thinner than ¼", but bits specifically sized for other thicknesses require special ordering.

When buying bits, consider that you will be cutting a few thousand linear feet to make strips for a single boat. Quality should take precedence over cost, and keeping the bits sharp is important but not difficult. Sharp bits cut cleanly, reduce tear out, and given the amount of cutting you will do, reduce strain on the router motor. A few passes over a medium- or fine-grit diamond sharpening stone on the inside flat surface of the cutters are sufficient.

The equipment setup for milling the strip edges is not difficult or complicated. A table mounted router, fence, and at least three feather boards are all that is necessary. Long infeed and outfeed tables are a luxury, the lack of which you can compensate for by proper handling during cutting.

Routing operations using a table-mounted router are usually performed by feeding the work against the rotation of the bit. Viewed from above, the router bit rotates counterclockwise and you feed the stock from the right to the left. The bit rotation tends to pull the stock into the bit, keeping the work against the fence. You can mill strips in this fashion, but the problem is that significant tear-out can result when the grain changes slope. Cedar is not very strong between grain lines and will crack or tear out, especially while cutting the more fragile cove edges.

Back routing, sometimes called climb cutting, reduces tear-out to nearly zero, and produces a superior quality milled edge. With this method, the work piece is fed *with* the rotation of the bit. When properly set up and carefully executed, back routing will produce nearly perfect bead and cove strips regardless of changes in grain orientation. But you must be careful. Back routing with a hand-held router is extremely difficult to control, with the router suddenly wandering off line, potentially ruining the work. Or, on a router

71

GANG-CUTTING STRIPS

Slicing planks into enough strips to build a guideboat requires passing more than a thousand linear feet of wood over the blade of a saw. We can reduce that amount by one-half using gang-mounted blades on a table saw to cut two strips at a single pass (Figure 8.1).

The blades used for gang cutting are thin kerf blades, with typical kerf widths of nominally $\frac{1}{16}$". These 7" to 8" blades are usually used in portable circular saws, but with the correct size arbor hole, adapt quite nicely to the table saw. Using two blades separated by a spacer in a gang-cutting configuration produces the same total kerf waste as the standard 10" table saw blade, but you produce two strips rather than one.

There are a few considerations in the design of a blade spacer for gang cutting. The total thickness of the spacer and any shims has to be a little more than $\frac{1}{4}$" (for $\frac{1}{4}$" strips) to compensate for the difference between the kerf width of the teeth and the thickness of the blade disk. If you made a spacer exactly $\frac{1}{4}$" thick, the actual distance between the teeth of the adjacent blades would be less than $\frac{1}{4}$".

The spacer should also be round, with a centered $\frac{5}{8}$" arbor hole. Its diameter should be the same as the saw's arbor flange to prevent distortion stresses on the blades when you tighten the arbor nut. Machining a metal spacer is a luxury; making a solid wood spacer is a practical and satisfactory alternative.

We do not recommend using $\frac{1}{4}$" strips after cutting them with the table saw unless you give them a final planing. Cutting strips to exact thickness without planing requires using precise spacing between the blades and the fence. We have previously described cutting strips a little thicker than $\frac{1}{4}$", followed by planing to precise thickness.

You may use any common hardwood for the spacer. Its thickness should be such that when inserted between the blades, the resulting strip will be around $\frac{9}{32}$" thick. This is not a precise dimension—a ruler measurement is sufficiently accurate at this point. The diameter of the arbor hole is usually $\frac{5}{8}$"; you can use a Forstner bit in the drill press to drill the hole. Counter boring the arbor hole first leaves a dimple in the bottom of the counter bore that is used as a center point for the lead drill of a circle cutter, which is adjusted to the same diameter as the arbor flange. Once you have cut the spacer from the blank, the arbor hole may be completed. Drilling in this sequence assures that the circumference of the spacer is concentric with the arbor hole.

A new zero-clearance insert on the table saw is required to accommodate the twin blades. A simple alternative to making a new one is to turn an existing insert around end for end and cut the twin slots along the side opposite the standard blade slot. With the blades and spacer mounted, lower the blades and install the insert. Capture the insert with the fence just over the edge to prevent the insert from possibly becoming dislodged. Turn on the saw and slowly raise the blades to cut the new clearance slots.

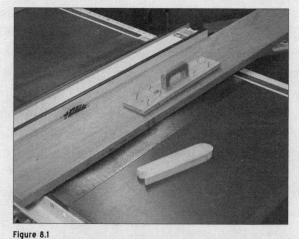

Figure 8.1
Table saw setup for gang cutting strips.

Adjust the fence so that the inner strip width will be the same as the outer one, and make a test cut. Both strips should be equal thickness, and close to $\frac{9}{32}$" thick. You may adjust the outer strip thickness by shimming between the spacer and a blade. The picture above shows a $\frac{3}{4}$" cedar board being gang cut. It also shows a sacrificial push stick, along with a shop-built feed helper. The helper is a piece of $\frac{1}{2}$" plywood pierced by eight small finishing nails driven at a forward angle. The nail points just penetrate the plywood and securely bite into the surface of the board, permitting both forward and lateral pressure while feeding.

table, back routing can grab the work piece and propel it with near rifle-like force. To set up properly, adjust the feather boards to keep the stock firmly against both the table and the fence. When fed into the cutter, there is no tendency for the bit to grab. In fact, you must push or pull the stock through the entire length, so you are in full control.

CUTTING THE BEAD

Before beginning the edge milling, set two strips aside. These can be damaged or low quality, poor color strips and need not have any edge treatment. They must be full-length since you will use them as alignment battens for the ribs, and later as anchors for the bungee cords used for clamping the actual glued strips. They will ultimately be discarded and not become any part of the boat.

Cut the bead edge first so that it will then bear against the feather board when you cut the coves. If you cut the cove edges first, the pressure of the feather board against the fragile cove edges will damage them. Install the bead bit in the router and initially adjust its height visually so that there is a smooth transition between the surface of the table and the curve of the cutter. Then visually adjust the fence so that the apex of the curve is tangent to the fence. These adjustments will be refined later by routing a short piece of actual strip.

Now place a piece of strip against the fence so that it spans the cutter, and is long enough to extend at least a foot on either side. Rotate the cutting edge out of the cutting position so that the strip will lie against the fence on both sides of the bit. Place one feather board flat on the table to bear against the strip, centered at the cutter and pushing the strip against the fence. Place the other two feather boards vertically against the fence so that they push down on the strip. These should be located just before and just after the cutter opening in the fence. See Figure 8.2.

With the power off on the router, push the test piece through the feather boards. It should be a snug fit, and require some effort to pull back out. Check the

feather boards, making sure they are not cocked and all of the fingers are bearing against the strip. Remove the test piece and turn on the router. Feed a few inches of a strip into the cutter, holding it securely. If there is any tendency for the strip to move on its own, stop and readjust the feather boards to provide more pressure. You will have achieved the ideal adjustment when the strip must be pushed into the rotating cutter, and will not move when you let go of it.

Figure 8.2
Router setup for back routing bead and cove edges.

Examine the test piece. The bead should be centered, with no shoulder. If there is any shoulder, adjust the vertical height of the bit to correct it. The top of the bead should be round and in alignment with the flat uncut portion. There should be no flat area on the top of the bead.[2] If there is a flat, the fence must be moved back so that the bit cuts deeper. If the bead is below the level of the uncut edge, you have removed too much stock and you must move the fence forward. Figure 8.3 illustrates some bead cutting problems.

With the router and feather boards properly adjusted, turn on the router and feed a strip into the cutter. When about two or three feet have passed the outfeed edge of the router table, change your position to pull the rest of the strip through. Keep the strip level with the table as you pull it, using one hand between the outfeed feather board and the edge of the table to keep the strip flat on the table, and letting the finished end fall to the floor.

73

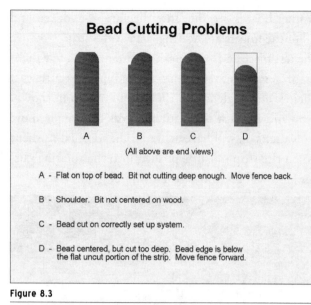

Bead Cutting Problems

A   B   C   D

(All above are end views)

A - Flat on top of bead. Bit not cutting deep enough. Move fence back.

B - Shoulder. Bit not centered on wood.

C - Bead cut on correctly set up system.

D - Bead centered, but cut too deep. Bead edge is below the flat uncut portion of the strip. Move fence forward.

Figure 8.3

Bead cutting problems. (Drawn by Dick Millet.)

If you push the entire strip through and have no out-feed table or other means to keep the strip level, the flexing of the strip as it drops to the floor will lift it off the surface of the table slightly, even against the pressure of the feather board. The result is a bead that is not centered, and all the setup and test runs will have been wasted. Be careful sliding your hand along the strip to gain a new grip. Slivers are possible, and can be surprisingly painful. Leather gloves work well here.

It is a good idea to cut all of the beads once the router is set up. It takes time and patience, with several test cuts, to get the fence, feather boards, and router working in harmony. Changing to cove cutting is best left until all of the beads have been cut.

Some builders prefer to keep the strips in the natural order as they cut them from the plank. This permits book-matching strips on each side of the boat, eliminating the need to sort through a pile of randomly stored strips to select one of just the right color. This approach works well for strips that are naturally full length, but it becomes increasingly difficult to maintain the order when shorter strips are scarfed together to provide the needed length.

We know of at least one professional builder who mills his strips, then sorts and arranges them side by

side on a very long and wide table. He thus achieves the final color matching and strip layout for the entire boat, and handling the strips after this initial sorting is minimized. He then mounts the strips on the hull in the sorted order. Certainly, this refinement requires an amount of open space not likely found in the average amateur builder's shop.

CUTTING THE COVE

The setup for cutting coves is the same as for cutting the beads, with the obvious exception of the router bit. Once the bit is changed, the adjustments of the bit height, fence location, and feather boards are the same as for bead cutting. Run test pieces on strips with the beads already cut. The ideal cove is centered on the strip and has very small but perceptible flats about 10 mils wide on the edges. These dull edges will be less fragile than if you cut the cove deep enough to form a knife-edge.

We have noted that the advice given by both amateur and professional builders on how to cut coves varies. Some say to cut them shallow, leaving a significant thickness on the edges. This excess must later be faired off, reducing hull thickness. This is an impossible job on the inside of a guideboat, given the interference of the ribs.

Another recommendation is to cut the strips initially thicker than ¼" so that when the coves are cut to the proper depth, the additional thickness will leave a flat on the cove edges. The problem here is strips that are thicker than a precise ¼" will have shoulders left when the beads are cut.

Both of these alternate milling methods may be acceptable for kayak construction where you cannot see the inside of the craft or for canoes where the absence of ribs makes it easy to fair properly. For guideboat construction, cove edges that resemble the edge of a very dull knife are sufficiently sturdy to resist breakage if handled carefully, and reasonably easy to fair from both the inside and outside of the hull.

Before cutting the coves, set two beaded strips aside. These should be full-length good quality strips, which you will later mount as the sheer strips. A cove on these strips is not necessary; in fact, we do not recommend it. You will be stripping the boat with the beaded edges up from the sheer to the bottom board, and the sheer strip will see a lot of epoxy drips when the outside of the hull is fiberglassed. Having a coved sheer edge complicates the clean up and may compromise the design location of the sheer.

Once you have made all of the adjustments, run a full strip through and verify the quality of the cove. Figure 8.4 shows some potential problems.

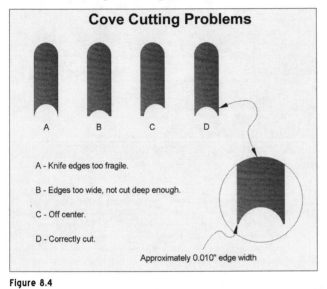

Figure 8.4

Cove cutting problems. (Drawn by Dick Millet.)

When pulling the strip through the router, be very careful handling it. Grip the center portion of the strip with your thumb and fingertips to prevent too much pressure on the cove edges, which may crack them. When the milling is complete, carefully lay the completed strip safely aside off the floor on a bench, across sawhorses, or on some other safe storage support.

Some shops use two routers set up to simultaneously cut the bead and cove edges. The advantage is a savings in time, but at the expense of requiring a more extensive set up and doubling the intensity of the noise. A dedicated router table is required, which once set up and adjusted, is used for no other purpose. Unless you plan to build multiple boats, you will not need such an arrangement.

Occasionally, back routing will lift a grain line from the strip without tearing it out. The nearly straight grain in red cedar with the weaker soft wood between grain lines is largely to blame, but dull bits exacerbate the problem. You can remove these strings, but do not try to pull them off, since they will only get longer and can potentially split the strip. Clip or break them off, or, if short, leave them alone. They will be buried in the joint, and will not cause any further problems.

1 Appendix 4 details the technique used to scarf the shorter strips together.

2 Some builders mistakenly leave a flat on the top of the bead to act as a glue reservoir. This can cause glue creep when the boat is exposed to the hot summer sun, which leads to unsightly fiberglass print through. Such excess glue also forms a weaker joint than one that is properly fitted and glued.

CHAPTER 9

STRIPPING THE HULL

With the ribs and stems mounted to the bottom board and the assembly fastened and aligned on the stock plank, it is time to cover the structure with strips. Here is where the boat begins to assume its classic shape, perhaps one of the most intriguing and rewarding steps in the whole project. After spending a considerable number of hours making laminated ribs and stems, cedar strips, and lots of sawdust, we will begin to see the hull appear as if by magic.

THE OLD AND THE NEW

The generally accepted method for planking a traditional guideboat was to lay planks from the bottom board, working upward to the sheer strake. The edges of each lapped plank were beveled to a knife edge, bedded in a sealing compound, and screwed to the ribs. Clinched copper tacks through the beveled edges between the ribs completed the joinery. That was how it was done—no variation, no glue, no bead and cove edging, just simple planking with lapped beveled edges. Grant improved the feathered edge bevel by using a stepped bevel, eliminating the knife-edge, which helped to prevent splitting. His unique bevel, seen in cross-section in Appendix 1 on Plate V, was called the "Grant lap."

In the modern stripped reproduction, however, some variation is possible. In fact, there are at least four ways to strip the hull with thin edge-milled cedar strips, not counting the variations possible with simple edge-beveled strips. Should we strip from the bottom board to the sheer, or from the sheer to the bottom board? Which edge of the strip should be exposed as the hull is stripped: the bead or the cove? Let us look at some considerations.

The drawings of the *Virginia* describe a typical Adirondack guideboat. Our goal has been to accurately reproduce this boat in form and function by using modern materials, as suggested by John Gardner. We strictly adhered to the dimensions in the drawings to make the laminated ribs. We accurately reproduced the bottom board indistinguishable from the original, and we mounted the ribs at precisely the design spacing. The rocker of the bottom board was also curved the same amount as the original.

With the framework almost ready for stripping, we must now duplicate the shape or curve of the sheer. Gardner defined the curve of the sheer in the form of offsets in Plate II. But he cautions against trying to reproduce the boat from these measurements, as they were only intended for study rather than construction.

To some extent, the shape of the bottom board influenced the shape of the sheer when the traditional boat was seen in profile. The flare on the ends of the garboard plank also affected this shape, with more flare raising the ends of the sheer to a higher termination on the stems. In actual practice, the builder would shape the sheer by eye, sighting and adjusting the curve along a batten until it was fair. To be more precise, he could measure the position of the faired sheer line along one quarter of the boat at each rib and later copy it to the remaining three quarters. As mentioned above, these sheer measurements are given in the tables of Gardner's Plate II. Because these data were intended for study purposes, we will use the data only to estimate the approximate locations for the sheer strips on the ribs, and fair them as needed.

There are two measurements in the Gardner data that are absolute and accurate for the sheer of the *Virginia*. One is the location of the end of the sheer on the stems, and the other derives from the depth measurement amidships. If we mark these points on the stems and rib 0 respectively, we will have defined the low point and the end points of the sheer at the design locations. Using the study points on the remaining ribs as guides only, we can get a fair sheer line, duplicating the original. Stripping can begin here with no further consideration given to shaping the sheer (Figure 9.1).

Figure 9.1

Stripping from the sheer to the bottom board.

Each added strip will follow the previous, until you reach the bottom board. The strips will then run over the rolling beveled edge to a greater or lesser extent, with the center portion completed before the bow and stern areas. Short strips will be required to fill the remaining areas. The final stripping pattern will appear to have been cut from a large expanse of strips to a shape that is defined by the bottom of the boat. This is not aesthetically difficult to accept.

The hull may also be stripped beginning at the bottom board and progressing to the sheer, as was the practice in traditional planking (Figure 9.2). A significant difference here is that the traditional hulls were planked with the framework in an upright position; our boats were stripped with the framework inverted.

In stripping from the bottom board to the sheer, the first strip covers the entire length of the bottom board's rolling bevel, with subsequent strips placed from beneath the previous one. The compensation for the flare at the bow and stern is in the form of one or two "cheater" strips, which are short tapered strips, added to relax the severity of the bending with this method of stripping. As you add more strips, it becomes more difficult to achieve a tight joint, since the newly added strips must assume a progressively more severe bend in the bow and stern areas. The addition of cheater strips is usually not required when stripping from the sheer to the bottom board, since the flare compensating strips become the short filler strips added to complete the hull closure along the ends of the bottom board.

Figure 9.2

Stripping from the bottom board to the sheer (note the strips stored on both sides of the stanchions for easy access as well as the strip holder mounted on the bottom board, which makes gluing easier).

Defining the sheer on a hull that has been stripped from the bottom board to the sheer is similar to the first method described above. The lofted sheer points can be marked on the ribs before they are covered by strips, then transferred by measurement to the outside of the hull as you approach the marks with the last strips. When stripping is complete, clamp a thin batten to the hull to fair the marks and draw a line on the hull along the batten to outline the sheer. You may then cut the rough sheer line with a portable jigsaw. Final sheer refinement and clean up is performed later after fiberglassing the outside of the hull.

Having built hulls using both stripping methods, we have decided that stripping from the sheer to the bottom board is easier. The biggest advantage is that you do not have to fit cheater strips. You will also get an assist from gravity when you are positioning strips from above. The procedure we will detail later will describe stripping from the sheer to the bottom board.

Should you mount the strips with the bead up and exposed, or should the cove be the leading edge? There are adherents to both methods among canoe and kayak builders. Since there are no bottom boards in these boats, closure of the bottom of their hulls requires the strips along each side to meet in some way at the center. In the center, the strips are lying flat, or nearly flat, on the building form. Fitting these final strips may be easier with the coves leading, but laying glue into a horizontal cove or on top of the bead of the next strip is challenging. On the other hand, with the bead leading, it is more difficult to fit the joints, but easier to apply glue to the cove of the next strip to be installed. Experience dictates here.

In a guideboat, the only thing you really need to consider regarding the orientation of the strips is the clamping arrangement you will use to insure snug fitting joints between strips. Once glue is applied and the joint is made, pressure must be applied to the new strip to maintain a firmly fitted joint until the glue sets.[1] This requires some form of clamp pressing down on the exposed leading edge of the new strip.

You can accomplish this with the use of bungee cords wrapped around the entire stripped area, with the hook ends over the strip edges. Or, some builders use packing or duct tape to do the same thing. We have also used short lengths of stripping to push the glued strips into place, clamping them to the ribs with 2" spring clamps.

Regardless of the method used, there should not be any damage to the leading edge of the strips. If the coves lead, you must protect them during clamping. Do this by laying ¼" dowels or short pieces of scrap

stripping in the cove before installing the clamping. With the bead leading, there is no need for any additional protection. The cove of the next strip covers the occasional dent on the beads caused by the placing or removing of bungee cords with their hook ends. This is the method that will be described later.

FAIRING THE RIBS AND STEMS

The ribs are rectangular in cross section (i.e., the width is 90° to the edge). To get the strips to lie flat against the ribs and stems, you must fair them to the proper contact angle, as illustrated in Figure 9.3. This is really a rolling bevel, the angle of the bevel depending on the position on the hull where the strip is to be mounted. The old masters used a spoke shave to shape all of the rib edges before they applied any planking.

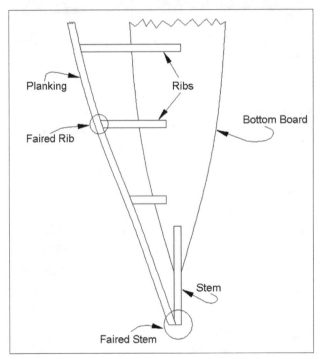

Figure 9.3

Diagram illustrating the need to fair the ribs and stem for the strips to fit flush. (Drawn by Dick Millet.)

This was an exercise in true craftsmanship, requiring a well-tuned spoke shave, a steady hand, and a good eye. You can still do the rib and stem shaping that way, of course, but we have devised an easier method. We lay no claim to originating this; it is so simple that other builders must have used it in the past, although we have seen no reference to it. Simply use one rib and the last strip as a guide for a sanding stick to shape the next rib, working from about rib 4 or 5 to the stem. We describe the sanding stick in Chapter 3, and show it fairing a rib in Figure 9.4. Before detailing its use, some discussion of the inner stems is in order.

Figure 9.4
Using the sanding stick. Work from rib 4 or 5 toward the stem (to the right as shown in the photo).

Before you can mount the sheer strips, both the ribs and stems must be shaped along an area sufficiently wide so that the strips will lie flat when mounted. This area should be a little wider than is necessary for a single strip—perhaps a half strip or so more. The reason for this is the area immediately behind the bead of a mounted strip cannot be shaped for the next strip once the previous strip is mounted. The cove edge of the next strip will not fit well, if at all. Doing a bit more than is strictly required for a given strip eliminates this problem, and shaping for the next strip is simplified (Figure 9.5).

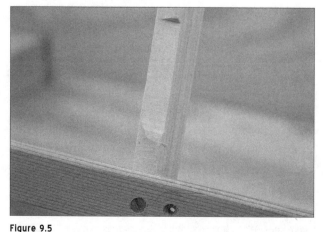

Figure 9.5
Rib shaped for mounting the sheer strip.

To shape the ribs, lay the narrow edge of the 60-grit sanding stick on the previous strip (the alignment batten when shaping for the sheer strip), with the sanding surface contacting the rib to be shaped and the plain surface contacting the rib behind it. Start at rib 4 or 5, and work toward the stem. Carefully sand until the aft outside corner is a knife-edge. Only a few strokes will be required on the ribs farthest from the stem. Be careful not to sand beyond this point, or you will have a gap under the rib when the hull is completed. Sand high enough on the rib so that the shaped area is nearly two strips wide. When the present rib is shaped, move the sanding stick to the next rib and lay the plain end of the stick on the rib just completed, and repeat the shaping operation.

Shaping the stem is similar to the ribs, but there is too much wood to be removed by simply sanding. A spoke shave, rasps, even a drawknife (careful!!) can be used to hog off the leading corner of the stem. We found a large round Microplane to be very effective for removing the major portion of the wood. Whatever tool is used, sight along the cutting edge, and keep it in line with the previously mounted strip. Approach the line drawn along the leading edge of the stem (described in Chapter 7), but leave about $1/16$". With the plain end of the sanding stick guided by the last rib, finish the shaping by sanding to the line (Figure 9.6).

Figure 9.6
Stem shaped, ready for mounting the sheer strips. The two strips shown are the alignment battens.

THE SHEER STRIPS

Of the sixty or seventy strips in the boat, the first strips mounted at the sheer are the most important. As you strip the hull, all strips follow the curve of the sheer strip. Thus, the profile of the boat is defined, as well as the stripping pattern. Most importantly, you must mount the sheer strips symmetrically about the center rib to preserve fore and aft hull symmetry, and both sides must be identical.

In the previous chapter, we suggested setting two beaded strips aside without coves cut on them to be used for the sheer strips. Measure the lengths of these strips and mark their centers. It is also a good idea to make a mark on rib 0, such as with a dark pencil line the length of the outside of the rib. Imagine the frustration applying a glued strip with the center mark on rib 0[1]!

Position a sheer strip with the center mark on rib 0, with the beaded edge up. Align the bottom edge about $\frac{1}{16}$" below the marked sheer position,[2] and temporarily spring clamp the strip to the rib. It may be helpful to position a few other spring clamps further along the strip to help hold it in position. Spring the strip around the ribs and make sure it will fit fair to the stems. When you are satisfied with the fit, drill a countersunk pilot hole through the strip and into rib 0, and screw it home.[3]

Using a few spring clamps and working from rib 0 to one stem only, position the strip on the ribs at the approximate location of the marked sheer points on the ribs. Position the end of the strip on the stem at the defined sheer location, and clamp it to the stem. Sight down the strip from the stem to rib 0, and make any clamp adjustments to bring the strip into a fair curve. The strip may or may not touch all of the sheer points marked on the ribs—a fair curve is more important than hitting all of the points. This operation should be done with great care, since the remaining three quarters of the sheer stripping will be referenced to this first quarter.

Now you may install the remaining screws. Drill and install one screw before moving to the next, being careful not to shift the strip: mistakes can be fixed similarly to adjusting rib feet, but it will require removing most of the strip to do it. Do not use any glue on the ribs when mounting the sheer or any other strips. It is unnecessary and would be a mess to clean up later.

When you get to the stem, put some glue on it and hold the strip in place while you drill the pilot hole and drive a screw. Immediately wipe off any excess squeezed out glue, paying close attention to the area on the stem behind the bead. You must remove all excess glue from this area or hardened squeeze-out will prevent the cove edge of the next strip from making a tight joint. This is a common problem on any type of stripped hull, but you can easily prevent it. Make a useful tool for this purpose by sharpening the end of a thin stick to a knife-edge, much like a chisel but with a longer bevel. Work the sharpened end of the stick in behind the bead to wipe out the squeeze-out before the glue has a chance to set. A paper towel or slightly dampened sponge is a big help here for wiping the removed glue off the stick.

We now have the definition of the sheer on one quarter. The next task is to copy this curve to the other three quarters. An easy way to do this is to use a story stick—a piece of stripping or other similar piece of wood about 3' long.

Spring clamp the other end of the sheer strip into approximate position. Now set the end of the story stick on the already mounted portion of the sheer strip at rib 1, and let the upper part of the stick lay against the bottom board. You have essentially measured the straight-line distance from the sheer to the bottom board at rib 1. Mark the stick where it touches the edge of the bottom board, and move it to the same rib position on the other end of the sheer strip. Adjust the clamps, moving the sheer strip up or down, until the mark on the stick aligns with the edge of the bottom board, and clamp it to the rib. Repeat this every three or four ribs, and finally clamp the end to the stem at the proper location.

Verify the fairness of the curve and then drill, countersink, and screw the strip to the ribs, and screw and glue it to the stem as you did on the other end. Rough trim the ends of the strip about ⅛" beyond the end of the inner stems. The trim is left a bit long here because cedar will shred and chip when crosscut. If you trimmed flush with the stem, the chipping would show on the finished hull. You will do the final flush trimming later using a sanding stick when the stripping has been completed. If you use a Japanese pull saw with gentle pull strokes from outboard towards the stem, chipping and splintering will be minimized.

Attach the sheer strip for the opposite side the same way. In fact, you can work it along with the first side, using the same marks on the story stick. Make certain the ends of the strips align evenly on the stem. This is important not only with the sheer strips, but also with all of the other strips. Any misalignment will carry through the remaining stripping, and the hull will look crooked when viewed head on.

STRIPPING THE HULL

With the sheer strips mounted, we can now build the major portion of the boat. We will add approximately twenty-five to thirty strips to each side, essentially completing the hull. The temptation here is to rush the job, not so much in the interest of speed, but to see what the covered hull will look like. Your patience will be rewarded in due time, and more so for a near perfect hull.

Before gluing on that next strip, a few preliminary notes are in order. First, there is the decision on the final finish. Will the boat be painted completely, painted partially, varnished completely, or a combination? Contemporary guideboats are finished several different ways according to the desires of the builder or his client. One of our boats was varnished inside and out; the other had the outside of the strips painted, with all trim and the inside varnished.

We have already discussed the depth to which you should set the screws holding the strips to the ribs. You should also consider the location of the strip scarf joints. You can hide the joint on the inside if the strip

is mounted so that the joint is under a rib. You will still see it on the outside of a varnished boat, but a painted hull will hide all. You can also vary the screw pattern. On one of our boats, we drove the screws into every other rib, alternating the order on every other strip. This resulted in a screw pattern approximating the look of the screws on an original Grant boat. Since the other boat had a painted exterior, we used screws at every rib for every strip.

Our deviation from the originally designed single piece stem in favor of a two-piece stem presents a minor problem. The inner stem has a ¼" wide flat area on the leading edge. The cedar strips on each side of the hull will be trimmed off flush with this flat area, with the final width of the flat ideally being ¹³⁄₁₆". This is the desired width, since a hardwood outer stem of standard thickness is the same: ¹³⁄₁₆". Even though the strips are each ¼" thick, when added to the stem flat area width one might expect the total to be ¾". But the strips are trimmed at an angle determined by their position on the hull, and the width of the angled cut surface will vary. The overall result is that the final flat surface for mounting the outer stem will vary from around ¹³⁄₁₆" to ⅞".

Some of the ends of the cedar strips will need to be faired off slightly after the outer stem is mounted to bring the hull and outer stem into a smooth transition. This is of no consequence, either structurally or aesthetically. However, to do the fairing you must first remove the screws holding the strips to the stems. The glue will hold the strips in place, and there need not be a concern with strength. You will then replace the screws flush with the faired strips, and construction continues.

If you are going to fill the screw indentations and paint the hull, there is no need to replace the screws at all and you may fill the holes with a filler of choice. Note that when drilling for the original screw placement, the holes should be located as far back as possible without coming through the inside of the inner stem.

Now we can finally get to it.

82

Select the strip to be mounted. We assume that you have already determined the color and grain pattern. Carefully bring the strip to the hull and place the cove over the bead of the sheer strip in its approximate position. You can hold it temporarily in position with a few judiciously placed spring clamps. Dry fit the strip, making sure it will extend a few inches beyond the stems, and that the coved edge will fit tightly over the bead at the stems. If there is a scarf joint in the strip, position the inside of the joint under a rib so that it will be hidden when seen from inside the hull.

Once you are satisfied with the fit, make a mark on the bead with a dark pencil at the rib 0 position. This mark will align with the pencil mark identifying rib 0 when the glue is added and the strip is ready for final placement. Trying to shift a misplaced strip into position once you have glued it is not easy and is best avoided. The pencil marks on rib 0 and the center of the strip prevent misalignments.

The next strip will cover the pencil marks on the bead and rib. If the strip ends extend well beyond the stem, it is prudent to mark the approximate location of the stem on the strip. Any glue spread beyond these marks will be wasted, remaining with the off cut.

Now remove the strip and support it on the framework with the cove up. A convenient and simple support is two or three spring clamps placed on some widely spaced ribs, with the strip lying behind the clamps. Alternatively, you can place scrap wood supports on the bottom board to hold the strip while you apply the glue.

It takes a bit of practice to apply the glue to the cove of a strip some 18' long while getting the correct amount dispensed and steadying the strip with one hand, but you will readily master it. The glue dispenser could present some problems if the wrong type is used. Stripping the *Virginia* requires about a quart of glue. It is not practical to try to dispense it directly from the quart bottle. A more convenient dispenser is a half pint (sometimes called 250 ml.) plastic bottle

with a tapered dispensing tip, and a tiny plastic cap (which is misplaced most of the time). The hole in the tip is too small as purchased, so drill it out to $\frac{1}{16}$" or even a bit larger. Try the smaller diameter first before going to a larger hole.

Fill the glue-dispensing bottle about three quarters full, and squeeze a bead of glue into the cove of a piece of scrap to verify proper dispensing. The bead of glue should be about $\frac{1}{8}$" wide. It is possible to get the proper width with just about any size hole, but it may be too slow to be efficient. The right size hole, coupled with a comfortable amount of hand pressure on the bottle, will enable dispensing of the proper amount of glue with good control and adequate speed.

Spread a few handfuls of #3 x $\frac{1}{2}$" screws on the bottom board, and have the drill and screwdriver at the ready near one end of the boat. Hang a few bungee cords over and along the bottom board ready for immediate use. As more strips are mounted, you will need additional bungees.

Hold the strip upright with one hand, and squeeze a bead of glue into the cove the entire length between the marked stem lines. Leave the glue bottle on the bottom board near one end of the boat. Move back to rib 0, and turn the strip over into position. Align the mark on the top of the bead in the center of the strip with rib 0 (it should also have been marked) and mount the strip. Work the strip down on the sheer strip on a few ribs fore and aft, rocking the strip in and out a bit to seat it. Place a spring clamp on the strip at rib 0, and work toward the glue bottle, seating the strip and clamping.

When you approach the inner stem, squeeze some glue onto the side of the stem, and press the strip into it, putting downward pressure on the end beyond the stem. Make sure there is a good tight joint at the stem, both onto the stem and downward onto the sheer strip. Holding the strip in position, drill a pilot hole through the strip into the stem, and then screw it home. Recall that you left the drill, screws, and screwdriver in a convenient position to be able to reach them with one hand holding the strip. Do not place any other screws yet. Move to the other side of rib 0 and work toward the other end, seating the strip, clamping, and screwing the end into the stem.

Secure the strip by wrapping bungees between each rib and around the strip and the alignment batten, as shown in Figure 9.7.

Figure 9.7
Bungee cords used to clamp the first strip to the sheer strip. The lowest strip seen here is the alignment batten.

Note the presence of glue squeeze-out from the strip just mounted in Figure 9.7. It is important to get a little squeeze-out, which indicates that the joint is fully glued. If the amount squeezed out develops runs, the glue bead was too wide. Conversely, the lack of squeeze-out indicates too little glue, suggesting that a bit more should be applied for the next strip.

When you have completely clamped the strip with bungees, go back and try to wiggle it in and out once again before the glue has a chance to set. Getting a good tight joint is very important to the overall craftsmanship of the hull and will reduce the need for filling gaps later on. Remember, the goal is to mount the strips so that they look like they grew that way.

With the strip secured by the bungees, drill pilot holes for the screws. Be careful at the higher numbered ribs—the screws should go in perpendicular to the hull surface, which will be at an angle into the rib.

Now trim the ends of the strip about ⅛" beyond the stems, which will allow the ragged cut edge to be removed when fitting the outer stem. It helps if the cutting stroke of a pull saw is to the inside of the hull. Clean out any squeeze-out between the bead of the new strip and the inner stem as soon as possible. When the glue has set to the rubbery stage as indicated by the squeeze-out, you can remove the bungees. You may use a paint scraper to scrape off the squeeze-out at this point, but it is not structurally necessary. It just looks nice.

The inside is a different story, however. Removing hardened squeeze-out from the inside after the hull is righted is not as easy as removing it before it is fully cured, especially in the cramped area between rib 12 and the inner stem. If there is any squeeze-out on the inside of the inner stem, it will benefit from some attention also. A useful tool for scraping hardened squeeze-out on the inside is the Pro-Prep scraper with a convex blade.

Select another strip previously color matched to the one just installed, and mount it on the other side. Make certain the ends of the strip at the stems are perfectly even and lined up with the previous strip on the other side. Alternate from side to side, installing two to three strips to each side. This is to avoid stressing the assembly unevenly and possibly inducing a warp. Fair the ribs and stems as you go, using the sanding stick to finish the bevels.

When approaching the bottom board, strip completely over the rolling bevel. It is difficult to get good clamping here—pressing down firmly by hand while drilling and setting screws is acceptable provided you do it carefully. Figure 9.8 shows one way to clamp the last strip along the bottom board. Remove a rib mounting screw and drive it through a hole in a short piece of scrap stripping into its original hole, which then presses the scrap piece down on the last strip. The clamping force with this method is fairly low, and could probably be improved upon with a little ingenuity. We leave it up to the reader to try.

Figure 9.8
Clamping the last strip.

1 The screws used to fasten the strips to the ribs are not a substitute for clamps. The screws hold the strips snug to the ribs to maintain hull shape, but additional downward pressure from clamps is required for good fitting glue joints before driving the screws.

2 This allows for a good cleaning after the hull is fiberglassed.

3 If the hull is to be painted, the screws should be driven slightly deeper. The screws will later be covered with filler before fiberglassing.

CHAPTER 10

FAIRING, FILLING, AND SANDING

Fairing is the drawing of a smooth curve given several points, or the refining of a rough line or surface to a smooth one. Our stripped hulls (Figure 10.1) will now need this smoothing. Any hull built using flat strips or planks joined along their edges around ribs or forms will have an unfair surface because of ridges at the joints. In this chapter, we will install the outer stems, smooth the outer surface of the hull by removing the ridges between strips, fill any gaps, and make a smooth flowing surface from stem to stem.

Figure 10.1
Rough-stripped hull.

We must take a short detour in our building of a reproduction *Virginia* to accommodate these design changes (improvements?) not seen in the original. We described them in detail in earlier chapters. First, the outer stems must be fashioned and installed, and then the outside of the hull will have any gaps and cracks filled. The last operation before fiberglassing will be to sand the hull smooth.

The traditional guideboat builders used a one-piece stem, and a few modern ones still do. When the planking was finished, the shape of the hull was com-

plete. The installation of an outer stem will finish the shape for our reproductions.

THE OUTER STEMS

In Chapter 2, we described the outer stem variations found on modern boats. They can be built up from laminated spruce similar to the ribs and inner stems, or made from a single piece of hardwood carefully selected for durability, grain, or figure. Some boats have a combination, where builders laminate the inner portion attached to the hull, and mount a solid hardwood cutwater outboard.

Regardless of the structural configuration, all of the outer stems share common characteristics. They are tapered across most of their width, matching the total width of the planking at the inner stem inboard, tapering to about ¼" at the extreme outboard edge. There is a short section at the top that is full thickness with no taper. A brass stem band along the outer edge running from the stem cap to the bottom board and merging with the bottom shoes completes the outer stems. The brass work is not required at present, and we will describe it in a later chapter.

On one of our boats, we used fully laminated outer stems; on the other, we used solid cherry. Aside from the selection of the wood, we tapered both according to the original design. You can see cross sections of the outer stem in Gardner's Plate XIV. The task at hand is to shape the outer stems to match these cross sections.

Begin by roughing out the ¹³⁄₁₆" thick blank with a band saw or jigsaw, leaving the top end to extend about 3" above the sheer. Cut about ⅛" wide of the curve on the inner edge to allow for fitting. Sand the outer curve to the line with a disk sander. The final curve of the inner edge will be finished when you fit the stem to the hull.

Draw the *TOP-STEM TAPER* line on both sides at the estimated position shown on Plate XIV in the sketch in the upper left corner titled *GRANT STEM CAP*. Also, draw two lines along the outer (leading) edge ¼" apart and centered. Clamp the blank to the bench, and using bench and block planes, Microplanes, sanding sticks, spoke shave, trained beaver, etc., form the taper on one side. Do not cut inside the ¼" area or beyond the inner edge. Also, do not do any shaping above the top stem taper line. Turn the stem over and shape the opposite side exactly the same.

You must now clean up the inner stem leading edge and the ends of the strips. You should have trimmed the strips slightly beyond the edge of the inner stem. It is this excess that you will now remove, providing a smooth and fair mounting surface for the outer stems.

It is best to trim the excess cedar flush with the inner stem by sanding. Trimming with a saw will leave a jagged edge on the cedar, due to the splintering properties of the wood. It is challenging to hand-sand this surface so that it does not become slightly rounded. There is no way to easily construct a jig or guide to hold a sanding block or stick in perfect alignment at right angles to the centerline of the hull, but careful use of a wide sanding stick can produce a satisfactory surface.

To use the sanding stick, stand aside the hull with the blank end of the stick braced against your hip and visually aligned square with the stem. Stand still and do not move your hip while stroking the sanding stick across the stem, as shown in Figure 10.2.

Another effective, if not perfect, approach is to use a belt sander very carefully with a medium-grit belt. Standing in front of the stem, hold the machine so that it hangs downward and the travel of the belt is vertical. Lightly touch the belt to the area to be

trimmed, and move it up and down against the stem by bending your knees while keeping the sander aligned. Take light cuts, all the while keeping the sander moving. Near the top, you will have to use your arms to raise the sander. Again, try to maintain the alignment square with the centerline of the hull.

Figure 10.2
Fairing the strip ends and inner stem with a wide sanding stick.

This operation can be daunting, with no room for error. The goal is to sand off the excess cedar flush with the leading edge of the inner stem without removing any of the stem, all the while keeping the sanded surface square with the centerline. Using a fine rather than medium grit may be somewhat safer, but slower. Figures 10.3a and b show the before and after views of the fairing.

Figure 10.3a
Leading edge of inner stem as stripped...

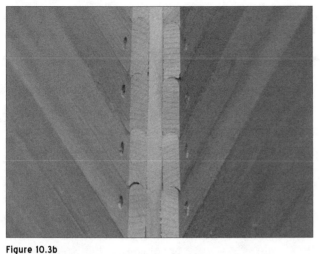

Figure 10.3b
...and sanded fair.

With the strip ends sanded flush with the leading edge of the inner stem, you may now fit the outer stem. In order to accommodate any irregularity in the curve of the inner stem due to sanding, a pattern or template is used. Tape a piece of poster board to the side of the hull so that it sticks out beyond the sanded stem surface. It may be convenient to use the original outer stem pattern, but you may have to use a second one for the other end of the boat.

Hold the poster board flat against the hull while tracing the curve onto it from the sanded side. Then cut the line out with a utility knife, and use the pattern to trace the outline of the curve onto the inner edge of the outer stem. When cut and sanded to the line, the outer stem should be a good fit to the sanded surface of the inner stem. The stem will be slightly narrower than the thickness of the inner stem plus strips, but this area will be faired smooth later.

Attach the outer stems to the hull with epoxy, with screws through the inner stem holding it in position. You may leave these screws in, or remove them and plug the holes. Make the decision on the screws before actually drilling for them, since you should first drill counter bores to plug later if you are going to remove the screws.

Five 1½" long galvanized Phillips head deck screws will suffice if the screws are to be removed. You may

use flat head brass screws, countersunk flush with the surface of the inner stem and left in.[1] The correct size pilot hole is a must, and waxing the threads before driving any screws is recommended. The epoxy may bind the screws, and waxing could make it easier (or even possible!) to remove them if necessary.

You will also need a screw drill, an extended screwdriver bit so that the screws may be driven from inside the boat, drill bits for the body clearance of the screws and one for the pilot holes, and a ⅜" Forstner bit for the plug holes. If you contemplate plugging, you will first use a small diameter drill for drilling marker holes to locate the Forstner bit. The following description assumes that you will remove the screws and plug the holes. Since it will be necessary to drill from inside the overturned hull, if you have not already done it, remove the internal bracing originally installed to immobilize the framework for stripping.

Begin by marking the outside of the inner stem in five places, roughly equally spaced. Drill small marker holes through the inner stem from the outside at the five marks, being careful to drill square to the stem surface and aligned with the hull centerline. The screw will ultimately come through this hole and into the outer stem. If the hole is square to the inner stem and true to the centerline, a mating hole drilled square to the curve of the outer stem will align in a straight line and driving the screw will be easy. If the holes are misaligned, driving the screw will be difficult and it may break.

With the marker holes drilled, drill the counter bores about ¼" deep into the inside of the inner stem. This may be difficult in the cramped area of the inner stem. When the counter bores are completed, increase the diameter of the marker holes to the size of the pilot drill (*not* the size of the clearance hole just yet).

The next step is to clamp the outer stem in position. This is challenging since there are no convenient clamping surfaces. Figure 10.4 shows web clamps holding the dry-fit stem in position for drilling the holes from

89

inside. Clamp a thick batten across the rib 12 extensions to provide a mounting surface for the clamps.

Figure 10.4

Clamping the outer stem in position for drilling the screw holes from the inside.

With the outer stem held in position, run the pilot hole drill bit from inside the hull into the outer stem just enough to place a mark. A very useful drill bit to use here is one made specifically for screw drills. It has a hexagonal shaft for mounting in the chuck, with a much smaller diameter twist drill bit on the business end. You can use this bit with a magnetic socket commonly used in screw drills for the rapid change of screwdriver bits. If the space and drill configuration permits it, you may drill the pilot holes directly into the outer stem. This will insure a straight screw hole later. If full depth drilling is not possible, drill as deeply as you can.

In any case, at least make a drill mark on the outer stem. Remove the stem and drill or deepen the pilot holes where marked as necessary, keeping the drill bit square with the curve of the stem. If all goes well, the holes in both the inner and outer stems will be aligned. Now widen the holes in the inner stem to the clearance hole size. It is a good idea to confirm the alignment of the screw holes by mounting and screwing down the stem dry. This also cuts the screw threads and sets up the stem for the next operation. Do not forget to wax the screws first.

With the stem screwed onto the hull in its final mounting position, there is one last detail to attend to before removing it and gluing it on permanently. The top of the stem has yet to be shaped, and may be done before it is permanently mounted or after. In either case, it is convenient to lay out the shape of the top and the stem cap rabbet while it is dry mounted. Careful work is required here, since you must consider the thicknesses of the deck planks and deck center capping strip. See Gardner's Plate XI for the detailed drawings of the deck and stem cap area.

The point of reference is the end of the sheer where it fits to the stem. There were measurements given for this point on the detailed Gardner stem drawings in Plate VI, but a point based on actual construction is much preferred. Extend the sheer line by drawing it on the side of the stem, maintaining the proper fair slope. (If this point is different on the opposite side of the stem because the sheer strips were misaligned when mounted, you must first correct the sheer.) This line represents the top surface of the deck planks, which will be recessed into the gunwale. The top of the recessed deck planks is the sheer line.

Now draw another line parallel to the first and ⅛" above it. This line represents the top surface of the deck center capping strip. Referring to Plate XI, draw the raised and rounded tip of the stem. You should make a template of this stem tip for use on the other end of the boat, and for use later in making the brass stem cap.

You may now remove the stem and complete the final shaping. Refer to Plate XIV, the drawing labeled *GRANT STEM BAND,* for dimensional details of the stem cap rabbet.

Mix about an ounce of resin with the appropriate amount of hardener.[2] With an acid brush, thoroughly coat the inside of the outer stem and the ends of the cedar strips with the mixture. It will soak into the cedar almost immediately. Keep adding epoxy until no more will soak in. Also, check the inside of the outer stem for any dry spots and recoat as necessary.

When no more will soak into the ends of the cedar strips, thicken the remaining epoxy mixture with colloidal silica. You may add wood flour (extremely fine sanding dust, see Chapter 3) at this time to provide a darker color for the glue line. The consistency of the mix should be about like mayonnaise and should *not* run off the mixing stick. Wipe the excess soaking coat off the gluing surfaces, and spread the thickened epoxy liberally on the inside of the outer stem.

To mount and align the stem, use a couple of screws driven so that their points stick out of the inner stem about ⅛". If desired, a web clamp may be repositioned while you drive the screws home. Drive the screws from inside, but do not over-tighten them. Over-tightening the screws may cause them to break, or force the glue out of the joint. There should be some squeeze-out of the glue along the entire joint, but over-tightening can starve the joint. Figure 10.5 shows a completed outer stem. Plugging the screw holes is done after the hull is righted.

Figure 10.5
Outer stem installed.

FILLING AND SANDING THE HULL

With the installation of the outer stems, you must fill defects and gaps and sand and smooth the entire hull in preparation for fiberglassing. If the hull is to be painted, you must also fill and smooth the stripping screws. In this case, a simple water based product such as Durham's Rock Hard Water Putty may be used. This filler is easily sanded and can be used anywhere that will be covered by paint, including the screws holding the strips to the ribs. If you plan a bright finish, leave the screws unfilled.

For crack filling, we recommend colored epoxy similar to the glue used to attach the outer stems, thickened to a peanut butter-like consistency. A common mistake is to mix sawdust and strip mounting glue and call it filler. It will be called something else when it cures—an unsightly yellow streak that calls attention to itself will forever be under the varnish.

Most of the cracks in the hull result from breakage of the fragile cove edges during stripping. Rough handling of the strips following edge routing and during sorting and selection often results in broken cove edges, as does careless handling during fitting and glue-up. You avoid gaps resulting from poor fitting with careful attention to the clamping and screwing of the freshly glued strips. But despite your diligence in all of these operations, there will likely still be a few cracks and gaps.

Regardless of the type of filler chosen, we found that we could apply it with a simple tool, one used in an unrelated field and slightly modified. A ¾" wide stainless steel cake-decorating spatula with the rounded end carefully ground off flat served well. The ground edge and sharp corners were smoothed with sandpaper, creating a narrow flexible putty knife.

The best time to do the filling is before any sanding. This gives ample opportunity for removal of the epoxy stain surrounding the filled crack without a lot of extra sanding later on. After the first round of sanding, you may find a few additional defects, but filling them is easy and straightforward.

91

Mix the water-based filler according to package directions. For an epoxy filler, mix a small amount of the proper resin/hardener ratio, and thicken it with colloidal silica. Add wood flour to color it, and be sure the consistency is like peanut butter. Apply the filler with the modified spatula, being sure to press the mixture into the crack. Immediately scrape off as much of the excess as possible from around the defect. Any excess must be sanded off later, and removing it while soft is preferred to sanding, sanding, and more sanding.

Removal of excess epoxy around a filled defect is important if you are going to varnish the hull. When you add a thixotropic agent like wood flour or colloidal silica to mixed epoxy, the mixture does not change chemically, rather, the effect on the epoxy is merely mechanical. Imagine you are at a sandy beach building a sand castle. The wet sand is stacked and sculpted, and holds its shape because it is wet. Now lay out a paper towel and place a handful of wet sand on it. The water in the sand immediately wets the paper.

A similar thing happens when you fill a crack in a soft wood like cedar. No matter how much thickening agent you add, some of the epoxy will wet the cedar. The longer it remains on the wood, the deeper it will penetrate. It will eventually cure in the wood. When you apply the wet-out coat of epoxy to the fiberglass over the wood, the filled area that is already cured blocks the even absorption of the epoxy. A light colored stain remains that you cannot get out. Removing as much of the excess epoxy filler as possible before it cures prevents this stain. The water-based filler does not exhibit the soak-in problem as does epoxy, but we recommend the immediate removal of the excess to reduce the amount of sanding required.

When the filler has cured, scrape the area with a cabinet, Pro-Prep, or carbide scraper. A paint scraper here may be too rough. The goal is to remove the staining that surrounds the fill as well as to level and smooth the filled area. You may not be able to remove all of the stain, but getting most of it off will leave less for sanding. There is also a danger that if you do not scrape

beforehand, the excessive sanding necessary later could leave flat spots or an otherwise unfair surface.

With 80-grit sandpaper mounted on the random orbit sander and the sander attached to a shop vacuum or dust collection system, sand the hull smooth. Keep the sander moving slowly (rapidly moving the sander back and forth can leave swirl marks) and do not operate it at its maximum speed. Cedar is soft, and 80-grit sandpaper on a random orbit sander can be quite aggressive. When sanding the concave areas near the bottom board, tilt the sander very slightly to use the outer edge of the paper.

If any filling stains remain, attack them with the slightly tilted sander. Concentrate on the stain but keep the sander moving over a broader area to prevent a flat spot. Do not forget to sand the bottom board, and do not try to sand over the edge of the cedar that forms the transition between the bottom board and the hull sides. The random orbit sander will round it over, making installation of the bottom shoes difficult. The edge can be lightly sanded with 120-grit by hand, but only enough to break the sharpness.

The ends of the strips at the outer stem will be higher than the stem, and must be sanded fair. The screws that fasten the strips to the stems interfere and should be removed before fairing. You can reinstall them when fairing is complete if you will be varnishing the hull; otherwise, you may simply fill the holes for a painted hull.

When the first sanding is complete, vacuum the hull and look for any areas that you may still need to fill. Repeat the filling, scraping, and sanding as necessary. There should be few, if any, additional gaps that need filling. One can become paranoid about filling hairline cracks between strips on the outside of the hull. These small cracks will fill with epoxy when the fiberglass is wet out.

Once the hull has been filled and sanded to 80-grit, change to 120-grit and sand the entire hull once again. It should not take very long, since you have knocked down the ridges between strips with the first sanding. Do not move the sander rapidly back and forth; take your time and move the sander slowly.

Vacuum the hull when you are done sanding. To remove any residual dust, wipe the hull down with a clean damp (*not* wet) sponge used with frequent rinsing. After drying, the hull is now ready for the application of the fiberglass.

1 A caution here: brass screws are not nearly as strong as steel, and can easily break under the heavy torque required to drive them into hardwood. An alternative when using brass screws is to drive steel screws of the same thread shape and size first to cut the threads, and then replace them with the brass.

2 For complete details on the handling, mixing, and use of epoxy, see Appendix 3.

CHAPTER 11
FIBERGLASSING

Nineteenth and early twentieth century guide-boats leaked. Initially a new boat was sound, the builder having sealed the lapped planking joints with a bedding compound, usually a mixture of varnish and white lead. With the hard use some of these workboats got, the joints would eventually loosen and water would seep in. Wood swells when wet and shrinks when dried, so it was common to submerge a boat that had been stored over the winter to allow the water to swell the planking and tighten the joints. This is still done today. We know of a pair of reproduction bateaux in the Adirondacks that the owners allow to fill with rainwater, only to be baled out in preparation for tours and demonstrations.

WHY DO WE FIBERGLASS?

The finish on the hull could minimize leaking, or at least postpone it. Guides preferred their workboats painted rather than varnished, which, besides making the boat less conspicuous on hunting expeditions, would help to protect the wood from the water. Prompt repair of minor damaging bruises and scratches, and periodic maintenance went a long way toward keeping feet dry.

It may be said with virtual certainty that if the old masters had had access to fiberglass and epoxy, they would have routinely applied them to the hull. The penalty for such waterproofing is paid with the addition of a few pounds of extra weight. But, for boats kept at hotels for guest use that never had to transport a trophy deer or be carried to the next lake, fiberglassing would have been a requirement.

Many, if not most, modern reproduction guideboats have an outer covering of fiberglass. This is especially true of strip-built boats. However, we have found that the few people still building pine-planked traditional guideboats, builders who strictly adhere to the original designs and methods, do not use it. On a boat that will see limited summer use, a coating of a good marine paint or varnish will probably keep the boat dry. To insure a long life for the coating, a boat without fiberglass should not be left in the water for extended periods.

Strip-built canoes, kayaks, and similarly built ribless guideboats require a layer of fiberglass on the inside of the hull as well. The composite lamination of wood and fiberglass significantly increases the structural rigidity and strength of the craft, dispensing with the need for ribs. With the fiberglass cloth applied such that the strands of the cloth run parallel to the keel line and at right angles across the boat, the transverse strands inside act as thousands of "ribs."

Because fiberglassing the outside of a ribbed guideboat hull is done only to seal it and not to strengthen it, the cloth may be of a lighter weight than would normally be used on a composite hull. The usual or normal weight cloth used on canoes and kayaks is 6 oz. per square yard, known simply as "6 ounce cloth." Variations include a double layer on the outside bottom, either of the same or different weights. For a guideboat, a single layer of 4 oz. cloth is sufficient. We did not consider 2 oz. cloth for our boats, but we know of no technical reason not to use it. The problem with 2 oz. cloth is that suitable widths are harder to obtain since builders in the strip-built small boat community do not normally use it.

BUYING EPOXY AND FIBERGLASS

We recommend you buy your epoxy and fiberglass from the same vendor, preferably one whose primary business is building strip boats and supplying boat builders. A vendor may not be relied upon to answer your technical questions if he sells only the epoxy or only the fiberglass, and does not use them in his or her normal course of business. A supplier who also builds boats professionally is infinitely better equipped to be a reliable source of not only products, but information.

We do not recommend the use of automotive fiberglass and polyester on boat hulls. Automotive fiberglass is usually supplied with polyester resin and methyl ethyl ketone peroxide catalyst. It was used for marine work for several years before epoxy became available. The epoxy we use today is superior in its adhesion to wood, is readily available, and produces a much better result.

The mixing ratios of hardener to epoxy resin vary from manufacturer to manufacturer, and generally range from 2 parts resin to 1 part hardener (2:1) to as much as 5:1. You must follow the ratio stated by the epoxy manufacturer exactly.

Different epoxies have different qualities, not only in their application and curing times, but also in the quality of the final cured coating. As some epoxies cure, they form a waxy by-product called "blush" on the surface which must be removed before the next coat is applied. Other brands are free of blush, eliminating that annoying extra work. We will discuss blush more a little later in this chapter.

Since it is difficult to fully explain the fiberglassing process in general terms, we will base our description on a specific product; one that we are familiar with that has produced consistently good results. We have chosen to use the products manufactured by Phoenix Resins and marketed as MAS Epoxy to describe the process.

The first rule for buying fiberglass is to insist that it be supplied rolled on a cardboard tube and shipped in a cardboard box. Paying a few dollars extra for this kind

of packaging will pay off in the end. Fiberglass cloth intended for small boat building is a simple weave, and the strands are quite slippery against one another. It is easily distorted when handled improperly or excessively. The strands are normally at right angles to each other, and must be kept that way. Folding the cloth for shipment can easily distort it, leading to pulls, gathers, lumps, and other imperfections when it is epoxied.

When you receive it, open it only enough to verify it is what you ordered. Do not unroll it. If it is from a reputable supplier whom you trust, do not even open it until you are ready to use it. When you are ready to begin fiberglassing, put on a pair of latex gloves and carefully open the box. Never handle fiberglass cloth barehanded. This is not to protect your hands, but to protect the cloth. Any little bits of rough or calloused skin on your hands can easily cause pulls and gathers in the cloth, which will cause problems later.

The day before fiberglassing, vacuum the hull, wipe it down with a damp (NOT wet) clean cloth, and allow it to dry overnight. DO NOT wipe the hull down with a tack cloth or solvent: any contamination can negatively affect the curing; in fact, acetone is a solvent for mixed epoxy and will soften cured epoxy.

Carefully unroll the cloth down the bottom board (Figure 11.1), keeping the roll centered. It is very helpful to have a gloved assistant here. Do not pull the cloth; if you have to get more cloth to the end of the hull, roll it back up, move it to position, and then unroll it. Keep it centered over the hull and rolling out straight, and keep the transverse strands at right angles to the bottom board. Do not try to get it to lay flat and tight just yet—you are simply measuring it out here. When you have enough unrolled to get to the other end, have your assistant cut it from the roll in a straight line across its width. Immediately replace the wrapping paper it came in, and safely stow the remaining cloth, if any, in the box.

Resist the temptation to run your gloved hand over the cloth. Use a wallpaper smoothing brush to smooth it out, sweeping from the bottom board to the sheer, and make sure that the longitudinal strands run straight and parallel with the bottom board and the transverse strands run at right angles to it.

Figure 11.1
Rolling out the fiberglass cloth.

If you have to shift the cloth, lift it as much as possible before pulling on it, and do it carefully. Again, use the brush to smooth it, and make sure of the orientation of the strands. If the strands are not running parallel and across the boat, there is a good chance you will have wrinkles and gathers at the sheer.

To remove any pulls, where the strands in a small localized area are distorted from a straight line, brush the area back and forth rapidly with a stiff clean dry brush. You can also use the corner of the wallpaper smoother brush.

The opposite of a pull is a gather, where the strands bunch up tightly in a small area. If left there when the epoxy is applied, a lump forms that will need to be sanded off later. These are a bit more difficult to remove. Use your gloved fingertips to try to spread the strands out to a normal configuration. You may have to tug on the edge of the cloth, but just at the strands that are affected.

With the cloth smoothed and covering the entire hull, trim the edges to within an inch or two of the sheer (Figure 11.2). At the ends, hold the cloth against the boat with one hand and trim with the other, again leaving an inch or two of cloth overhanging past the stems. To trim the stem areas, hold the cloth up so

that it lies against the hull and trim it down to near the bottom of the stem. Make sure the strands remain at right angles during trimming.

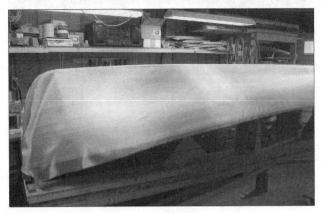

Figure 11.2
Fiberglass cloth on the hull, trimmed and ready for epoxy.

EPOXY CONSIDERATIONS

You will find in Appendix 3 an explanation on how to safely handle, mix, and clean up epoxy. We strongly recommend you review the information before beginning any epoxy work. Such general information, if given here, would detract from the description of the actual work at hand, namely the application of epoxy to the cloth on the boat.

Gather up the tools and safety equipment you will need for the wet-out (Figure 11.3): epoxy resin, hardener, a few squeegees (rectangular plastic pieces for spreading epoxy, usually available from your fiberglass supplier), disposable 2" bristle brushes, mixing cups and stirring sticks (wood strips about ½" wide and ¹⁄₁₆" thick are ideal), latex gloves, and at least Tyvek sleeves, although a Tyvek suit is highly recommended. You will be standing beside the hull and reaching over it to the bottom board to spread epoxy, so the chances of getting your arm wet are very good. Also, in reaching to the bottom board, you may get the front of your shirt wet. The Tyvek suits are really inexpensive, costing much less than a new shirt.

Do not forget some paper towels, and have the jugs and dispensing area free of clutter and the surface under the epoxy jugs covered with cardboard, not newspaper. Epoxy will drip, and newspaper is easily soaked with the uncured epoxy, gluing it to the bench top or floor. Cover the floor under the boat with cardboard.

Figure 11.3

Some of the supplies needed for fiberglassing the hull. Pictured are MAS epoxy resin and slow hardener, calibrated pumps, plastic squeegee tool, latex gloves, bristle brush, short nap roller, mixing sticks, and cup.

You must also consider the shop's environment. It should be comfortable and its temperature and humidity should be within the range recommended by the epoxy manufacturer. The general consensus is to have the shop warm to begin with, and let the temperature cool down as you are wetting out the cloth. For example, if you are applying epoxy during warm weather conditions, wait until later in the day when the temperature begins to drop to do the application. The widely accepted theory is that the cooling will contract the air in the pores, drawing epoxy into the wood rather than expanding it and forming bubbles if the temperature is rising. A more plausible explanation for the formation of bubbles under fiberglass is the displacement of air by wet epoxy settling into voids in poor glue joints between strips.

Another option often discussed among strip-boat builders is precoating the bare wood hull with a coat of epoxy and letting it cure before applying the fiberglass cloth. Doing so is not a structural requirement, but the practice has its adherents. When the question was posed to a leading epoxy manufacturer, the answer was that precoating was not a requirement but merely a matter of personal choice. One of our boats was precoated; the other was not. We saw no significant difference in the final results.

Mixing epoxy is another area where strict conformance to the manufacturer's guidelines is required. Epoxy must be mixed, mixed well, mixed some more, and then some. Using the mixing stick described earlier, mix vigorously in one direction for a while, then scrape the sides and bottom of the cup, and vigorously mix some more in the opposite direction. Do this several times, so that the total mixing time is a good two minutes—a *real* two minutes. Complete mixing cannot be over-emphasized. Many of the problems reported with epoxy can be traced to inaccurate measuring and/or improper mixing.

When the epoxy is completely mixed, it will be full of bubbles. This is of no concern since bubbles in a freshly mixed batch of MAS epoxy are normal and they will quickly dissipate when the batch is used on the hull.

The cloth is ready, the epoxy is about to be measured and mixed. How will you do the wet-out? Do you use a brush, a squeegee, or a roller? In point of fact, you can use them all. Use the squeegee to spread the epoxy over the broad areas of the hull, and move or spread the excess around. Use the brush in areas that are difficult for the squeegee to get at, such as around the stems, and for pressing down wet cloth here and there, for example, along the sheer or at the stem ends. Use the roller for fill coats after the wet-out coat has hardened.

Speaking of stems, do not try to fold one end of the cloth around to the other side of the boat. You will spend the better part of the day trying to get it to lay flat, largely without success. It is a lot cleaner to let it just run straight off the end of the hull, and trim it off even with the stem later on. The wood at the extreme outside of the stems will be covered with epoxy anyway, and a brass stem band will be installed over it.

MAS epoxy, and most other brands, consists of the resin and two hardeners—slow and fast. There are other variations for special conditions, but for general use, some fast hardener along with the slow is all that you need.

MAS epoxy, when mixed with slow hardener, does not blush. As we mentioned before, blush is a waxy coating that forms on the surface of some brands of epoxy. It must be completely removed by washing and rinsing before the next coat is applied or it will cause problems. It will clog sandpaper, and varnish will not adhere well to an epoxy surface that still has traces of blush. We do not recommend using an epoxy that generates blush, since removing it is an additional step that you can easily avoid by using one that is blush-free. MAS will not blush even when you mix it with a slow hardener and then add up to about 25% fast (always maintaining the 2:1 ratio). If you use the fast hardener alone it will blush, but we will never use a mixture of resin and only fast hardener for wetting out fiberglass or filling the weave.

The MAS slow hardener is just what it says it is—slow. It is a very comfortable epoxy for the novice, since there is plenty of time to apply a full 6 oz. batch without the danger of it starting to cure before you are ready. This is the ideal situation for wet-out, since a good penetration of the wood before it cures provides a deep bond of the cloth to the hull.

You will be applying a wet-out coat, and two or three fill coats. In order for one coat to chemically bond to the previous coat, the previous coat cannot be fully cured when the next coat is applied. This is true with any coat; if your fingernail will dent the surface, the epoxy is not cured hard yet and no sanding is necessary. If it has cured hard and you see no dent, you must roughen the surface to provide "tooth" for the mechanical bonding of the next coat.

Consider the above discussion about chemical bonding vs. mechanical bonding on a sanded surface. Depending on the curing requirements and characteristics of your epoxy, we strongly recommend that you give yourself enough time to follow through to the last coat. Suppose you did the wet-out. The hull is now glassed but rough, and requires a few more coats to fill the weave. If you cannot add the fill coats at the proper time, you will wind up having to sand the wet-out coat. But that coat

is extremely rough, and sanding will cut the glass. Choosing a slow hardener for the wet-out coat will leave the epoxy still a bit soft after an over night cure, and fill coats can be done the next day without sanding. Some brands of epoxy cure a lot faster than MAS with slow hardener, so it is essential that you adjust your timing accordingly.

Using MAS epoxy with slow hardener, and with the shop at a comfortable 65°F to 70°F and nominal humidity, the wet-out can be done on one day and the fill coats the next. By adjusting the hardener for the fill coats to 25% fast and 75% slow while still maintaining the 2:1 ratio, you can apply two, or possibly three, fill coats the day after wet-out.

Getting to know your epoxy is important for success, but what if you have never worked with it before? Using a small hull mockup consisting of strips attached to a section of plywood and covered with some scrap fiberglass, mix a small batch of epoxy and do a wet-out. See how long it takes for the epoxy to "kick off" (begin to gel), how long it takes for it to cure enough to do a fill coat, and generally learn how to measure, mix, and handle it. You might even continue with this test piece and apply fill coats as well (Figure 11.4). The time and materials invested could mean the difference between a nice boat and a mess.

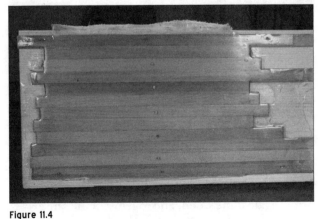

Figure 11.4

Fiberglass and epoxy test panel. The fiberglass and epoxy are applied to scrap strips of cedar that are glued and screwed to a board.

DOING THE WET-OUT

With everything ready and time allotted, mix 6 oz. of epoxy, consisting of 4 oz. of resin and 2 oz. of slow hardener. Pour a small puddle of epoxy on to the bottom board near one end. Spread it around on one side of the hull with a squeegee, but do not press hard—you just want to spread it, and you do not want to drag the cloth. Work towards the stem. When you get to the steep side, you may want to use a disposable brush in addition to the squeegee. Be careful not to let it run off the hull. Wet the cloth out all the way to the stem, on both sides of the hull. Do not create a problem by trying to wrap the cloth around the end of the stem.

With the cloth wet down on one end, work towards the other end (Figure 11.5). The work will go quickly along the main part of the hull. From time to time, like between batches, look closely at the sections you have just done. If there are dull whitish looking areas, indicating that the epoxy has soaked deeply into the wood and starved the cloth, add more epoxy to these areas.

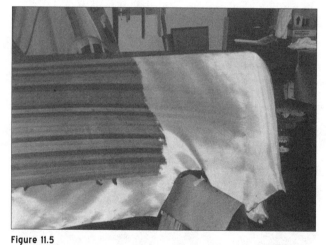

Figure 11.5
Hull wet-out nearly complete.

After applying a few batches, you can start the squeegeeing (what a word!!) process. The object of squeegeeing is to make sure the glass is pressed down firmly against the wood, and to redistribute any excess epoxy. Hold the squeegee at a little higher angle and press a little more firmly than when you are just spreading, but do not press hard enough to scrape epoxy out of the glass.

With some epoxies, the foamy stuff that results should be removed and discarded. MAS has stated that all of their product can be used, even if foamy. You can spread the foamy excess to dry areas. By the time it has gelled, the foam will have dissipated and cleared. This assumes that you use the slow hardener for the wet-out coat. With a faster curing brand of epoxy, removal of the foamy epoxy may be required.

When the hull is completely wet-out and squeegeed (Figure 11.6), periodically walk around it and look for any sags and runs. You should not see any on a wet-out coat, but if you do, use the squeegee to spread them out. Check for any bubbles or where the glass may have pulled away from the stem or sheer. While the epoxy is still sticky, you can work out the defects with a squeegee. Press them down, and try to get the cloth to stick.

Figure 11.6
Fiberglass wet-out complete.

If you have bubbles, attack them as soon as they are spotted: the more liquid the epoxy still is at this point, the easier it is to press them out. If you have a particularly ornery bubble, try slitting it along its edge, being careful not to cut into the wood. Work some epoxy into the slit to get the air out, and press the flap down. If you cut into the wood, it will leave a scratch mark under the glass. After a few hours, it will no longer be necessary to check for sags, runs, or other defects.

Now for some clean up. To remove the latex gloves, grab one at the cuff with your thumb and index finger and peel it off inside out. Then do the other one.

Do not turn them right side out yet; there is uncured epoxy on the inside. If you want to use them over again, wait until the epoxy is cured, like the next day, before turning them right side out. Latex gloves usually have talcum powder inside them to make them easier to put on. You will lose this slipperiness when you try to reuse them, but dipping your hands in the sawdust bin before putting them back on will work almost as well as the talc.

To clean up any uncured epoxy, white vinegar works well. The epoxy hardener is an amine, which is alkaline. Wiping it with the vinegar, which is an acid, neutralizes it. In any event, use waterless hand cleaner to clean your hands when you are ready to quit. NEVER use a solvent on your skin!! It dilutes the epoxy and allows it to soak rapidly into your skin. The potential for contact dermatitis is real, and chronic exposure can be downright dangerous.

THE FILL COATS

If you used a slow hardener and MAS epoxy for the wet-out coat, let it cure overnight. It will still be slightly soft in the morning, but this is the ideal time to trim along the sheer and stems and add a fill coat. Cut off the overhanging cloth flush with the sheer and along the stems with a sharp utility knife. Do not run your hand over the freshly cut area—fiberglass cloth with hardened epoxy on it can be quite sharp.

With the trimming complete, you are ready for the fill coats. For these you can use a roller, with a 2" disposable bristle brush here and there. The roller covers are half of a standard 9" cover. The nap is very short (on some labels it appears as "mohair"), and can be obtained from your epoxy supplier or sometimes from the paint department in large hardware or paint stores. Be sure that the covers are labeled for use with epoxy. Cut them in half (a band saw works well for this) and mount a section on a short roller frame. Do not bother with the usual paint tray—you do not need it.

For fill coats, you may hasten the cure somewhat by using some fast hardener along with the basic slow. Mix 4 oz. of resin, with 1½ oz. of slow hardener and ½ oz. of fast. If your pumps are working burp-free, this is four pump shots of resin, three shots of slow hardener, and one shot of fast. The resulting 25% fast/ 75% slow hardener mixture will cure faster than the 100% slow hardener wet-out coat (MAS epoxy assumed). Mix it for a full two minutes, as described previously. If your pumps are burping, you can use the calibrated plastic cup for measuring.[1]

Pour a puddle on the bottom board near one end, and have at it with the roller. The roller will probably soak up most of the first puddle. Spread it around, using a painting stroke much like painting a bedroom wall. Try for an even coat, and do not get it too thick. You will not fill the weave on the first coat—do not even bother to try. Also, do not worry about the foamy stuff; by the time the epoxy gels, the bubbles will be gone.

When you have rolled on the first 6 oz. batch, go over the entire area with a dry brush, tipping off any bubbles and dragging up any runs or drool. Do not try for a varnish-like finish; just keep the epoxy on the boat and not on the floor. You will not get all of the bubbles, but they will soon go away. If a lot of runs start to develop, you rolled it on too thick. Roll on the next batches, alternating between rolling on a coat and tipping off.

You can drag the brush over areas already brushed when chasing runs. The brush marks will level off in a few minutes. Go over the whole boat with a dry brush periodically throughout the day until there are no more runs to drag up. Let it cure until evening, and do another coat. By this time, you should be quite comfortable mixing and handling epoxy. Repeat the process the next day, and the filling will be done. We have found that three fill coats are sufficient when using the 4 oz. fiberglass (Figure 11.7).

101

Figure 11.7

Fully epoxied hull, ready for sanding.

SCRAPING AND SANDING

The next operation you must perform on the fiberglassed hull will be to sand the cured epoxy in preparation for paint or varnish. Sanding removes epoxy. When you remove epoxy, you may expose the fiberglass in places. You can paint or varnish exposed fiberglass, but if you varnish it, the exposed areas become visible in direct sunlight.

There are a few ways to prevent the exposure of fiberglass during sanding. If you apply enough epoxy initially, the problem will likely not develop. But how much is enough? The amount of epoxy put on to fill the weave is usually given as a number of coats. Saying "three coats are enough to fill the weave" is an imprecise statement, since there is no way of defining the final thickness of a "coat." Variables such as epoxy characteristics as a function of manufacturer, environmental conditions when you apply it, the thickness at which you apply it, and if you can keep the runs on the boat when they form rather than letting them drip off onto the floor all contribute to the final epoxy thickness. Only experience will tell the builder how many coats are enough.

If, after you sand the hull, you see a significant number of spots of exposed glass, another coat is called for.

A few dime-size spots here and there are of no consequence and will not be noticeable.

If you wait until you complete the sanding to determine if the epoxy is thick enough, the main problem you encounter will be just one of time. The epoxy must be allowed to cure hard before sanding, usually a few days to a week, depending on the epoxy used. If an additional coat is required, then sand the hull and apply the coat. You will then have to wait some additional time for curing before final sanding can begin. Only the experience gained with building your first boat will determine if that additional coat of epoxy should be applied during the normal sequence of filling the weave.

Before righting the hull, it is a good idea to do the preliminary surface preparation in anticipation of painting or varnishing. If there are any runs, use a cabinet scraper to take them down before sanding. Scraping runs rather than sanding them is preferred, since it is impossible to keep a sander on the run only and not off the surrounding area. Trying to sand off cured runs virtually assures the exposure of the fiberglass weave.

Scraping is easiest when the epoxy is still "green," that is, soft enough to be dented by a fingernail, and not yet cured hard enough to sand. This optimum time for scraping can be as short as several hours to as much as two or three days after the final coat, depending on the epoxy curing characteristics and ambient temperature. Sanding is not done until the epoxy has cured hard, which is usually a few days after the scraping. You do not have to scrape the surface down to a dull scraped sheen; just remove the high spots and let the sander do the rest.

If you notice a cloudy area developing as you scrape or sand, stop. The epoxy is still too soft, and you are smearing it. Scraping and sanding generate heat, and heat softens the epoxy, causing it to smear. If you are sanding, the softened epoxy will plug the sandpaper, causing more heat, more smearing, etc..... That cloudiness will not go away if you add more epoxy, and it will show up under varnish. The fix is to let it cure hard, then scrape and sand it off. Sanding may take off enough epoxy to require adding some back on.

Do the rough sanding with the random orbit sander and 80-grit sandpaper, with the sander hooked up to the shop vacuum. Sanding epoxy is dusty and potentially toxic, and some form of dust collection is an absolute necessity. If there is no way to collect the dust, a good-fitting dust mask and latex gloves are essential, followed by a shower after sanding. There will be dust all over the shop unless you are able to do the sanding outdoors.

Keep the sander moving, but do not swing it rapidly back and forth. Moving it slowly along the surface will prevent sanding swirls. Be very careful sanding the sharp edge formed by the side of the hull and the bottom board. It is very easy to sand off the fiberglass along this joint. Work the sander flat on the bottom board and let it extend beyond the edge. Do not tilt it to move it off the bottom board and onto the side of the hull.

When sanding the hull near the bottom board, again let the sander extend a bit beyond the bottom of the hull without rolling onto the bottom board. You can lightly sand the sharp edge of the hull/bottom board joint later by hand, just enough to dull the gloss. If the cloth becomes exposed slightly it is of no concern here—just do not cut through it to the wood.

The surface after sanding with 80-grit is not ready for varnish, but do not sand to the 120-finish grit until just before varnishing or painting. If you choose to use epoxy to glue the outwales on (Chapter 12), you will get it on the outside of the hull in places during installation. The final sanding will remove this excess epoxy.

1 See Appendix 3 for a description of how to calibrate a plastic cup for measuring epoxy.

CHAPTER 12

INSIDE CLEANUP AND GUNWALES

You have built the hull and it is finally time to get a better look at the inside. Those several squats under the support structure to peer at the upside down innards of the boat are about to end. You will soon be rewarded with your first look at a work-in-progress classic. But before righting the hull, some thought must be given to how you are going to support it in the upright position.

RIGHTING AND SUPPORTING THE HULL

A favorite support of strip-boat builders is a pair of slings. These can be any sort of two uprights separated by a distance sufficient to cradle the boat between the gunwales, with a strip of scrap carpet fastened to the top of each upright (Figure 12.1). The slings can be free standing, or designed to be used with the existing support structure after removing the hull and stock plank.

Figure 12.1
A typical sling. 2 by 4s gusseted together and mounted on a sawhorse.

Slings permit you to tilt the boat for easy access to work on the inside. If the slings are wide enough, you can invert the entire hull. Also, a padded horizontal support can be screwed to the uprights to support the gunwales of the inverted hull when painting or varnishing. With this type of rigid support, it is easy to work on the bottom shoes, stem bands, etc.

You should press an assistant into service to help in righting the hull, but you can right it single-handedly if suitable rigging is available. In one of our shops, the inner stems were detached from their supports on the strongback. We then placed ropes attached to ceiling hooks around the hull at both ends, which we used to lift the hull clear of the stock plank. We tied off the ropes, holding the hull above the support structure (Figure 12.2). We worked the stock plank free of the stanchions supporting it and removed the stanchions. Next, we placed the slings under the hull and screwed them to the strongback, and lowered the hull into the slings. It was then a simple matter to right the hull in place.

Figure 12.2
Hull hung from shop ceiling. The stanchions and stock plank have been removed.

Figure 12.3 shows the rib ends trimmed. When trimming the rib ends, leave about a quarter of an inch extending beyond the sheer. You will do the final trimming and shaping of the ends after you install the gunwales.

Figure 12.3
A first look at the inside. The rib ends are trimmed to within ¼" of the sheer, and slings have replaced the building stanchions.

The first order of business after righting the hull (and admiring it!) is the clean up of the epoxy runs on the sheer. There will be some hardened drips of epoxy on the edge of the sheer strip, which you should remove before cleaning the inside. The coarse side of a 4-in-hand rasp takes the lumps down quickly, but you must use care with the top of the sheer strip. When you approach the strip, switch to the fine teeth. Do not go all the way into the wood—we will get the last remaining epoxy when the gunwales are installed and the ribs are trimmed to their final shape. One caution here: do not even think about using a Microplane to clean up the sheer. The fiberglass will dull it useless with just a few strokes.

You sanded the ribs, stems, and bottom board before they were mounted. You planed the strips smooth when you sized them, and screwed them tightly to faired ribs. You scraped most of the dried glue squeeze-out from the strips between the ribs during stripping. You now have to clean up the remaining glue and sand between the ribs.

Most of the inside of the hull is concave, and is best cleaned of dried glue with a curved scraper such as the Pro-Prep, properly sharpened. A paint scraper can also be ground with a curve and sharpened. The gentle

curves of these scrapers also do a fine job on the convex areas just above the bottom board. Be careful not to cut too deep—just remove the squeezed out glue along the strip joints. Do a section between two ribs at a time; it is easier to mark your progress. You can easily vacuum out the dried glue chips and scrapings. Dampening the wood with a sponge will reveal any additional glue that must be scraped off. If you fitted the strips tightly, there should not be much to remove.

After you have removed the glue, the strips need to be sanded. In strip-built ribless hulls, sanding is a mundane, even boring, chore. In a ribbed guideboat, it is a challenge. Common random orbit sanders have disk sizes too large to fit between the ribs. The triangular pad detail sanders are effective, but slow. Finishing sanders do not fit the hull contours and tend to mar the sides of the ribs. Hand sanding borders on painful, both from the sometimes-awkward body positioning required and from the mental fatigue of sanding…sanding…sanding….

Then there is the dust collection, or lack of it. The Fein detail sander has an optional accessory dust collection system via the shop vacuum, but small finishing sanders are normally not so equipped. There is no dust collection with hand sanding, of course, but you may vacuum dust periodically. Without dust collection, a properly fitting dust mask is a requirement in the interest of safety.

The ideal sander for the inside of the hull would be a variable-speed random orbit type with about a 3" diameter hook and loop disk, vacuum dust collection, and an extension foam pad that allows sanding of contours. Metabo makes such a sander: the model SX E 400 (refer to Chapter 3). Sanding disks and a vacuum hook-up are available only as OEM accessories, the machine being too new for other after-market sources. We found that cutting disks from bulk rolled hook and loop paper (80 and 120-grits) is slow, but economical.

Power sanding the strips inside the boat between the ribs should not be difficult, since the ribs hold the strips fair. Contrast this with a ribless boat, where strips may be "stair stepped," requiring extensive sanding and fairing to shape the hull and correct misaligned strips. You should avoid excessive sanding between the ribs since the sanded surface could finish below the edge of the ribs.

If you had planned to remove the screws that hold the outer stems while the glue cures, now is the time to do it and plug the holes. It is better to cut the plugs from flat sawn spruce rather than using hardwood dowel plugs. Plugs cut from wood with the grain running across the plug, rather than along its axis, will be much less noticeable under varnish. Dowel plugs have end grain that is accentuated when finished.

Removing the stem screws is relatively easy with a long screwdriver bit in the screw gun. Inserting the plugs is a little more difficult, and trimming and sanding them may seem impossible. We use a narrow bench chisel to pare the plugs flush, followed by sanding with a thin flexible sanding stick. The stick is sliced from the edge of an ash board, about 30" long and thin and flexible enough to easily fit the inside curve of the stem. A 6" length of 120-grit sandpaper glued to the surface on one end completes the tool. You may have to narrow the stick to fit against the inside surface of the inner stem.

With the sanding nearly complete (some touch-up will be required later), it is time to plan the construction and installation of the various components that will complete the boat. These are the gunwales, decks, seats, brass work, and the finish. Gardner's drawings in the Durant book are highly detailed with dimensions and cross-sectional views of these parts. A description of their construction and installation follows in this and subsequent chapters.

GUNWALES

On a traditional guideboat, the gunwales protect the edge of the sheer strake, stiffen and strengthen the hull, and provide a mounting surface for the rowlock "straps" or plates. Gunwales on wooden rowboats less elegant than the guideboat are often dismissed as simple strips of constant dimension along their entire length, fastened to the sides of the boat with screws. But the Grant gunwales (or "wales," as they were known to the early builders) have important design considerations that cannot be overlooked.

Gardner's Plate IX shows the cross section of the gunwales at several frame (rib) stations. The shape amidships provides sturdy stock for mounting the rowlock plates. The angle of the outside surface is such that when the oars are placed in the water, the oar pins make a right angle with the oar shaft for maximum transfer of power. The gunwales are thinned in both thickness and width from about frame 4 to the stems, the gentle taper allowing them to be mounted dry (in most cases) without steaming and lending an aesthetic accent to the graceful lines of the hull. A decorative bead on the lower edge completes the design.

Gunwales may be made of several species of wood, although hardwood is preferred for durability. Durant states that Grant used the readily available Adirondack woods: cherry, oak, or ash, with spruce used on lighter boats. We opted for cherry. It is commonly available, and coordinates with the remaining trim used throughout the boat. Ash would be a second choice, but it suffers from discoloration (a fungus?) when the finish is worn or otherwise damaged. On one of our boats, we epoxied and screwed the gunwales to the hull. We did not consider oak, since it contains varying amounts of tannic acid, which is thought to react with the alkaline amines in the uncured epoxy, resulting in a weakened joint. We considered spruce too soft.

For a 16' boat, the gunwale blanks should be about 18' long. If that length of cherry were available, transporting and milling it would be challenging. Scarf-joining shorter lengths is much easier. We ripped three pieces about 1¼" wide from a straight-grained 12' cherry board and cut one piece in half. We scarfed each 6' half to a 12' piece using an 8:1 scarf ratio, yielding the two rough blanks.

A strong well-made scarf is important here, since the joint will be under strain as you fit the gunwales to the hull. Cut the scarfs with a sled on a table saw (Figure 12.4), reproducing the same cutting angle on both pieces. Make the cuts with the narrow edge of the stock on the sled, with the wide side held against the angled fence. The glue line on the outside surface of the finished gunwale will then be vertical, and hidden by the rowlock plate. Save the off-cuts; you can use those wedge-shaped pieces for clamping cauls when gluing the joint to direct the clamping pressure square to the joint. Do the gluing on a flat surface to insure a straight and accurate alignment of both pieces (Figure 12.5). A crooked gunwale blank is useless and may as well be cut up for seat frames.

Figure 12.5
Gluing gunwale scarfs. The wedge-shaped off-cuts are used as cauls to direct clamp pressure squarely across the joint. Waxed paper protects the tabletop from squeezed out epoxy.

Figure 12.4
Scarf cutting sled. The inside of the angled fence has sandpaper glued to it to prevent the stock from slipping. The base has a hardwood strip that rides in the miter gauge slot.

Figure 12.6
Completed scarf joint (this one is cut at a 5:1 ratio). Note its placement relative to the rowlock plate.

Use slow-curing epoxy to glue the scarf after first wetting the mating surfaces with unthickened epoxy and allowing it to soak in. After a few minutes, wipe off the excess and make the joint with thickened epoxy. Use clamps to hold the joint firmly, but not tight enough to cause excessive squeeze-out. Epoxy glue lines should be slightly wider than a conventional glue joint made with the common woodworking glues. Let the joint remain clamped overnight, after which you can clean up squeeze-out with a scraper. A light sanding completes the joint, and then the gunwale blanks are cut or planed to the final dimensions of 1 3/16" wide x 3/4" thick (Figure 12.6).

You may now shape the gunwale, but do not try to bend it around the sheer just yet. Allow the epoxy to cure for at least several days before bending, and then only after shaping. Trying to bend the unshaped rough gunwale will insure the need to make a replacement.

Shaping the gunwales is not a complete exercise in freehand planing, although it is fun to speculate about exactly how Grant would have done it. The well-practiced hand and eye of the old masters probably could have turned out a shaped pair of gunwales before lunch. It took us a bit longer.

On the ribs, mark the number of each rib on the top of the trimmed end. A soft pencil works well on the end grain. These marks are indispensable as references when laying out the gunwales, seat positions, yoke cleats, etc. On the gunwale blanks, mark the outside surface boldly and unmistakably. Doing this may prevent shaping the wrong edge later on.

The rowlock plates that will ultimately hide the scarf joint are located between the forward ribs 2 and 3. Using a flexible measuring tape (a cloth tailor's tape works well), measure the distance along the curve of the sheer from midway between forward ribs 2 and 3 to the center of the boat at rib 0. Lay out this measurement on the outside of the gunwale blank, beginning at the scarf joint and going toward the center. Mark this point on the blank "Rib 0." With this mark as the reference, make sure the gunwale blank is long enough to extend somewhat beyond both stems. Since the gunwales are now non-symmetrical with respect to the scarf joint, draw arrows from the rib 0 mark indicating forward and aft, and mark the top and bottom surfaces similarly. It is also recommended that each gunwale be marked as to its final location on the boat—port or starboard. All of these marks may seem redundant, but avoiding having to remake a gunwale because you cut the taper on the wrong edge makes the markings worthwhile.

The reference surfaces of the gunwales are the top and outside faces. These are square with each other and are not tapered. The task is to remove wood on the inside and bottom surfaces such that gentle tapers are formed. The taper on the inside surface is also angled with a rolling bevel. After marking reference points, you will rough out the tapers with a jig or sabre saw, then hand plane them to final shape.

Plate IX shows the cross sections of the gunwales from amidships to rib 4, then at ribs 8, 10, 12, and the stem. Measure the distances along the sheer from rib 0 to each of these ribs and mark the gunwale blank at corresponding locations by drawing vertical lines at the measured locations. Do this for both ends, and identify each line with its corresponding rib number.

Referring to the Plate IX cross sections, mark each vertical line with the height measurement shown, referenced from the top of the gunwale. For rib 12 and the stem locations, do not make any adjustment for the deck in the measurement. Use the actual dimension given on the drawing. Cutting the recesses in the gunwales for the deck is done after they are mounted.

Now connect the points with a line. You should have a straight line from the rib 4 mark to the rib 12 mark that tapers along the bottom of the blank; the line will then run to the stem end parallel to the top. Even though the stem location can be marked on the gunwale blank, do not cut it off. Shape the gunwale blank all the way to its end. You will cut and fit the excess to the stem when the gunwales are mounted. Cut on the waste side of the taper line, and plane to the line.

The taper on the inside surface is a bit more complicated because of the rolling bevel. Once the layout is completed, it becomes an exercise in planing between two lines that define the beveled taper, similar to how the bottom board rolling bevel was shaped.

Wrap the rib location lines around to the top and bottom of the gunwale blank, and mark their rib numbers. Make marks at the measurements for the width at each rib location on the top and bottom surfaces, measuring from the outside surface. You can see these dimensions on the Plate IX cross sections. It cannot be overstressed—*make sure you are marking the correct surface.* Connect the marks with lines on both the top and bottom. You should have reasonably fair lines; not perfectly fair, but sufficiently accurate for initial shaping. Mark the waste side of the lines with X's or anything else that will positively identify the waste. Since the bottom of the gunwale is wider than the top, you may use the bottom line as a cut line. Stay on the waste side of the line, and check that you indeed have the bottom up before making the cut. Plane the remaining waste off between the lines to create the rolling bevel. Note that the rolling bevel runs the length of the gunwale. The bevel is constant between the fore and aft rib 4s.

109

There is one final component of the Grant gunwales that is fairly easy to make: the bead along the bottom edge. At first glance, one would think a router could easily cut the bead. The problem with a router is that you probably do not have a suitable bit, and if you did, cutting the work pieces on a router table would be extremely difficult, given their length and tapers. We resorted to a very old technique that worked exceptionally well—the scratch stock. This simple tool is really a small shaped scraper. Some scrapers have the blade mounted in a holder; we converted a little-used cabinet scraper and it performed admirably. In fact, we also used the same scraper, with an additional shape ground in it, to shape the seat risers.

To get the shape we needed on the scraper, we used a chain saw sharpening bit in a Dremel high-speed grinder to cut two semicircular notches, and then partially ground the outer notch off. We did not do any other sharpening. Figure 12.7 shows the final tool.

Begin with slow shallow passes until the general shape is established; then full scraping strokes will cut the bead to its final shape.

The gunwales are now ready for dry fitting. They will be fastened with screws and may be left in place, or removed after the deck beams are fitted and, if desired, epoxied back on.

Figure 12.7
A scraper blade ground to produce the seat riser and gunwale bead shapes.

FITTING AND MOUNTING THE GUNWALES

The curve of the sheer indicates that a fair amount of force will be required to bend the gunwales into conformity, even with the tapered ends. Steaming both ends back 3' or 4' to facilitate bending may be advisable. The decision to steam depends on your confidence in the quality of the wood chosen for the gunwales, and the quality of any scarf joints. On one of our boats, the gunwale ends were steamed; on the other boat, we bent them dry. Do not get any steam or heat at the scarf joint, since the epoxy may soften and fail when the gunwale is bent.

Align the rib 0 mark on the gunwale with the actual rib 0 and clamp it in place, using a clamp on each side of center as shown in Figure 12.8. Place two more clamps a few ribs away, and align the top of the gunwale with the top of the sheer. We advise using padded clamps to protect the relatively soft inner surface of the sheer from denting.

Figure 12.8
Clamp the gunwale to the sheer strip with padded clamps to avoid marring the interior.

Drill a pilot hole for a screw through the gunwale into rib 0, making sure you place it so that it does not hit the screw holding the sheer strip to the rib. With ¾" wide strips, the strip mounting screw should be centered ⅜" below the top of the sheer. Locating the gunwale mounting screws at the center of the gunwale will clear the strip screw. As the gunwales taper further away from rib 0, the strip mounting screws will eventually have to be removed to avoid the interference. This occurs near rib 8.

Continue driving screws into the ribs, alternately moving the clamps on each side away from center. Maintain the bending pressure with the clamps so that the screws are not depended upon to draw the gunwale tight to the sheer. Do not drive a screw until you clamp the gunwale tight to the sheer.

When you reach rib 5 or 6, it is time to consider fitting the ends of the gunwale to the stem. The situation here appears daunting, given the relatively stiff piece of hardwood required to make tight compound angled butt joints between two stems about 18' apart over a compound curved surface, while also getting all the joints tight. You also cannot let the raw gunwale extend beyond the stems to mark it for cutting. To fit the gunwales, and other seemingly difficult fitting problems, one would think that the master builders would have some simple methods figured out. If they did, they incorporated them into the woodworking skills learned in the shop, but they never recorded them. The modern builder is left to his own devices.

First, you will have to cut a compound angle on the gunwale ends. Just guessing the location and the angles will insure the need for filling the error gaps later. Fortunately, you can get a more accurate estimate of these parameters by using an ancient tool—the story stick. The stick is made from a piece of soft wood, like pine or cedar, cut to the same cross-sectional dimensions as the end of the gunwale, and long enough to reach between the stem and a little beyond rib 8. Cut a compound angle on the very end of the stick, approximating the angles with a sliding bevel or even by eye. Place the stick along the sheer, noting whatever corrections you have to make to the angled cut at the stem. Fit the angle cut for a tight butt joint, using the 60-grit sanding stick to make the adjustments.

Once the end of the stick fits precisely against the stem when the stick is aligned with the sheer, clamp it to the sheer as if it were the actual gunwale. Make an alignment mark on the stick at rib 8, with a mating mark on the top of the rib. Remove the stick. Bend

the gunwale to rib 8, and copy the mark from the top of the rib to the gunwale. Lay the stick on the gunwale, align the marks, and copy the angles (Figure 12.9). Do not simply extend the angles to the gunwale or the cut will be short. Make sure the cut lines begin and end at the same locations as on the stick.

Figure 12.9
Fitted story stick aligned on the gunwale at the reference marks.

Carefully cut the end off the gunwale with a fine-toothed saw, being careful not to break the waste off and cause a splinter. Stay between ⅛" and ¼" outside the lines, and refine the fit with the sanding stick. The heel of the angle cut will need to be rounded somewhat to fit the strip/stem joint. Finally, complete the initial installation of the gunwale. It still needs a bit more milling for the decks, after which you will remove it so that you can fit the deck beams. You have yet to cut the notches for the deck beams, but they must await the cutting of the deck recesses.

DECK RECESSES

Plate XI shows a recess cut into the gunwale and sheer (Figure 12.10) to accept the edges of the deck planks, which are thinned to ⅛" at the sheer. Besides cutting the recesses, this section will also describe the clean up of the end of the inner stem.

No dimension for the location of the start of the recess along the sheer is given, but scaling an estimate from the drawing yields a distance of about 1½" forward of rib 10. Mark this location on both gunwales across the beam of the boat by laying a batten across both sides.

There will be a difference in the location of the mark with respect to the number 10 ribs because of the over-lapping rib halves. You may ignore this purely nit-picking detail.

Figure 12.10
Close-up of deck recess cut into gunwale.

Scribe a line ⅛" below the top of the gunwale, from the start of the recess to the stem. Saw or chisel the tops of ribs 11 and 12 to ⅛" or a little more below the sheer for clearance when cutting the recess. Make a shallow cut into the sheer/gunwale at the starting mark. The cut should be square with the boat centerline. Since only ⅛" of material has to be removed, be careful to not exceed this depth, but rather leave it a bit shallow to allow for final shaping of the bottom of the recess.

It is easiest to remove the waste with a spoke shave, and with a sharp chisel at the ends. Do not exceed the depth of the recess as indicated by the scribed line. In fact, it is probably wise to leave final shaping of the bottom of the recess until you install the deck beams. The deck curvature, slight as it is, may then be continued fair with the deck beams using the sanding stick.

The top of the inner stem complicates the forward end. You may shape the recess up to the stem, and then trim the stem to the depth of the recess with a fine-toothed handsaw. Finish the clean up with a chisel (Figures 12.11a and b). When the gunwale shaping is complete on both ends, remove the gunwales, making sure they are still properly identified as to port, starboard, fore, and aft.

Figure 12.11a
Before cutting recess and clean up.

Figure 12.11b
Recess cut, stem trimmed, cleaned up.

CHAPTER 13
DECKS

It is interesting to speculate on how decks came to be. Did they evolve from seats? Were they a cover to keep duffel dry? Were they added to stiffen the hull? Most likely, all of the above are true. Guideboat decks are thought to have originated as simple planks fastened across the gunwales. Some were inset flush with the sheer strake; others placed above it. Later, builders designed decks to add structural strength with as little extra weight added as possible.

Two people can carry the boat easily by lifting under the decks for short portages, and the beached boat can be entered by climbing over the deck. These tasks demanded rugged construction, and the Grant design for the decks provides both the requisite light weight and ruggedness.

Building the decks is an exercise in the precise fitting of curved members, but done in a logical sequence, it is not difficult. Plates X and XI show the drawings for the decks.

DECK BEAMS

If you had the foresight (or the instincts of a pack rat) and kept the off-cuts from the bottom board, you have sufficient ½" pine to duplicate the Grant deck beams. Although pine is Lewis Grant's choice for the deck beam in his sketches in the Durant book, fitting the carlins and gunwales requires inserting and removing screws a few times. A harder wood, such as ½" poplar, may be a more appropriate choice. On one of our boats, we used epoxy in addition to screws to fasten the deck structure, thus reducing the potential for loose screws in the pine.

Begin by making a deck beam template using the dimensions given in Plate XI and cut four rough blanks from the ½" material. Extend the blanks a few inches beyond the ends, maintaining the curve. Note that only a single deck beam drawing is shown. A second beam is required forward of the first, and since no dimensions are given we assumed that the same template could be used. As with the first beam, allow a few inches overhang. Finish the curved edges by sanding to the cut lines.

You will cut notches in the sheer strips that will mate with interlocking notches in the ends of the deck beams (Figure 13.1). Since the beams shown on the Gardner drawings are 1" high, we would expect a notch ½" deep in the sheer, with a similar size notched end in the deck beams. Plate X shows the location of the aft deck beam as lying midway between ribs 11 and 12. No dimension is given. Once again, the location of these scribed (footless) ribs brings up some trivial questions. Were the ribs mounted forward or aft of the rib station line? Were they in alignment across the boat, or staggered like the footed ribs? It makes no difference whatsoever: mount the deck beam midway between the ribs, making sure the distance from the stem to the notch location is the same on both sides.

Do not simply cut a notch blindly between two marks on the sheer. Mark the outside of the sheer for the notch location, then drop lines down that are square to the sheer. Finish laying out the notch by connecting the lines ½" below and parallel to the sheer. The accurate layout and cutting of these notches will keep the deck beams square with the sheer, insuring a good fit of the deck planks later on.

Figure 13.1
Aft deck beam notch, port side.

Figure 13.2
Deck beams and gunwales fitted. The slightly curved plane defined by the deck beams and gunwales is faired with the sanding stick.

Cut the sides of the notches only to the ½" depth line, keeping the saw inside the lines. Make sure to hold the saw square to the centerline of the boat. A plank across the sheer, with its edge aligned with the cut marks, will help to keep the saw aligned. Scribe the fiberglass between the cut lines with a utility knife along the depth line, and simply push the waste inboard. The piece will snap off quite cleanly.

You may clean up the matching notches across the boat with the sanding stick spanning the distance between them, using the notch on one side as a guide for the other.

Cutting the notched ends and fitting the deck beams into the sheer notches is an exercise in patience. If you lay the deck beam in the notches, mark the outline of the notch and cut it to the line, it will not fit because of the decreasing distance between the sides of the boat as you descend from the sheer to the bilge. This is a convenient starting point, however, for final corrections and fitting with rasp and sanding stick.

Once you fit the beams, trim the excess outside the hull flush and temporarily reinstall the gunwales. Now you can place gunwale-mounting screws into the ends of the deck beams. You may need to fair the bottom of the deck plank recesses to the curve of the deck beams. This will be a very slight angle, and may be left until the deck planking is fitted. You can fair minor irregularities along the curve of the deck plane with a sanding stick (Figure 13.2).

The deck structure at this point should have the deck beams and gunwales fitted and screwed down without epoxy. It will be necessary to remove the forward deck beams to work on the carlins, and the gunwales will be removed later in order that they may be epoxied on, or at least sealed with unthickened epoxy.

CARLINS

The carlins form the curve along the inner edge of the decks, support the coaming (deck circle), and add considerable strength across the boat at the decks. Traditional carlins were made from sawn spruce crooks, but we chose to use spruce sawn from planks. We did not laminate stock for the carlins, although that would certainly be possible. They would likely be stronger than simple sawn pieces, but the actual effective difference is minimal considering the location and fastening method. Using epoxy in addition to screws to mount the carlins, deck beams, and gunwales provides adequate strength.

At first glance, the complex shape of the carlin would seem to defy a method for its manufacture.[1] It is a curved member with angled surfaces which, to be effective, must accurately fit the sheer and the deck beams. Plate X gives detailed drawings of the shape.

Despite its complexity, the shaping can proceed from a single reference surface. That surface is the edge that

114

mounts to the inboard deck beam. With a suitable blank initially clamped or screwed to the beam, you will shape the remaining surfaces sequentially. We find that a disk sander is extremely useful for working the convex curved surfaces, along with a drum sander for the concave surfaces.

A rotary Microplane in the drill press makes quick work of some of the hollowing operations, but careful handwork with a curved rasp would be just as effective, if slower. It is in making the carlins that you realize a deep appreciation for the skill of the old traditional builders—accurately shaping the carlins from spruce crooks entirely with hand tools would discourage lesser workers.

The best place to start is to make a template—not of the carlin, but of the blank. Lay a piece of illustration board across the inboard deck beam and resting on the sheer. A triangle will be cut from it, the long (reference) side being the deck beam from a few inches beyond its center to the sheer, then along the sheer to rib 10, and then back to the starting point beyond the deck beam center.

From below, trace along the sheer and deck beam, and make marks a few inches beyond the center of the deck beam and another at rib 10. Include the location of rib 11 by tracing around the top of the rib. Remove the tracing and connect the marks from the deck beam to rib 10. The tracing represents the shape of the rough blank. Note that the side along the sheer is not straight, but very slightly curved.

Cut out the template, including the notch for rib 11, and fit it into the junction of the tops of the deck beam and sheer. Make any necessary refinements so that the template is a good fit. You should have a triangular piece slightly curved on the shortest side, which extends a few inches beyond the deck beam center with a notch around the top of rib 11, and fits the sheer and deck beam surfaces smooth and flush.

Select a piece of clear 2-by spruce, put a straight, square, and flat reference edge on it, and cut out the

blank. The notch for rib 11 is a bit of a guess, since it is not just a simple hole that is cut open from the edge. The hole is angled by an amount the same as the angle between the sheer and rib 11, and also the angle the side of the boat makes with the vertical. Careful layout here is essential.

When you are confident that the layout is correct, drill a ⅜" hole through the blank. Open the hole to make the notch by cutting into it from the edge. The notch will be refined after the next step to compensate for the angle the side of the boat makes with the deck. If the notch turns out to be too loose, you may fill the void with epoxy later during final installation.

Cut two clamping notches in the blank as shown in Figure 13.3. Do not cut the deck beam clamping notch too deep—there should be about ¾" of blank stock remaining.

Figure 13.3
Carlin blank clamped to sheer and deck beam.

Clamp the blank to the sheer and deck beam, making sure the deck beam is completely covered by the edge of the blank. At this point, the blank should fit the sheer along the bottom edge of the blank, and be offset away from the top of the sheer. The width of the gap at the top is a measure of the amount of wood that you need to remove from the bottom of the blank. Measure the width of the gap, remove the blank, and scribe this width along the *bottom* of the blank. Disk sand or rasp the waste off.

The shape of the removed waste is triangular, tapering from the width of the gap scribed on the bottom of the blank to the top edge of the blank. The goal is to remove wood so that the short edge of the blank fits snug against the sheer as well as along the deck beam.

With the deck beam completely covered by the blank, the top edge of the blank should be a little higher than the edge of the sheer. You may have to deepen the rib 11 notch. A rat tail file works well here. When the fit is acceptable, transfer the center mark of the deck beam to the blank, and trim the excess from the end of the blank. The trim line is not square with the top of the blank, but vertical. The resulting trim cut will be slightly angled with respect to the top of the blank. When fitting the other side, you may have to trim the butting ends back a bit more for installation clearance. Figure 13.4 shows both blanks fitted.

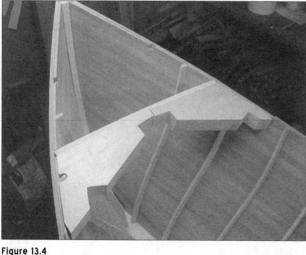

Figure 13.4
Both carlin blanks fitted and screwed to the deck beam, ready for shaping.

With the blank clamped to the sheer and deck beam, drive two screws through the deck beam into the blank, as shown on Plate X. Be careful of screw length and placement—the screw nearest the center of the deck beam will be shorter than the outboard screw. The outboard screw should be located so that it will ultimately be in the shaped carlin.

Next, we need a template of the deck circle curve so that you can cut the inboard curve of the carlin. You can draw it on illustration board according to the dimensions and measurements shown on Plate X. Here lies another nit-picking detail. The measurements are given to the outer edge of the deck circle, which is ¼" thick, and not to the carlin. The layout is further complicated by the fact that the deck circle is thinned to ³⁄₃₂" as it approaches the end at the sheer. Rather than try to accommodate this minor detail, we added ¼" to the dimensions shown, made a half-template, and continued with the carlin. Figure 13.5 shows the template in use.

Figure 13.5
The carlin curve template.

Lay the template on the mounted carlin blank, positioning it so that it makes a smooth transition to the inside of the sheer. Align the center of the curve with the center of the deck beam and ½" away from it. Trace the template and remove the blank, but do not cut it yet. The cut is not a simple square cut, but is angled so that the surface of the carlin to which the deck circle is fastened is vertical to the water line. See the sketch titled *SECTION DECK CENTER* in Gardner's Plate XI. To determine the angle, lay a sliding bevel on top of the deck beam and let the blade hang down loosely. Tighten the locking screw without disturbing the blade. The resulting angle on the sliding bevel is the angle to which the band saw table should be set to make the cut.

Cut the concave inside curve and clean up the saw marks with some sanding. To form the outside convex curve, use a compass to scribe the curve 1" away from the inside curve and cut it at the same angle as the inner curve. Remount the carlin, and fair the top with the sheer and deck beam (Figure 13.6). A sharp low-angle block plane may be useful here providing grain direction is favorable. The sanding stick is also a big help. After fairing the top, trace the bottom of the deck beam on to the back of the carlin, and remove it.

Figure 13.6
Inner and outer curves cut, top faired. Note the gap between the deck beam and sheer, the price for cutting the deck beam too short.

The last step in shaping the carlin is to curve the bottom surface to conform to the curve of the bottom of the deck beam. There should be a traced curve on the back of the carlin from the last step. To define the curve on the front, use the compass to scribe a line along the inside curve 1" down from the faired top surface. Now remove the waste between the front and back lines, forming the bottom curve. A rotary Microplane in the drill press is effective here, but you can also use a rasp or manual Microplane. You will round the inside bottom edges for gripping comfort after the deck circle is installed. Figure 13.7 shows the completed carlins installed.

Figure 13.7
Completed carlins installed. A single screw into the gunwale holds the carlin against the sheer.

BREAST HOOKS

The breast hook is the smallest piece of the boat. It is shown in the Durant book in a few of the Lewis Grant sketches as simply a "block." Grant identifies it as a "pine block with hole to let out water under deck when boat is bottom-side-up and to fasten end of deck center strip." The Durant text essentially repeats Lewis Grant's description. Gardner's Plates IX, X, and XI show it, and it is identified in Plate IX as a *BREAST HOOK BLOCK.* We have chosen to identify the piece as well by its nautical name, "breast hook," based on its placement and its additional function joining the sides of the boat at the stems. It also ties down the inboard end of the brass stem cap. A notch in the forward end forms what is known as a limber against the inner stem, which is open to the space under the deck by way of a small hole through the stem cap. Any water that may collect under the decks when the boat is overturned can drain through the limber hole. This feature is unique to Grant and also to Riley Parsons, who worked with him and then opened his own boat shop in Old Forge, New York.

Shaping the breast hook is best done on the end of a blank long enough to hold safely while milling the side angles and the notch. Note that the sides are tapered slightly as well as angled. There is nothing critical here, and the average builder should be able to easily shape it to fit, as shown in Plates IX, X, and XI.

117

You can make a template to define the bow angle and notched end. First, cut and fit the angles on the blank, then cut the notch, and lastly, cut the piece off the blank to the final dimension. Be sure to leave enough wood behind the notch for the deck cap strip and stem cap screws.

You should install the breast hooks at this point, even though the gunwales and deck framing have yet to be permanently mounted. Mounting the piece is somewhat awkward if only screws are used; we preferred to install it with epoxy. The purpose of the curved cutout on the bottom edge is unknown, although it would provide a landing surface for the screw heads. If you only use epoxy to mount it, you do not need the cutout. Once you have installed it, use the sanding stick to adjust the fairing of the piece with the gunwales.

DECK CIRCLES (COAMING)

Coamings were not a universal feature of other builders' boats, although they are found on boats of the Grant design (Grant called the pieces "deck circles"). Their purpose is to deflect water splashing on the decks, although it is unlikely that a guide or his passenger stayed significantly drier by virtue of the coamings. They do give the carlins and deck edges a finished look and add to the aesthetics of the decks.

At first glance, the coamings appear as simple flat thin boards, bent between both ribs 10 and screwed to the face of the carlins. However, to proceed from assumption to construction is to invite failure. Recall that the inboard edge of the carlins follows the convex curve of the inboard end of the deck. The coaming follows this curve while at the same time bending around from rib 10 along the carlin face to the rib 10 on the other side. The blank is therefore flat but with curved edges. Further compounding the job is the thinning of the coamings from a thickness of ¼" at the center to ³⁄₃₂" at the ends.

Begin by making a rough template. It will not define the final shape, but will give a good idea of what the blank should be cut to. Clamp a strip of illustration board to the inboard edge of the carlin, from the deck center to rib 10. Make sure there is sufficient width in the strip to completely cover the carlin along its entire length, with an inch or so beyond both top and bottom. Trace the bottom inside edge of the carlin to the template, and ¾" to 1" above the top of the carlin. Draw a vertical centerline. The template should be between 2" and 3" wide over its entire length, and be curved with the centerline square to the curve.

Now trace the template to a ¾" thick plank (we used cherry), making a tracing on each side of the center. Straight grain is not preferred here; a curved grain following the curve of the template is ideal for bending. Rough out the blank longer than required and re-saw it in half, and then plane each piece to ¼" thick (Figure 13.8).

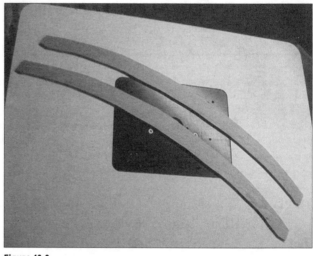

Figure 13.8
Coaming blanks resawn and planed, ready for thinning.

Thinning the blanks to ³⁄₃₂" at the ends is next. It is a good idea to thin only to ⅛", leaving the final thinning until after the blanks are bent. You may use a jointer with push blocks, tapering from near center to the ends. A sharp bench plane is also effective. The centers of the blanks should remain ¼" thick.

The blanks must be steamed or hot soaked in order to achieve the bends. We found that clamping the hot blank to the actual carlin was easy and effective (Figure 13.9), eliminating the need for a separate large and cumbersome bending mold. The ends of the blanks lie on top of the number 10 ribs, but after trimming and final fitting, they will spring into place.

Figure 13.9
Hot-soaked coaming clamped to shape over the carlin.

The ends of the blanks may crack during bending, especially if the grain there is weak and they have been excessively thinned. There is some twist at the ends, and they are being stressed directly along the straight grain. If a failure occurs, the broken piece can be fitted separately and glued in later. The repair will not be noticeable if the broken edges are preserved and the fit of the piece is accurate.

After the blanks cool and dry, remove them and set them aside until the deck planks are fitted.

DECK PLANKS

There was generally no ornamentation on guideboats. These boats were made to work, and superfluous ornamentation contributed nothing to their effectiveness. Decorative additions would take time for the builder to make, and would add nothing to the functionality of the boat. With the possible exception of the bead cut into the bottom edge of each gunwale, ornamentation was rarely seen on a guideboat. The one single place where the builder could indulge in a bit of artistic expression was the varnished decks. Wood was required for the decks. It mattered not whether that wood consisted of a few simple painted pine planks, or figured cherry or walnut glowing under varnish—it still had to be milled and fitted.

Deck planking was often highly individualized, to the point that one could identify the builder by the

structure of the deck. The *Virginia's* decks are typical of Grant's construction, being a single plank on each side of center separated by a small gap, which he covered with a tapered cap strip. Pine, oak, and walnut were typical, and we assume that Grant used pine for fully painted boats. In fact, on his #3 boat from 1904, pictured in Chapter 1 and observed first hand by the authors, he used pine for the decks.

Modern reproductions generally use attractively grained hardwood, as opposed to highly figured burl or crotch wood. Contemporary builders of traditional craft may opt for the pine, either painted or varnished. We chose to deck our boats in cherry (one has a contrasting wood for the cap strips) and then we varnished the decks.

The deck planks begin as boards or planks of sufficient dimension to cover an entire half of the deck from the tip of the gunwale at the stem to the aft end of the recess cut in the sheer. The length of a suitable plank is not a problem, but you may have to make up the width by edge joining narrower pieces. Do the joining after you mill the blanks to the correct thickness.

Begin by resawing and planing sufficient stock to 7/32" thick. It may be desirable to book match the stock to provide an attractive grain pattern on the completed deck. Edge glue pieces together to make up the required width, and let the glue cure overnight. PVA glue is sufficient here.

When the glue has cured, clean up the assembly and lay it over the deck framing. Cut a small notch to fit the piece around the stem on the top of the gunwale end. Note that there is a gap between the two deck planks, tapering from 3/16" wide at the stem to 1/2" wide at the carlin (Figure 13.10). With the notched plank clamped in place, trace the outline of the deck plank around the outside of the sheer from the stem to the end of the recess in the gunwale, and along the carlin. Cut the blank out about 1/4" oversize along the sheer and carlin. Clamp the blank to the bench top, and plane it to 1/8" at the sheer edge, as shown in Plate XI,

SECTION A-A. This thinning is important, since the deck planks will be forced to do what a flat solid board is not supposed to be able to do.

Figure 13.10

Deck planks installed. Note the tapered gap between the two sides.

When installed on the deck framing, the deck will be slightly concave fore and aft, but convex athwartships. This would seem to be impossible, but the thin portion along the wide area of the plank can be bent down to the gunwales quite easily.

After you have thinned the deck planks, you can do the final fitting. Trim the tail ends to fit the recesses in the gunwales. Clamp, and then screw the planks down in their final position. Plane and scrape the excess along the sheer flush with the gunwale, and rasp or Microplane the edges along the carlins, finishing by sanding flush with the carlins. Once again, do not glue anything yet—the only piece glued in thus far should be the breast hook.

DECK CENTER CAPPING STRIP

The last piece to be made for the decks is a capping strip that covers the gap between the deck planks (Figure 13.11). On varnished boats, builders sometimes make this strip from a contrasting colored wood. It is a simple piece, as shown in Plate X. Taper a ¼" thick blank to ⅛" thick at the end, and cut the piece out. A template is not required; a simple layout on the blank is adequate. Cut out the shape, smooth the edges to the layout line, and plane a bevel on the top edges. The piece could probably be beveled before reducing the thickness, but we did not do so.

Fitting to the deck is done with the deck planks screwed in place. Screw the capping strip down but be careful at the tip: the brass stem cap will extend over the capping strip later and be screwed into the breast hook, so screw location must be carefully planned. Drive the screws into the carlin and into the forward deck beam.

With the deck planks and cap strip screwed on, you can finish trimming the edge along the carlins. Trim only flush with the carlin—overly aggressive rasping can distort the carlin face. Also, it would be impossible to use a router with a flush trim bit because of the angle between the deck and carlin face.

Figure 13.11

Deck planks and cap strip installed and trimmed flush with carlin face.

COAMINGS REVISITED

The final fitting and shaping of the coamings (deck circles) completes the construction of the decks. Carefully trim the ends to fit snuggly against the sheer and ribs 10. The disk sander is very helpful here for making slight changes in the end angle or length. It will help to align a centerline on the coaming with the center of the deck during fitting. Spring clamps underneath the carlins temporarily hold the coaming in place, but if the bending was less than perfect, stronger C-clamps may be required to pull the coaming tight to the carlins. The goal is to get the coaming to lie flat against the carlins for its entire length, with no gaps. On the original boat, the ends of the coaming were inset into the siding as shown on Plate XI. We could see no structural need to do this somewhat difficult fitting task, and chose to mount the coaming ends flat to the sheer with no insetting.

With the coaming fitted and clamped in place, it may be useful to trace the bottom of the carlin edge on the backside of the coaming. If the amount of overhang is minimal, final trimming of the bottom of the coaming flush with the bottom of the carlin can be done with a Microplane or rasp. Otherwise, we recommend you trim the excess with a band saw after removing the coaming. Do not do the trimming with the coaming held in place only with clamps. You must screw the coaming into its final position before you do any trimming, or misalignment later is almost a certainty.

That said, screw it down with the clamps in place to firmly hold it against the carlins while inserting the screws. Do not try to pull the coaming tight with screws only—cracking is a real possibility. With the coaming screwed in, you can trim the bottom to final shape. Note that Plates X and XI show a non-dimensioned overhang of the coaming under the carlin. We opted to trim it flush with the carlin and round it over slightly, providing a more comfortable grip when carrying the boat by lifting under the decks. The top of the coaming is block planed to a height of about ¼" above the cap strip, tapering slowly to flush with the deck at its ends at ribs 10. Rounding over the top of the coaming completes the deck (Figure 13.12).

Now that you have completed the deck parts and structures, you may, if you like, take apart the whole assembly and glue it with epoxy. Certainly, this was not done in the original *Virginia* and it is not crucial. But, would it have been done in the old traditional boats had epoxy been available? Perhaps, but one can only guess. The advantage in using epoxy is that it seals the wood in the joint, preventing moisture from becoming trapped in the joints and encouraging rot. The disadvantage is the difficulty in removing parts for replacement. However, having to replace damaged parts is rare and a capable boatwright can deal with the epoxy if a repair is necessary. In any event, the decision on whether or not to epoxy is one to which you should give some careful thought.

Removal of the decks and gunwales is simply a matter of removing screws. The deck cap strip comes off first. Before removing the deck planks, make a story stick for each deck that will locate both the screws for the ends of the brass stem caps and the location of the limber holes. To do this, lay a piece of stripping on the deck along the center gap touching the coaming and extending to the stem. Make a mark on the strip at the center of the breast hook and at the limber hole. Identify the marks and whether fore or aft deck, and set the strip aside. As we said, you will use it later for locating holes at the correct locations in the brass stem cap.

The fiberglassed hull should have been sanded to 80-grit by this point. This sanding also provides a surface for a mechanical bond when you apply epoxy glue. For the gunwales, coat the inner surfaces with unthickened epoxy and allow it to soak in for a few minutes. Use a slow hardener for the mixture,[2] and brush on more epoxy if any areas seem to be dry.

After a few minutes, wipe off any excess and coat the surface with thickened epoxy colored with a little wood flour. Reinstall the gunwale, starting at the center, clamping and screwing sequentially towards the ends. Mounting the gunwales is easier than before, since you have already cut the screw holes. Remove only excessive amounts of squeeze-out with a putty knife, sharp stick, etc. It is best to leave the removal of the remaining squeeze-out until after the epoxy cures.

The deck beams should be set into their notches with epoxy right after you install the gunwales. The notches will be filled with epoxy from the gunwales, and if too much time elapses before the deck beams are installed, the cured epoxy in the notches will make a simple task annoyingly difficult. Coat the deck beams and carlins with epoxy, and screw the deck planks down. Make sure squeezed out epoxy does not plug the limber hole.

121

The cap strips are the last to be glued on.[3]

When the squeeze-out has partially cured (still soft), you may cut or scrape most of it off with a paint or Pro-Prep scraper. Wait another few days for the final hard cure of the remaining squeeze-out before attempting to sand the joints. You can use a cabinet scraper here to reduce the need for sanding.

Plates X and XI show cross sections through the carlins and deck beams, with the inside lower edges rounded. This was done to create a comfortable grip when carrying the boat upright. You can easily form the rounded shape with a round Microplane or curved rasp, followed by sanding.

The decks are now complete (Figure 13.12).

Figure 13.12
Finished deck.

RIB ENDS AND GUNWALE CLEANUP

A few details remain to complete the gunwales. The ends of the ribs require final trimming and shaping, and there may still be some epoxy on the sheer remaining from the fiberglassing of the outside of the boat. If you epoxied the gunwales on, there will be some additional squeeze-out you need to take care of. Figure 13.13 shows a rib end and gunwale area as it appears at this point.

Scrape the excess epoxy from the top of the gunwale, being careful near the area around the rib end so as

not to chip the top of the rib. The rib end is now ready for the final trim (Figure 13.14).

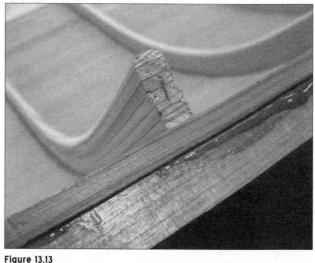

Figure 13.13
Epoxy squeeze-out and raw rib end.

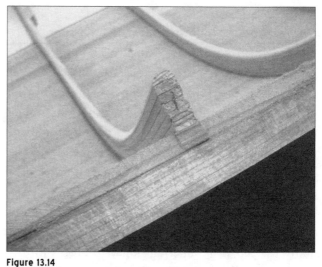

Figure 13.14
Excess epoxy scraped from gunwale, rib end ready for final trim.

You can use a flush-cutting saw to trim the rib end flush with the gunwale. The top of the gunwale may now be sanded; once again be careful at the top of the rib (Figure 13.15).

The next step is to round and smooth the rib end. The sanding stick is very useful here for the rough shaping, followed by hand sanding to complete the task. You may also lightly sand the edges on the top of the gunwale and sheer strip to break the sharpness (Figure 13.16).

Figure 13.15
Rib end trimmed, ready for sanding flush with the top of the gunwale.

Figure 13.16
Rounded and sanded rib end and gunwale.

123

If you epoxied the gunwales on, now is a good time to turn the hull over and clean up the squeeze-out from the underside. Finish up by sanding the bottom of the gunwale to remove the sharp edge.

1 Lewis Grant, in notes on a sketch he made for Durant's *The Adirondack Guide-Boat,* refers to the shape of the carlin as a "cow horn."

2 This may take overnight to cure, but it produces a better soaking into the wood pores than a fast-curing mix.

3 We know from experience that a rainy day will cause the deck capping strips to swell and distort if they are not sealed when installed. We had to remove them, allow them to dry thoroughly for several days, and reinstall them with epoxy.

CHAPTER 14

SEATS, CLEATS, AND RISERS

When one thinks of a rowboat, a flat-bottomed boat built from pine planks with seats made of boards comes to mind. The mental picture of a more elegant craft brings to mind the classic form of the guideboat, complete with light, delicately fashioned, but sturdy caned seats. But those seats were not always lightweight. The early guideboats, really workboats, had rowboat-style seats, which, when carry weight became an issue, gave way to the much lighter caned seats.

By the late nineteenth century, builders preferred caned seats; with fore and aft seats fixed and the middle seat removable, and some with backrests, depending on the placement in the boat or the desires of the customer. Plate XIII details the seats in the *Virginia.* We duplicated these seats with a minor deviation, described later, that makes their construction a little easier. This change, without any visible alteration to the final product, has to do with the mortise and tenon joinery. In keeping with the wood we used for the gunwales and decks, the seat frames and rising cleats are made of cherry.

SELECTING THE CANE

You may cane the seats in natural cane or modern plastic. The natural cane is obviously more traditional, but plastic cane has its adherents who claim that it is stronger, resists stretching, and is easier to work with. Natural cane may also be obtained already woven into sheets. This type of cane is easily pressed into routed grooves in the seat frame, eliminating the need to weave individual strands through drilled holes. We leave the choice of cane to the builder: we chose to weave the cane, one of plastic and the other natural.

No consideration was given to using pre-woven cane, which is a relatively modern innovation commonly seen on commercially available canoe seats. You will find caning instructions later in this chapter.

The seat frames begin as raw stock, cut and milled to the dimensions shown in the Plate XIII drawings. Cut the athwartships rails a few inches longer than the finished dimensions shown in order to accommodate minor variations in boat width. Likewise, cut the side rails a few inches longer in order to form the tenons.

MIDDLE SEAT

Construction of the middle seat is straightforward. Cut the mortise and tenon joints using a 5⁄16" tenon as shown on Plate XIII, *MORTISE AND TENON.* If you do not have a dedicated mortising machine or mortising attachment for the drill press, you may cut the mortises by drilling out most of the waste followed by clean up with a sharp chisel. In all likelihood, the old masters used a mallet to drive a mortising chisel, an art that has lost ground to modern power tooling.

After you have cut the mortises, size the tenons to fit. The important thing here is to center the tenon, maintaining the flush alignment of all of the frame pieces when assembled. Loose-fitting joints may result and are acceptable, provided you choose to glue the assembly with thickened epoxy.

Dry assemble the frame and align the cross rails with the athwartships rails to the dimensions shown on Plate XIII. Make alignment or witness marks across each joint so that you can maintain the dimensions during gluing by lining up the marks.

A flat surface used as an assembly station is a big help during seat-frame glue up.[1] Your shop's normal tool surfaces, such as the router table or table saw, are ideal provided you protect the surfaces from epoxy glue squeeze-out. Ordinary kitchen waxed paper works well, with pieces slid under the glued joint during assembly. Use lightweight bar clamps across the top to hold the assembly aligned—avoid excess pressure here. The bar clamps are easily applied, and can be set so that the assembly is not misaligned.

Follow the usual procedure to glue the seat frame together with epoxy. Using a slow curing hardener or no more than 25% fast, coat the gluing surfaces with the unthickened mixture and allow it to soak in for a few minutes. Coat the inside of the mortises, but not to excess. Be sure to liberally coat the end grain around the base of the tenons, adding more if dry spots appear that indicate a complete soak in. An acid brush works well for applying the unthickened mix. After a few minutes, wipe off the excess epoxy on the tenons. It will be awkward to wipe out the mortises, so do not use a lot of unthickened epoxy here. Now thicken the remaining epoxy and add a little wood flour for coloring.

Spread the thickened mix on all surfaces of the tenons, including the shoulders. Also, dab some into the mortises. Be sure that there is enough excess epoxy inside the joint to act as a gap filler in loose joints. After laying the assembly on the flat table top with wax paper under the joints, align the witness marks and clamp across the joints with the bar clamps. Make sure the surfaces of the joined rails are flush. There should be squeeze-out all around the joint, insuring that an adequate amount of epoxy fills the internal gaps. Do not disturb the assembly, and let it cure overnight.

The next day, remove the clamps and peel off the wax paper. The epoxy may still be a bit soft, which is an ideal time to clean up the excess squeeze-out. You can do this with a sharp chisel, being careful not to dig into the wood. To get the remaining excess, a cabinet scraper works well, scraping diagonally across the joint. Do not overdo it, or there will be a dip in the finished frame. The inside corners can be cleaned out with an ordinary pocketknife, cutting flush along each rail into the corner to dislodge the chunk. A few passes with the scraper finishes the corners. Complete the job by sanding both sides of the joints.

Grant's penchant for reducing weight bordered on the obsessive and the seat frames were no less objects of his attention. His rails are narrow by modern seat frame standards, and he thinned the length of the athwartships rails beyond the frame proper, further removing a few more ounces of excess wood.

You should thin the ¾" thick rails to the dimensions given in the cross sections in Plate XIII. You can do it easily by nibbling the waste off with the table saw blade set to the appropriate height and repetitively passing the rail ends over the blade. A stacked dado set will do the job in less time, if you ignore the setup time.

Shape the inboard ends of the thinned sections to a convex end on the main part of the frame as shown in Figure 14.1. A die grinder fitted with a ¼" carbide bit or rotary file, round Microplane, rat tail file, etc., are all effective for the job.

Figure 14.1
Shaped seat rail.

Finish the curve with sandpaper wrapped on a dowel, and sand the section. Round the rail edges over, making sure the rounding flows smoothly into the thinned section.

Gardner's attention to detail matches Grant's proclivity for weight reduction. His drawings of the seat frames include the caning holes. Unfortunately, the hole spacing is *not* given. From the dimensions, hole count, scaling, and some careful arithmetic rounding, we found that a ¾" spacing between the hole centers was about right. This is a standard spacing found on chair and canoe seats. The holes are assumed to be ⁷⁄₃₂", since that is the only hole size shown on Plate XIII, on the drawing of the stern seat. The common hole size in modern chair and canoe seats is usually ¼", but the slightly smaller size worked well.

Layout of the holes is next. Most caning instructions have you place a hole at the center of the athwartships rails, and mark off equally spaced holes on either side until you reach the side rails. The only seat in Gardner's drawings that has a hole at the center is the stern seat; the bow and center seats have an even number of equally spaced holes, centered on a space. We must say here that the hole layout as shown has no measurements establishing the accuracy of the drawing. We found that the hole count and layout as shown, using a ¾" spacing between the hole centers, provide a guide to a perfectly acceptable seat when caned.

The distance across the seat between the holes on the fore and aft athwartships rails should be a multiple of ¾", or more simply stated, the side rail holes should begin and end with the same ¾" spacing at all locations.

After you have laid out the holes evenly and centered them over the seat frame, you can drill them. An awl pressed into each mark will guide the drill bit, which you should feed very slowly until you start the hole. A brad-point bit works well, but a ⁷⁄₃₂" brad-point bit is not a common size. The solution is to use a ³⁄₁₆" brad-point bit to drill the holes through, and then widen them to ⁷⁄₃₂" with the more common standard twist drill bit.

The holes have sharp edges, which can damage the cane over time, that should be softened. Just a touch with a countersink bit will take off the sharpness. A little more elegant alternative is to round the edges with a brass-piloted ⅛" radius round-over bit in a table-mounted router. The brass pilot fits the holes, and rounding over all of the holes on both sides takes but a few minutes. Simply position the hole over the spinning bit and move the frame as if you were swirling it.

The rising stops, shown in the drawing above *SECTION D-D* on Plate XIII, are easily cut from leftover stock but cannot be attached to the seat frame until the rising cleats are made and installed (see Rising or Seat Cleats below).

BOW AND STERN SEATS

The modern woodworker might find it a challenge to cut the mortise and tenon joints for these seats as shown on Plate XIII. The old masters probably hogged out the angled mortise with a stout mortising chisel and mallet, a technique less practiced in today's power woodshop.

It is impossible to cut the mortise and tenon joints for the middle seat with precision using power tools at the angles shown for the bow and stern seats. With a slight modification to the joint, however, we will be able to use our power tools. Rather than angle the mortise, we simply angle the tenon. By cutting the tenons a little long across an angled shoulder, we can then square them to the shoulder, and hence to the mortise. Figure 14.2 shows a full-size layout of the stern seat, including the detail of the angled tenon.

127

Figure 14.2
A full size drawing is helpful for making seat frames.

A full-size drawing is extremely helpful for laying out the stock needed to make the seats. You can lay out the raw stock on the drawing, and mark the cut lines with accuracy. Mark the center of the athwartships rails, align the stock on the drawing, and mark for the mortises. The side rails can be similarly marked for the angled tenon shoulders. When the angles are drawn on the raw stock, it is a simple matter to set a sliding bevel to the angle and transfer it to a table saw miter gauge to nibble the waste to form the tenon. Be careful here: you must reverse the miter gauge angle to cut the opposite shoulder on each end.

The rest of the assembly follows the regimen used for the middle seat: dry assemble, make alignment marks across each joint, epoxy, etc.

SEAT BACKRESTS

When the guide used his boat for his own personal use without passengers, a seat backrest was only added weight. To accommodate "sports," or perhaps for a bit of elegance when ladies were aboard, a backrest was added to the stern seat (Figure 14.3).

Figure 14.3
Grant bent bow backrest.

The backrest shown on Plate XIII was standard equipment on the Grants' boats at the time they built the *Virginia*. The vertical rail extensions fit into the corner of the extended side rails of the stern seat, and rested against the coaming. Backrests in contemporary boats are optional, but are usually included in the interest of historical accuracy.

The bent bow frame is built from steam-bent stock. The only way to steam bend such a tight curve in a solid piece of wood is to bend it after freshly cutting it from the tree. The modern kiln-dried wood available to the average woodworker only bends grudgingly when steamed or hot soaked, so the bow must be built up with thin laminations.

To build the bent bow frame, cherry (or other hardwood of your choosing) laminations are cut, hot soaked, and bent around a form built from 2-by stock (Figure 14.4). The eight laminations are ⅛" thick, about 1½" wide, and 56" long. After the laminations thoroughly dry out, glue the frame up with epoxy. It is important to make sure the laminations are tight when glued—there must be no gaps (Figure 14.5a). To help in the gluing, use shaped cauls, shown in Figure 14.4, along the curve. After curing, remove the raw blank from the bending form (Figure 14.5b) and clean off excess squeezed out epoxy.

Figure 14.4
Bent bow shaping form and gluing cauls.

Shaping the final form of the recurved bent bow requires care in laying out cuts, and frequent referral to the drawing in Plate XIII. After you carefully band saw the sides to approximate thickness, the bent top portion of the bow is shaped with the disk sander, rasp, and Microplane. The cross piece is then fitted and installed as shown in the drawing: make sure that the distance between the bottom ends of the frame are as designed and that these ends will fit between the extensions on the bow seat frame. Notch the bottom ends to fit the seat frame and hold the backrest in place. A slight angled flat is required on the inside of the bottom ends to fit against the seat frame. After a final sanding, you are ready to drill the caning holes.

Figure 14.5a
Gluing the laminations.

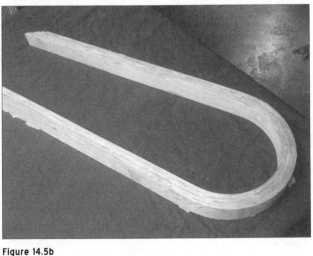

Figure 14.5b
Raw blank.

As previously mentioned, John Gardner was a stickler for accuracy and detail, which is strikingly evident on the drawing for the bent bow backrest. Although no dimensions are given for hole spacing and layout, we found that if the holes were spaced at ¾" along the vertical and curved portion of the frame and centered on a line ⁵⁄₁₆" in from the inner edge, the hole count on the drawing worked out perfectly. For the holes on the cross piece, there must be fifteen equally spaced to provide a match for the fifteen holes in the curved top portion.

To lay out the holes, first make a template for the top. This is simply a half circle drawn with a radius that is ⁵⁄₁₆" greater than the inside radius of the curve, for a total of 4¹⁄₁₆". Place a mark on the edge of the curve at the very top center. This is the position of the center hole. Mark the edge of the curve at ¾" intervals. There should be seventeen marks, representing all of the holes along the curved top. Lay the template on the frame and mark the holes. Then draw a line on each vertical rail from the end hole on the curve down to the crosspiece. These lines should be ⁵⁄₁₆" in from the inner edge and mate with the line of hole marks on the curve. Lay out the holes by placing marks along the lines beginning at the last mark on the curve, and spaced at ¾" intervals. The last hole near the bottom should be just above the crosspiece. See Figures 14.6a and b.

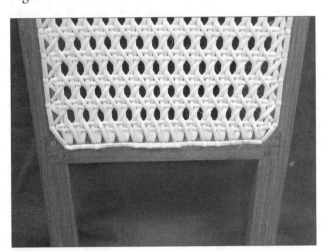

Figure 14.6a
Bottom detail.

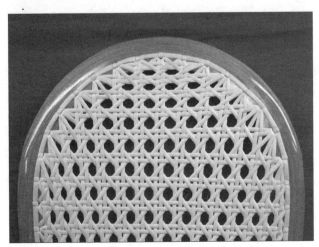

Figure 14.6b
Top detail.

129

Drill 7/32" holes at the marks, but be careful along the curve. The angle of the drill should follow the surface along the curve so that the holes are square to the frame at all points. For the crosspiece, there are fifteen holes, equally spaced. These holes are much closer than the main holes. Mark the center of the crosspiece and draw a layout line 5/16" in from the inner edge. Make marks at 7/16" intervals along this line, beginning at the center. There should be fifteen marks. Drill 7/32" holes, break the edges, and do any final sanding required.

Varnishing of the seat frames and backrest is conveniently done when the rest of the boat is finished, provided varnishing is planned. Varnishing the seat frames is common practice, even on painted boats, but they may be painted. Whatever your choice, the seats must have a finish applied before caning. The next chapter describes finishing the boat. Caning the backrests is very similar to caning the seats, which we describe next.

CANING THE SEATS

With the seat frames built and finished, it is time to cane them. This is a most pleasant diversion, free from the usual sawdust, noise, and sanding associated with boat shop work. A couple of hours in a comfortable chair with a few tools and you will have done a seat. The first one will take the usual extra time as you travel the learning curve, but the rest rapidly become routine.

Cane is available in two different forms, each in various sizes. There is natural cane, and the increasingly popular plastic cane. Natural cane is the choice for builders of traditional guideboats, but is not recommended for the first-time seat caner. While the finished product is quite attractive, the handling properties and soaking requirements of natural cane add another level of complexity that we can dispense with when using plastic cane. The instructions that follow will apply to plastic cane, and except for the soaking, you may also use them as a basis for caning with the natural material.

The two questions builders most frequently ask are: how much cane do I need, and what size? Suppliers (see Appendix 5) estimate that a 500' hank will cane two large seats, and a 1000' hank is enough for five seats. Obviously, you must consider the size of the seats, but the 1000' hank was sufficient for the three seats and backrest on our boats. We used the supplier's so-called medium width for all of the caning. A binder cane, which is simply a shorter length of a slightly wider cane, is usually supplied along with the main cane. We use this as a trim for finishing off the holes around the seat.

The tools required for caning are few and simple: a pair of small wire cutters for trimming the cane ends, about two dozen tapered hardwood pegs for securing cane ends during caning, a piece of paraffin or bees wax for lubricating the cane during the later weaving stages, and an awl for opening holes with several strands of cane already in them (Figure 14.7).

Figure 14.7
Everything you need for caning seats—a piece of wax, awl, cane, binder cane, pegs, and cutters.

Caning may be done in several patterns, but for boat seats, the most common one used is the seven-step pattern. It is the easiest to weave and produces an attractive result. Six of the steps consist of weaving cane in single overlaying patterns over the entire seat, with each new step repeating but in a different pattern. The seventh step is the binding, or trim.

We will describe caning of the stern seat. It is a bit more complicated than the simple center seat, but it will demonstrate the general procedure along with the details of caning a seat with angled sides.

With the seat frame right side up, place it so that the rear rail is away from you. We will refer to the parts of the seat frame as the rear or top, the front or bottom, and the left and right sides.

The cane has a top and a bottom: the top is slightly crowned and the bottom is flat. Whenever you are caning, the flat side is always down on the frame. Plastic cane is a continuous length, so we need to cut an amount that will be easy to handle. About 15' to 18' is convenient. If you hold the end in one hand and the loose cane in the other, and stretch your arms out as far as possible with the cane between them, you will have approximately 6'. Do this three times, and cut the length off the roll.

STEP 1

Push 4" or 5" of the end of the cane through the hole in the rear rail nearest the center from the top side, and secure it by pushing a peg into the hole. Push the other end through the hole directly opposite in the front rail and pull it through, making sure the cane will lay flat with no twisting. Do not worry about getting it extremely tight here; it will get tight enough during the later weaving steps. Secure it temporarily with a peg.

Move to the next hole to the left, and feed the cane up from below, over the rail, and to the next hole on the rear rail. You may now move the temporary peg in the front rail to this next hole. Keep working the cane back and forth, moving and inserting pegs as required. You will run out of holes on the rear rail, but still have holes left on the front rail. Run the cane from the front rail to the side rail, inserting it in a hole such that the strand of cane is parallel to the cane already placed.

Cane the other side of the frame the same way, using the same holes on the right side. Any time you need to trim an end, leave 4" or 5" on the underside of the

frame. Figure 14.8 shows a stern seat with Step 1 caning complete.

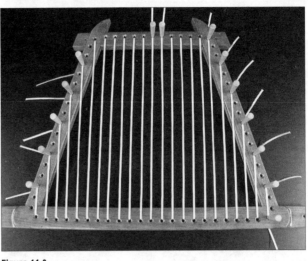

Figure 14.8
Step 1: Complete.

STEP 2

The next step is similar to the first. Simply lay cane back and forth from left to right over the Step 1 strands. There is no weaving here; the cane just lies on top of the strands (Figure 14.9). Some holes in the side rails will have two strands of cane in the same hole.

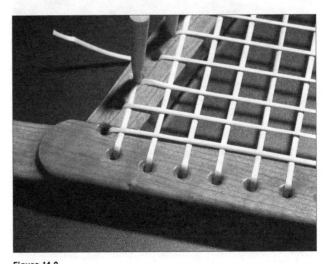

Figure 14.9
Step 2: Cane is placed right over the Step 1 strands.

STEP 3

Once again, cane right over the top of the previous step with no weaving. This time, however, begin with the cane inserted into the first hole without a peg—immediately to the left or right of the originally

131

pegged Step 1 center hole. If you look at the underside of the top or bottom rail at this point, you will see cane between every other pair of holes, where the cane was reversed for the next strand.

If you started Step 3 in the same hole in which you started Step 1, the cane would build up in the same pairs of holes underneath. Staggering the start hole for Step 3 eliminates this problem, and cane will then be seen between all holes on the undersides of the rails. You will appreciate this small detail when you tie off the cane ends later.

Try to keep the cane side by side with the Step 1 cane. This will make step 4 (next) a little easier (Figure 14.10).

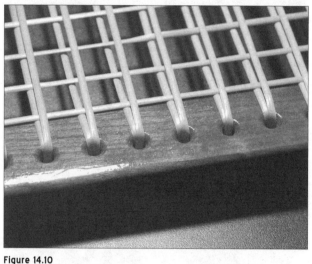

Figure 14.10

Step 3: Cane over Step 2, with some spread between Steps 1 and 3.

STEP 4

Now we get to do some weaving. Step 4 is just like Step 2, but this time we weave it. Look at Figure 14.11 for a visual cue about how to proceed. You can see from the photo that spreading the Steps 1 and 3 strands helps in Step 4. When weaving the Step 4 strands, always weave them the same way: if the first horizontal Step 4 strand was placed to run beneath the first horizontal Step 2 strand, all of the Step 4 strands should run beneath the horizontal Step 2 strands. As you progress during this step, you will find that the strands from the previous steps begin to tighten. This is normal. If it gets difficult to pull the strands through, you can lubricate the cane by first

pulling it across your piece of wax. Lubricate both sides of the cane for maximum effect. Figure 14.13 shows a completed Step 4.

Figure 14.11

Step 4: Weaving.

By now, you are probably running out of pegs, and the underside of the frame is looking pretty shaggy with all of the cut ends hanging down. A lot of these ends may be tied off and trimmed at this point. There must be cane going into or out of the holes immediately adjacent to the hole with the loose end. Feed the loose end over, then back under the cane next to it, forming a loop. Pull it tight and trim it off, leaving about ½" (Figure 14.12). Try to form the loop such that the final trimmed end will point inward, so it will likely be less visible when the seat is finished. Also, leave the trimmed cane about 1" to 1¼" long at this point. Mistakes do happen, and retying a piece of cane after correcting a problem is much easier when there is a sufficient length of cane to retie. You can final trim to around ½" later.

STEP 5

Here is where the classic caning pattern forms as we begin weaving cane diagonally across the seat. By now, the cane already woven has tightened up considerably, and will get even tighter as you weave Steps 5 and 6. Be sure to wax both sides before starting.

Begin at the upper right corner. Go under the horizontal strands and over the vertical strands, as shown

Figure 14.12
Tying off the loose ends.

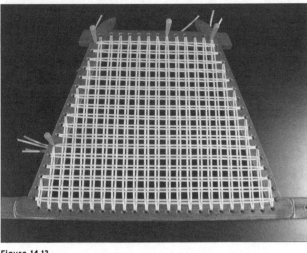

Figure 14.13
Step 4: Complete.

in Figure 14.14. Weave the cane through several holes, and then pull the cane all the way through. Be careful here—the cane has a tendency to twist just before the last of it is pulled through.

In the previous four steps, some of the horizontal and vertical strands met in the same holes in the side rails. In Step 5, and later in Step 6, two of the diagonal strands should be started or ended in these same holes (Figure 14.15).

Continue weaving cane from right to left and back and forth, filling in the area on the top left section the same way, until the entire seat is covered as seen in Figure 14.16. Do not be concerned yet about the multiple strand holes on the left rail. They will be done in the

next step and will match the right rail. Also, there may not be a diagonal strand from the right rail into every hole on the left. You may have to skip a hole now and then just to maintain parallel diagonals.

Figure 14.14
Begin Step 5 in the upper right corner, weaving under the horizontal and over the vertical strands.

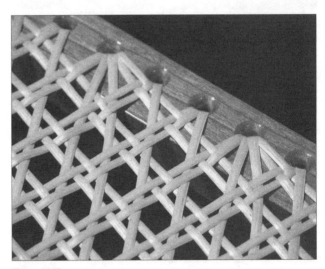

Figure 14.15
Two of the Step 5 diagonal strands in the same hole as all of the other strands.

STEP 6

Now start at the upper left corner, and weave over the horizontal strands and under the vertical—just the opposite of what you did in Step 5 (Figure 14.17). Any holes that were skipped on the left rail during Step 5 should be correspondingly skipped on the right rail during Step 6, and any holes that were doubled on the right rail should be correspondingly doubled on the left. Tie off and trim all loose ends.

133

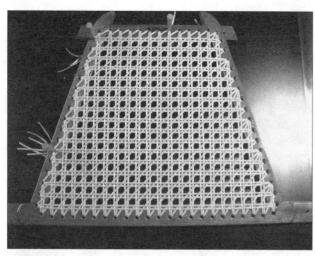

Figure 14.16
Step 5: Complete.

Figure 14.17
Step 6: Strands going from upper left to lower right.

134

STEP 7

The last step finishes off the caning with the binder cane. You will stitch it on with lengths of the same cane used for caning the seat. The goal is to lay the binder cane across every hole, making a neat finish.

Begin by cutting a piece of binder cane long enough to go all around the seat at the holes, with about 6" or 8" extra. Feed about 6" or 8" of regular cane up from underneath through a hole near the center of the rear rail. Fold it over and feed it back down through the same hole, forming a loop. Slip about 2" or 3" of the binder cane through the loop, and pull the stitching cane tight to capture the binding cane to the hole. Make sure that both the binder and stitching canes

are right side up. Feed the long end of the stitching cane up through the next hole, over the binding cane, and back down. Pull it through, stitching the binder to the hole. Repeat this all around the seat (Figure 14.18). You may need to poke the awl through a hole to open it enough to get the stitching through. Try to part the strands rather than pierce them with the awl.

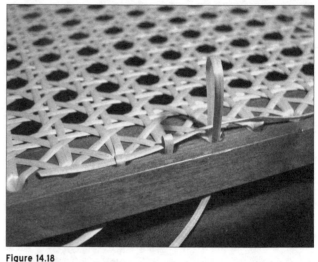

Figure 14.18
Stitching on the binder cane.

When you get back to near where you started, lay the binder cane over the starting end, and stitch both together for a few holes. Trim the binder neatly, and trim any loose ends. Wipe the wax residue off both sides with a clean cloth moistened with paint thinner. See Figure 14.19 for the completed seat.

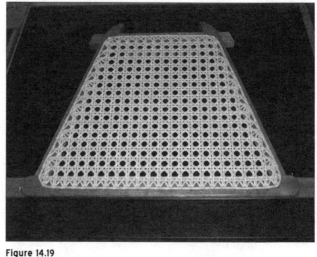

Figure 14.19
Completed stern seat.

Cane the remaining seats and backrest similarly. The middle seat is the simplest, since it is rectangular. For the bent bow backrest, be sure to use the hole layout shown in Plate XIII and described earlier in this chapter.

RISING OR SEAT CLEATS

The rising cleats are somewhat delicate, being the smallest size and length of wood (and the least weight) that could support a guideboat seat. Driving screws through them into the ribs must be done very carefully. There will be a slight curvature required to fit to the ribs at the fore and aft seat positions, which is achieved by simply drawing the cleat tight to the ribs with the mounting screws. Straight grain wood is much less likely to split, both when drawing it down on the ribs and later when installing the seat mounting screws. If cherry or walnut is used, be prepared to make some extra rising cleat stock.

Plate XII shows the rising cleat dimensions. The safest technique for making cleats is to start with a piece of board stock planed to ⅝" thick. You can then easily cut the shoulders on the edge of the board with a table saw and round the shoulder. When the shaping is complete, rip the cleat from the board, and begin another. The portion above the shoulder is rounded over with a shaped scraper, shown earlier in Figure 12.7. The scraper shape was ground by eye with a small grinding bit in the die grinder ending with the correct curve to fit the shoulder on the blanks. As you did when you scraped the bead on the bottom of the gunwales, begin with light passes, being careful to keep the scraper centered (Figure 14.20).

Once the outer portions of the round over have been established, you can scrape more aggressively to finish it. Change direction occasionally for the smoothest cut. Maintaining the correct shape on the ends of the work piece is difficult—use blanks a few inches longer than required, and trim the ends to length after shaping.

The rib positions of the rising cleats are shown on the bottom drawing on Plate XII. In Chapter 4, we described how to mark the rib drawings at the appropriate locations for the rising cleats. If not done already, transfer these marks from the drawings to the actual rib patterns. Then, holding the marked rib pattern against the respective rib, transfer the mark to the rib. When you have transferred all marks to the ribs, you can mount the rising cleats at the marks. If all goes well, the cleats will be evenly positioned on both sides of the boat and the seats will lie on the cleats at all four ends of the athwartships rails with no rocking.

Figure 14.20
Forming the seat riser on blank stock using a shaped scraper.

The screw holes for mounting the cleats to the ribs must be pre-drilled and countersunk into the cleat. It is best to do this with a Fuller bit, which combines a tapered twist drill with a countersink. Both the depths of the drill bit and countersink are adjustable with setscrews. Drill the center holes first so that the curvature to the ribs is established. Screw the center of the cleat down, and then drill and fasten the ends. A minor adjustment to the mating opposite side cleat may be made later if it is only fastened lightly with the single center screw. When the seat is ready for final installation, it can be placed on the risers and the cleat rotated slightly around the single screw so that all four rails of the seat fit flat on the cleats without rocking. The remaining screws may then be installed.

With the installation of the rising cleats, the seat frames may be completed. Trim the athwartships rails to center the seat, leaving some overhang between the sides of the hull and the rising cleats.

135

Angle the trimmed ends to follow the hull contour for a good appearance, with any sharp edges neatly rounded. With the center seat in position, clamp it to the rising cleats and position the rising stops so that the seat will not later slide from side to side. Mark the positions from below, and screw the rising stops into position.

The removable middle seats in our boats are held by rawhide or cord lacing securing them to the rising cleats. Screw the bow and stern seats to their respective cleats with thin round or flat head screws. To mount the seats, clamp them into position, aligning them evenly on the cleats. Mark clearance hole locations on the rails directly over the thickest portion of the cleat. Remove the seats and drill the clearance holes for the screws, and return the seat into position on the cleats, clamping it in place. Drill the pilot holes for the screws, using the correct bit size for hardwood for the size screw used. Coat the screw threads with a wax lubricant (bees wax preferred) and drive the screws home.

If at some point in the life of the boat you need to replace a seat rising cleat, it is not just a simple matter of screwing on a new one. The reason for this is the cleat is drilled for the screw holes at angles that are slightly different for each hole. To assure accurate placement of the holes, carefully drill out the screw holes in the ribs to ⅛" and plug with glued dowels. Trim the dowels flush with the ribs, and remount the new riser as previously described.

YOKE CLEATS

The carry yoke defined the guideboat as a carry boat. It supported the boat on the guide's shoulders, with the yoke arms in notched cleats fastened to the ribs amidships. The yoke cleats are shown fully dimensioned in Plate XII and are easily shaped from ½" stock.

The yoke cleats are not plumb when they are mounted, slanting outboard from the vertical. The bottom of the notches must be angled somewhat so that the yoke bearing surfaces of the notches are horizontal.

This is seen on Gardner's Plate XII, *SECTION A-A* of the *YOKE CLEAT* drawing. You can easily make this correction if the notch is initially cut square, but only to the depth of the outboard edge. This dimension is not shown on the drawing, but a notch depth of ⅝" is a good starting point. After the arms of the cleats are rounded to the shape shown in the drawing, sand them smooth and mount them to the ribs. Using a small (1¼" diameter) sanding drum in a screw drill and holding the drill level, sand the bottom of the notch to its final angle.

1 It may be easier to shape the athwartships rails before final assembly. Shaping the rails is described later in this chapter.

CHAPTER 15
FINISHING

There is a certain softness to an unfinished (as opposed to incomplete) object made of wood, be it a birdhouse, bedroom set, or boat. The natural surface of the wood is in full view, clouded perhaps with enough remnants of sanding dust to heighten expectations of what is yet to come. The craftsmanship of the builder is fully exposed. What happens next could mean the difference between a visually appealing piece and a botched job. Welcome to finishing.

For all of its strength and durability as a structural material, in some ways wood is really quite fragile. Left exposed to the elements, it is subject to oxidation, discoloration, warping, and can become the host to insects, fungus, and rot. It will absorb just about any liquid that comes in contact with it, leaving a stain when the liquid evaporates, if ever it does. Pity the plank that is a victim of petroleum—it will wear the stain long after its utility has ended.

THE WHYS, WHEREFORES, AND WHATS
Finishing wood preserves and protects it from the ravages described above, while imparting an additional level of beauty that can only enhance its overall appearance. We are blessed with a seemingly endless assortment of commercially available finishing products. Concoctions formulated by amateur chemists abound, ranging from mixtures of simple ingredients to complex brews of the exotic. Somewhere, at some time, somebody was sure to have tried fermented goat spit. We have poly- this and alkyd- that, dyes and stains, oils and varnishes, several grades of shellac (really, dried bug spit—where is the goat?), lacquer, epoxy, latex, enamel, urethanes, one-part, two-part,

oil-based, water-based, and waxes, all variously available as brushing liquid, spraying liquid, wiping liquid, gloss, semi- gloss, satin, and most of which are available in the ubiquitous spray can.

The master builders were not so blessed (or cursed); there was varnish, and there was paint, plain and simple. About the only choice they had was in the color of the paint. Given just these two products, builders painted some boats, varnished some, and combined paint and varnish for others.

For our *Virginia* reproductions, we chose to varnish one of them inside and out using several coats of a gloss spar varnish containing UV (Ultra Violet) protectors. The final inside coats were a satin-finish varnish, chosen to reduce the glare from the gloss base coats. We coated the other boat with epoxy inside, and then we varnished it with a high-gloss spar varnish with UV protectors. We painted the outside with several coats of a one-part polyurethane high-gloss marine paint.

Whether you choose to paint or varnish your boat is a matter of personal preference. Working guideboats, used for basic transportation as well as fishing, hunting, and transporting "sports" through the wilderness, were typically painted dark colors inside and out: mostly blues, greens, browns, and even black. Dwight Grant's boats were often a dark blue-black. Generally, builders used a different color for the inside of the boat than for the outside, and sometimes they painted the decks and gunwales in yet another color. Grant often painted the exterior stems in a color that contrasted with the hull. The dark colors of the boats helped them blend into their surroundings and kept the sportsmen from being too conspicuous as they pursued their quarry.

The *Virginia* is unusual in that it has a blue exterior and a bright orange interior, decks, and gunwales. The boat's original owner requested this unique color scheme in honor of his alma mater, the University of Virginia.

Varnished boats began to appear to meet the demand of sportsmen and others who employed them as pleasure craft. Although requiring more upkeep than a painted boat, varnished boats are perhaps nicer to look at, as they highlight the beauty of the wood and show off the intricate patterns of tacks and screws as well as the fine craftsmanship that is required for their construction. Many, but certainly not all, of the guideboats being built today, whether stripped or planked, are varnished.

Do not worry if you really cannot decide whether to paint or varnish your boat. Whichever finish you choose now, you can finish your *next* boat using the other!

A good finish begins with good construction. At this point, you should have all of the defects filled and sanded fair, the epoxy smoothed and faired, and the surface sanded to the proper grit.

Consider using a high solids (also known as high build) primer on hull surfaces to be painted. It provides a good bonding surface for the paint, and it will fill any swirl marks caused by rapid movement of a random orbit sander. If you are going to varnish the boat, make sure all of the screws are tight and flush with the wood surface, or, if you are painting it, the screws should be slightly countersunk and filled. We recommend powdered filler that is mixed with water, such as Durham's Rock Hard Water Putty, for filling over screws that will be painted.

Before opening that can of finish (or rounding up a goat), there is one detail that must be attended to. We have built a boat in some sort of shop, where we also cut and planed a lot of wood, and sanded many square feet of boat hull. The by-product of those past weeks or months of construction is everywhere—

DUST. It is on the walls and ceiling, on the floor, the light fixtures, under everything, in everything, and launched into the air when you walk around or open and close a cabinet or drawer. You must deal with it before starting the finishing process, or it will settle on the wet finish as tiny specks, detracting from the beauty of the completed boat. The excuse sometimes given that "it is really a non-slip surface" just does not fit with good craftsmanship.

Dust can be isolated, removed, or immobilized, and you should do all three for effective dust control during finishing. It is critical that the air be dust-free while the finish is drying, usually for a few hours. Regardless of whether or not you will varnish your boat in the same shop you built it, you should take some simple and reasonable precautions to make sure there is a minimum amount of dust in the shop air:

1. On the day before applying the finish, thoroughly vacuum the space where you will paint or varnish the boat. Vacuum all accessible surfaces—if you can see dust on *anything,* vacuum it, especially the entire floor. If you will be working in a basement or other location with exposed insulation, or in a space situated below foot traffic, consider stapling plastic sheeting above the boat. If you have an air filtration system in your shop, run it during vacuuming, for a few hours following, and from the moment you enter the shop on finishing day until the finish is dry. The gentle circulation of clean air provided by the air filtration system aids in drying the finish, especially the inside of the boat. Have everything you will need close at hand so you will not have to move excessively around the shop or open drawers or cabinets on finishing day.

2. Do not use paint or varnish, even if it is new, without first straining it into a separate clean and preferably new container fitted with a fine-mesh paint strainer. A simple conical paint strainer lined with two layers of women's hosiery material will work well. Similarly, do not return any varnish to its original container without straining it.

3. Keep your shop warm enough to insure adequate and timely drying of the finish, and do not attempt to brush on subsequent coats until previous coats have fully dried. As with epoxy, the manufacturer's recommendations for temperature and humidity should be followed.

4. If working in warmer weather, try to keep flying insects out of the shop. Make sure you screen open windows and doors (crucial for ventilation).

5. Use a new disposable foam brush for each coat. There are no loose bristles that can come off in the finish and no loose grit to contaminate the finish, each a common problem with bristle brushes. Be sure to get the type that has a plastic internal stiffener. One brand we found to be effective was made by JEN.

BEFORE YOU START

It may seem to be a trivial detail, but the clothes you wear while painting or varnishing can affect the quality of the job. What woodworker does not have at least a few flannel or wool shirts or sweaters to put on for taking the chill out of a cool shop? The soft nap of these materials is a dust magnet, and you will dislodge tiny lint fibers from the shirt or sweater by the simple act of wearing them. When you de-dusted the shop, some of the dust in the air collected on your clothing. Wearing your same favorite old shirt while applying the finish is an invitation for dust and lint fibers to fall off your sleeves and on to the finish. Shower, and wear a sleeveless or short sleeve shirt. A plain cotton T-shirt is ideal, and is virtually lint free.

Pet hair and dander can also settle on a wet finish. You should have removed all the residual cat and dog hairs during the shop cleanup, but stay away from your pets and keep them out of the shop on finishing day. Have everything ready, and mist the floor just before starting the next morning.

SPRAYING

Spraying a finish on the boat can produce the ultimate in finish quality. However, the formerly popular airless spray guns and conventional spray guns driven by compressed air have largely been replaced, both in the professions that demand high quality finishes and in the advanced amateur shop. Production shops that routinely spray finishes use specialized tools well out of reach of the modestly equipped amateur. There is an alternative, though.

The most popular type of spray equipment that is increasingly being used by amateur woodworkers is known as high-volume low-pressure, or HVLP for short. This system (Figure 15.1) consists of a multistage turbine providing the high volume of low-pressure air, and a bleeder type (continuous airflow) spray gun with an integral cup for holding the material to be sprayed. A relatively large diameter air hose connects the turbine to the gun.

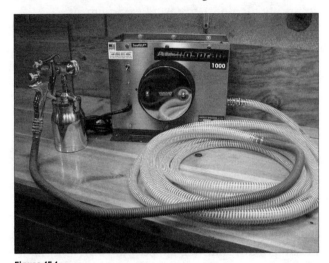

Figure 15.1
A four-stage HVLP spray system.

HVLP systems are capable of spraying a whole range of finishes, including the paint and/or varnish used in small boat finishing. Developed to reduce the amount of volatile organic compounds (VOC) released to the atmosphere, HVLP systems have transfer efficiencies approaching 90% or more, compared to about 50% for a conventional compressed air spray system.

With the high transfer efficiency of HVLP spraying, over-spray can generally be ignored and the inside or outside of a guideboat hull can be sprayed in a matter of minutes for each coat. One would think that the potential for achieving a high-quality finish, ease of

139

application, little over-spray, and the reasonable price of a system, would all contribute to its use as the method of choice for applying a finish. Ah, but there are some trade-offs....

Dust control is even more demanding. Spraying involves moving large quantities of air through the gun, where it picks up and atomizes the finish material and blows it onto the surface to be coated. The finish stays on the boat, but the leftover air can stir up a lot of dust in a hurry. We do not recommend spraying a boat in the same shop in which you built it unless you can move it to an area maintained dust-free specifically for spraying. Our experience has shown that enclosing a temporary spray area within the shop in a sheet plastic tent fitted with air filters and ventilation fans is a marginally effective, poor substitute for a dust-free work environment.

Then there is the clean up of the gun. Despite the salesman's claims of simple, easy clean-up, a thorough cleaning consists of an initial flushing of the gun with clean solvent, followed by disassembly of the gun, cleaning of the internals, and finally reassembly. It can literally take longer to clean the gun than it takes to spray a coat of finish on the boat.

In addition, you have to take the time to set up and mask the boat. Ordinary newspaper works well for masking, but it must be applied carefully. The masking tape has to be completely pressed onto the surface to be masked, or finish will seep under it.

In spite of these drawbacks, spraying can produce a nearly flawless finish, free of runs and brush marks, but it takes critical attention to dust control, preferably in a specialized facility or area maintained dust-free by design.

PAINTING

As previously mentioned, boats that were actually used for guiding by those who built or bought them were usually painted inside and out. Modern reproductions tend toward a varnish finish on both traditionally planked and cedar-stripped hulls. There are variations, of course, as exemplified by one of our boats. We varnished the inside, decks, stems, gunwales, seats, risers, and cleats over two coats of epoxy. We only painted the outsides of the strips, providing a pleasing complement to the varnish.

The choices of paint for marine use are many and varied. You may immediately eliminate bottom paint: guideboats are rarely, if ever, used in a marine environment requiring an anti-fouling paint. Two-part paints, designed for use below the water line on larger hulls that remain docked or moored for an extended period are also unnecessary for a guideboat, which is usually hauled ashore after a day of use. Although two-part paints produce results that are outstanding, their mixing, application, and safety requirements exceed the capabilities of the amateur builder. It is best to leave their application to qualified professional boat shops.

With what, then, do we paint our boat? Some amateur kayak builders have successfully used common latex house paint. However, we rejected it on our boat because of a lack of gloss. We finally decided on one-part marine high gloss Interlux Brightsides polyurethane. Although the manufacturer does not recommend it for continuous use below the water line, such as on a seasonally docked or moored boat, it is perfectly acceptable for day-use boats. This paint may be brushed or sprayed, making it appropriate for amateur builders, and it produces the desired gloss. We confirmed it to be compatible with epoxy before we applied it.

The epoxy fill coats were sanded to 120-grit on the outside of the hull, vacuumed, and tacked off. We thinned the paint slightly, using the thinner made and recommended by the paint manufacturer.[1] We used a new foam brush for each coat, sanding between coats as directed, with four coats ultimately required to completely cover the substrate epoxy. In retrospect, we should have applied a high-build primer first to fill random orbit swirl marks and other defects that remained invisible until coated with paint.

Dry sanding with 220-grit between coats was difficult. The paint, while dry, had not fully cured hard and the sandpaper plugged almost immediately. Wet sanding, which we did for later applications on both boats, was much more effective.

After curing for a few weeks, the hull was wet sanded with 240-grit sandpaper, dried, tacked off, and sprayed with three coats of paint using the HVLP system shown in Figure 15.1. There was no sanding between coats; we sprayed on successive coats while the preceding coat was still tacky. We did not clean the gun between applications, since the time between coats was only a matter of a few hours.

VARNISHING

Although varnishing can be time consuming and tedious, it will leave a fine furniture finish on your boat which not only highlights the beauty of the wood, but also the craftsmanship that went into building it. While it is by no means true that the only reason you would paint a boat is to hide defects, you should not varnish it if there *are* significant or noticeable defects in the hull (e.g., too much wood filler, joints that do not fit together tightly, unsightly imperfections in the wood, etc.). Clear finishes such as varnish have a nasty habit of highlighting such defects.

Varnishing a boat does not need to be the stressful experience it is sometimes made out to be. Online information, for example, can be daunting: there are perhaps thousands of discussions in forums on the Internet that deal with varnishing. Reading through just a small sample of them reveals that everyone has an opinion on the best way to achieve a flawless finish. Such a vast array of possibilities can confuse the novice or first-time builder and turn what was expected to be a pleasant experience into a complete nightmare.

Complicating the matter further is the perception that you can only achieve a flawless finish in an environment *completely* free of even the most minute dust particles. This is not the case, and unless you have the resources to create a perfect "clean room," do not worry about the errant dust particles and other tiny debris nibs that wind up on the varnished hull. They are going to appear no matter what you do. As we discussed before, dust control is important to minimize them, but rubbing out the finish is the only way to achieve a flawless varnish finish.

VARNISHING THE EXTERIOR HULL

The process we describe here will produce a finish we feel is difficult to improve upon. It is a bit time consuming and requires some elbow grease, but the end result is well worth the time and effort.

If you have not already done so, you will need to prepare the hull for varnishing. The epoxy should be completely cured and sanded smooth with 120-grit sandpaper. Do not go to a higher-grit abrasive, otherwise the varnish might not bond well to the epoxy.

After sanding, wipe down the hull with a tack cloth or a slightly damp rag to remove any remaining dust. Once the hull is dry, it will be time to begin varnishing (Figure 15.2). The goal is to apply a minimum of three coats of gloss marine spar varnish, although four or five coats are preferable. One of our boats has five coats of varnish applied to the outer hull for extra protection.

Use a good quality marine varnish such as Z-Spar Captain's or Flagship varnish (Flagship purports to have greater UV protection), or Epifanes. Before brushing the varnish on, add some Penetrol, available at most paint stores, or use a thinner made specifically for your brand of varnish. Determine the amount to add by the quantity of varnish you are working with. Follow the manufacturer's instructions for the correct mixture. The added thinner will slow the drying time slightly and help you achieve a more uniform, easily brushed on coat. Experience will dictate the correct viscosity of the varnish: too thin and you will have to deal with runs; too thick, and you will have difficulty brushing on a smooth, self-leveling coat.

Work one side of the boat at a time, down from the middle of the bottom board to the sheer. You can varnish the gunwales separately later along with the rest of the trim. Using a 3" or 4" foam brush, start at one end of the boat, about 2' to 3' in from the stem.

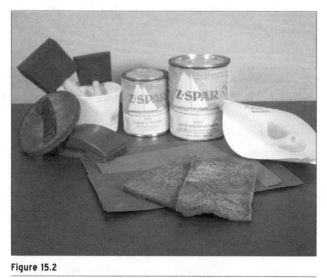

Figure 15.2

Some of the tools and materials needed for varnishing.

Apply a thin coat of varnish in long, smooth, horizontal strokes, holding your brush at a 45° angle. Work out toward the stem. Now go back and work another 2' or 3' section, working toward the area you just completed, allowing the brush strokes to overlap the varnish previously applied. Repeat this process all the way to the other end of the boat. It is important to leave edges wet to achieve smooth transitions between overlapping sections.

Smooth out any drips or runs before they become tacky, and work out any bubbles that may have formed by passing your brush over the surface at a 90° angle (called "tipping off"). Pay particularly close attention to the stems, to the first few inches below the bottom board, and to the hull sections closest to the bow and stern. These surfaces are at a 90° angle to the floor, and are where runs are most likely to occur.

Get in the habit of viewing the area you are varnishing from different angles, as runs are often visible at one angle but not at another. Holding a light at different angles can also reveal missed spots in the varnish. After you are satisfied with one side, proceed

to the opposite side. Avoid the temptation to go back and revarnish any missed areas or runs if the varnish is tacky—you will only create more problems. Instead, you can sand these areas smooth before applying the next coat.

The next few steps describe how to achieve a glass-smooth, virtually perfect final finish on the exterior of your hull. You *could* simply apply successive coats of varnish, sanding or rubbing with steel wool between each one, and call it a day after the fourth or fifth coat. But, given that what you have built can be described as a piece of heirloom furniture (that just happens to float), you are going to want to give it the best finish possible.

When the first coat of varnish is dry, roughen the hull a bit to prepare it for the second coat by going over it with an abrasive green or gray 3M Scotch-Brite pad. Do not rub through the first coat to the epoxy—all you want to accomplish here is to create a surface sufficiently rough to allow the second coat to adhere well.

If any runs, blotches, drips, or bubbles remain, sand them with 100- or 120-grit sandpaper, but go easy! You may want to use a light touch with a sharp cabinet scraper to attack the runs. The underlying varnish may still be tacky once the skin has been scraped off. These areas can be wiped with a rag dampened with thinner and allowed to dry thoroughly before sanding lightly. Using a new, clean foam brush, apply the second coat of varnish in the same manner as the first. Remain as vigilant as you were with the first coat to eliminate runs and bubbles before they dry.

The next step is important for achieving a glass-smooth final finish. Prior to the application of the third varnish coat, you must wet sand the hull. Begin by keeping handy a supply of soapy water (dishwashing liquid or Murphy Oil Soap is fine) as well as a container of clean, soap-free water, and a sponge. Attach a piece of 400-grit wet/dry paper to a sanding block. Dip the sanding block in the soapy water or apply the solution to the paper. Do not be afraid to put on a good supply of the soap solution, which will act as an effective sanding lubricant.

Begin at one end of the boat, and working toward the other, start sanding the hull. Keep it wet by dripping clean water from the sponge as you go. A spray bottle containing some of the soapy water also works well here. Sand in horizontal strokes, following the strip pattern, and stop every so often to re-lubricate and clean the wet/dry paper. Do the same to the other side of the hull.

When you are done, rinse the hull thoroughly with clean water to remove sanding and soap residue, and let it dry. Go back over any spots you might have missed, then take your Scotch-Brite pad and lightly work over any low spots, which will appear shiny when viewed at a low angle against the now dull wet-sanded areas. Tack off the hull or wipe it down with a rag dampened with mineral spirits.

When the hull is dry, apply the third and fourth coats of varnish. There is no need to wet sand between these two coats. Simply use the Scotch-Brite pad as you did between coats one and two. Wet sand again between the fourth and fifth, or final, coat. Apply the final coat of varnish to your hull just as you have the previous four. Check for runs and drips, and brush them out before they become tacky.

Next you will rub out the finish, the final step in producing a perfectly smooth hull. However, you will need to let the varnish completely cure and harden for approximately three to four weeks (Figure 15.3). In the meantime, you can jump ahead to the section on finishing the interior of the hull.

RUBBING OUT THE FINISH

At this point, your varnished hull is fully serviceable and, if you are so inclined, you *could* stop here. However, rubbing out the finish to a final, glass-smooth appearance is worth the extra time, and it will add one more element of fine craftsmanship to your boat. You can find various ways to do this described by a number of finishing experts in different venues.[2]

It essentially amounts to rubbing out the finish by first wet sanding the hull with successively finer grits, and then polishing with automotive compounds.

Figure 15.3
Varnished hull.

Begin by wet sanding the hull with 400-grit wet/dry paper affixed to a sanding block or wrapped around a sponge. Once again, use soapy water as your sanding lubricant. Go over the entire hull before proceeding to the next grit, working your way through 600-, 800-, 1000-, 1200-, and finally 1500-grit papers, thoroughly rinsing off the sanding slurry after each sanding. A final sanding with 2000-grit paper will make the polishing stage easier, but it is not essential. The first stage using the relatively coarse 400-grit is the most difficult, since at this point, there is the potential for the greatest number of dust specks and other defects. The following, finer grit stages are much easier, since all that will be removed are the scratches from the preceding stage.

To restore the hull to a glass-smooth, high-gloss finish, you will need to apply a series of automotive rubbing compounds (Figures 15.4a and b). You can do this by hand, with polishing pads and terry cloth towels, or with an electric buffer/polisher fitted with applicator and lambs wool buffing pads. Your variable speed random orbit sander can be modified to work as a buffer by fitting it with an extension foam pad first. If you mount the polishing pad on a hard-edged rubber disk on a heavy-duty polisher, be careful not to cut through the finish with the hard sharp edge.

143

Figure 15.4a
Applying a liquid polishing compound with an electric buffer/polisher.

Figure 15.5
Hull finishing products. Note the random orbit sander fitted with a foam polishing pad.

Figure 15.4b
A final wiping of the hull with a soft clean cloth, and the mirror finish is complete.

Figure 15.6
Exterior hull polished to a glass-smooth finish.

144

We find Meguiar's products, which are widely available at automotive supply stores, work well. Begin with Meguiar's #1 medium-cut cleaner. Follow this with #2 fine-cut cleaner, and then with #9 swirl remover. Finish up with #26 Hi-Tech yellow wax (Figure 15.5). Meguiar's polishing products are designed for application using a power buffer, and complete instructions for doing so are provided on the product container. Following these directions will produce a deep gloss that is perfectly smooth to the touch (Figure 15.6).

VARNISHING THE INTERIOR OF THE HULL

With the inside of the hull sanded, the decks installed, and inside wood ware (seats, risers, cleats, etc.) made,

fitted, and probably installed, another decision must be made. Should you coat the inside of the boat with epoxy? There are arguments for and against, with the final decision resting with the builder. On the plus side, epoxy will produce a more durable seal for the raw wood than just varnish alone. It will seep into unseen small gaps and crevices, adding additional structural integrity. It will bond with any epoxy used for filling.

On the down side, it must be sanded. Sanding the multiple irregular surfaces formed by the ribs, bottom board, and strips, to a surface finish equivalent to your craftsmanship on the rest of the boat is...well, impossible. The Metabo sander described in Chapter 3 and pictured in Figure 3.11 can do the bulk of the job, but sanding the details, such as where the ribs contact the bottom board and strips, is left to seemingly endless hours of hand sanding, or just left.

Do *not* coat the gunwales with epoxy if you have put the beading on the lower edges. Epoxy fills the bead channel almost level, requiring a lot of extra time and work to remove it. For that matter, while coating any of the trim with epoxy may seal the wood a bit better than just varnish, we found that, instead of epoxy here, a first coat of varnish thinned 50% and used as a base for succeeding coats is sufficient, and eliminates a lot of extra sanding.

There is a way out, however, where you can apply epoxy to the inside while minimizing the need for extensive sanding. The beautiful boat built by Dick Millet and shown as his CAD (computer-aided design) rendering at the end of Chapter 4 and on the back cover of this book, was epoxied on the inside, but the two coats of epoxy were applied with a bristle brush and then the excess wiped off with paper towels.[3] This technique worked well to seal the wood without leaving the characteristic bumps and runs inherent in the usual application of epoxy. A heavy coating is not required, since there is no fiberglass to be filled. The first wiped-on coat soaks the wood; the second leaves a smooth surface. Sanding only enough to dull the surface in preparation for varnish is all that is needed.

Although the choice is yours, you probably do not want a bright, high-gloss finish on the interior hull. On sunny days, the reflection off the gloss finish can be blinding. However, if you still want a gloss finish on the interior, simply repeat as much of the same process used on the exterior hull as you feel is necessary to achieve the desired finish. As you may have already guessed, the presence of the ribs makes finishing the interior hull a bit more challenging. You will need to pay particularly close attention to runs and drips and act quickly to brush them out.

It is important to varnish the underside of the decks to prevent moisture from invading the wood, particularly when you flip the boat over to drain it of excess water. It is much easier to do this while the boat is still

inverted from the exterior hull finishing than when it is upright. To increase penetration into the wood, begin with a coat of varnish thinned 50% with mineral spirits. Apply successive coats full strength, scuffing the surface between each one to insure adhesion. Three coats, including the initial thinned coat, are sufficient.

Now turn the boat to its upright position, and we can begin varnishing the interior of the hull. Do this prior to the final installation of any of the seat risers or the brass yoke protectors. Varnishing the interior of the hull is essentially the same process as varnishing the exterior, and once again, we recommend five coats for maximum protection and durability. If you decide on a satin or non-glossy finish, you have three options. The first is to apply a gloss varnish, just as you did for the exterior, but rub out the final coat to a satin finish. This is not difficult to do, but once again, requires a little extra time and work. We will explain this process shortly.

The second option is to apply a gloss varnish for the first three coats and a satin varnish for the last two coats. Both types of varnish should be designated for marine use, contain UV inhibitors, and be compatible.

Option three, which we do not recommend, is to apply all five coats with a satin or non-gloss varnish. The problem here is twofold. First, marine-grade satin varnishes are not available for use below the water line. Although the interior of the hull is obviously not below the water line, it will have standing water in it at times. Second, since satin finish varnishes are made primarily for inside use they do not afford any appreciable UV protection.

We adopted the second option for finishing the interior hull of the varnished boat described in this chapter. We applied two coats of Z-Spar Satin Sheen Varnish over three coats of Z-Spar Captain's Varnish. Epifanes Rubbed Effect Varnish is also a good choice. Both brands of varnish are available from suppliers listed in Appendix 5.

145

Whichever method you choose, be sure to thin out the first coat to 50% with a suitable thinner as recommended by the manufacturer. This insures a good penetration into the bare wood.

Should you decide to rub out the gloss finish to a satin finish (Figure 15.7), the process is simple, but once again, you will have to make sure the varnish has cured for at least three or four weeks (this may make the decision a little easier for you!). Once the finish is fully cured, lightly sand with 400-grit wet/dry paper, lubricated with soapy water. Wipe off the slurry and repeat the process with 600-grit wet/dry paper, again lubricated with soapy water. Remove the sanding slurry by rinsing thoroughly and wiping off any excess residue. Check for any glossy low spots, and dull them with the wet/dry paper or with a Scotch-Brite pad.

Figure 15.7
Interior hull with satin, non-gloss finish.

Next, using moderate pressure, rub out the entire surface with 0000 steel wool and either a good quality paste wax or soapy water (Murphy Oil Soap is a good choice here). If you use soapy water, wipe the surface dry when you are done. If the finish looks the way you want it to, this work is complete; you are ready for the next step. If it does not, rub it again until it does.

If you use wax, you will need to wipe it off first with a clean, soft cloth. Because enough of a thin

wax film will remain to cause smearing, you will need to remove it. Do this by sprinkling or spraying clean water on the surface and rubbing very lightly with a clean piece of steel wool. Wipe the surface with a clean cloth. You should be able to rub your finger along the surface without leaving a smear or streak.

DECKS AND OTHER TRIM

Before you fasten any of the brass work, apply the same gloss finish to your decks as you did to the exterior of the hull. The decks are a good example of the craftsmanship that has gone into building your boat and they deserve as fine a finish as the hull. Once again, be sure to apply the first coat thinned 50% as previously described to insure penetration into the bare wood. Apply a minimum of two, but preferably four, additional coats of varnish. Finish the decks as you did the exterior hull, wet sanding, buffing, and polishing to a glass-smooth finish. This is also a good time to varnish the gunwales, again building up five coats for protection and durability.

The only other items that require varnishing, whether your boat is painted or varnished, are the seat risers, seats, yoke cleats, and yoke. Do all of these in a similar fashion, beginning with a thinned-out coat of spar varnish, followed up with at least three additional coats of full-strength varnish. The choice to finish these items bright or satin is completely yours.

The risers and cleats should all be finished prior to installation (Figure 15.8) so that all surfaces are adequately covered. The seats should be finished before you apply the caning, and you should apply at least one coat of varnish in all the holes. If you will be using natural caning, we do not recommend varnishing it as some chair caners might suggest. Rather, it is better to coat the caning occasionally with a mixture of turpentine or mineral spirits and boiled linseed oil. This will keep the caning pliable and prevent it from becoming brittle.

Figure 15.8

Seat risers, yoke cleat, and middle seat finished and installed.

1 We highly recommend using the manufacturer's thinner for either paint or varnish. Experience has demonstrated that ordinary paint thinners may be incompatible with certain components of the paint or varnish, with disastrous consequences.

2 For example, Jeff Jewitt describes a rubbing out process in a magazine article, "The Quick, Modern Way to a Polished Finish," Fine Woodworking, no. 134: p 45–47. Michael Dresdner also describes a similar process in his book, *The New Wood Finishing Book,* Taunton Press, 1999.

3 A *lot* of paper towels!

CHAPTER 16

BRASS ACCESSORIES AND HARDWARE

You have worked a long time to get your guideboat to this point, and you have spent countless hours making and fitting the ribs, stripping the hull, building the stems, and attaching the decks. What seemed like an endless amount of sanding and varnishing is over, and the result is something you can truly be proud of. There remain a few important steps, however, which will further transform your boat into an even more beautiful craft.

Until now, you have been working almost exclusively with wood. In this chapter, you will be working with brass. Neither author would consider himself a metalworker; at first, we thought fitting our boats with shop-made brass accoutrements a bit daunting. The process, however, turned out to be fairly easy, and as you will see in the photographs, the results make a noticeable difference in the appearance of the boats. By now you should have developed plenty of patience and confidence in your ability—all you need is a little more time, some brass, a few different tools (many of which you may already have), and the realization that your boat is nearly done!

TOOLS

A band saw blade with 10 to 14 teeth per inch will make cutting the ⅛" plate brass almost effortless. We also found that the 7¼" blade used to cut strips on the table saw did an admirable job of cutting the brass for making the stem caps. A jigsaw with an appropriate blade for cutting nonferrous metals such as brass will also work. The common shop hacksaw is handy for smaller cuts or for cutting longer lengths of brass stock into shorter sections.

Figure 16.1
An assortment of tools necessary for the brass work.

You will be doing a little pounding on the stem caps and stem bands to get them to take a certain shape, or to flatten out certain sections. For this work, you will need a fairly hefty hammer. Do not use your carpenter's hammer, as it is probably too light to achieve the desired results. Instead, you will need either a heavy machinist's ball peen hammer, or a small hand sledgehammer. These provide the heft you need to flatten out the brass, and their heads are specially hardened, making them less likely to chip as a standard claw hammer might. A lighter wooden mallet is also useful for more delicate work, and will not excessively mar the brass.

For finishing work, you will also need some files. These are useful for smoothing edges, removing rough spots and tool marks, and for general shaping and finishing. You will use a flat double-cut file for rough work, and a single-cut file for smooth filing. Combination files are also available; these incorporate both a double-cut and single-cut surface into one file.

A round, or rat tail, file is also good for working the metal on concave surfaces, such as the underside of the stem cap.

Whichever file you use, be sure to keep a file card handy. Metal filings will build up on the surface of your files pretty quickly. As with sandpaper, the buildup will reduce a file's ability to cut, so a quick rubbing with a file card every so often keeps the file clean and cutting efficiently.

Use emery cloth for finishing the brass work after you have completed filing. Working progressively from a coarse to a medium to a fine grade will help you achieve a good finish on brass that has been roughed up from heating, bending, and pounding to shape. Your random orbit sander fitted with 220-grit paper can take a lot of the work out of the preliminary finishing.

A buffing wheel is the final tool needed for finishing brass work. By applying a polishing compound to the wheel, you can achieve a mirror-bright finish, which will help to set your boat apart from others. Buffing wheels work well on bench grinders, but if you do not have access to one, you can purchase a buffing wheel with a mounted shaft that will work almost as well with a power drill.

Finally, you will need a couple of good quality, high-speed steel (HSS) countersinks, suitable for use with #4, #5, and #6 wood screws (Figure 16.2). The head diameter for these screws ranges from just under to just over ¼", so a countersink with a ¼" body diameter will be sufficient. Purchase a couple; if one begins to wear out or is damaged for some reason, you can simply switch to the new one. Be sure to purchase these with an angle to match the taper on the heads of the screws you will be using. For brass wood screws, this taper is usually 82°. Although countersinks are available with multiple flutes, a single flute version such as the Series 61 or 62 manufactured by W.L. Fuller is all you really need, and you can use them in either a power drill or a drill press. These are relatively inexpensive and produce a clean, burr-free countersink in brass.

150

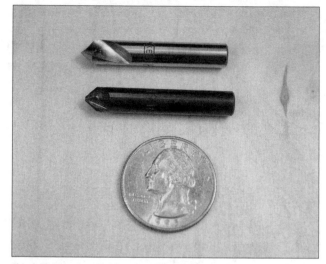

Figure 16.2
A pair of high-speed steel countersinks.

Remember, wearing eye protection is important any time you use tools, but especially so when working metal!

MATERIALS

We will talk in detail about working brass in the next section, but for now just mention the materials you need to purchase to complete the stem bands, stem band bottom sections, stem caps, painter (bow) ring, siding protectors (anti-chafe plates), shoe-irons, and yoke end bands.

For the stem caps and the bottom section of the stem bands, you will need one 12" x 12" sheet of ⅛" thick Alloy 260 brass. Expect to pay $20 to $30 for this. For the stem bands, you will need a total of 6' of ¼" square Alloy 360 free-machining brass, at a total cost of about $4 to $6. If you can find this in 3' lengths, you will pay less for shipping since shipping costs are higher for the longer lengths. However, do not purchase anything shorter than 3'.

To make the siding protectors, or anti-chafe plates, that fasten to the inside of the hull directly behind the yoke cleats, a small sheet of 0.020" thick Alloy 260 brass will suffice. You may find that 12" x 12" sheets are the smallest size available. This is more than enough for the siding protectors, but if you plan to also make foot plates, you will probably need a 12" x 24" sheet. Prices for this range from $7 to $14, depending on the size you buy.

If you choose to make your own painter or bow ring, you will need a small length of inexpensive (about $1.50 for 6') ⅛" diameter Alloy 360 free machining brass. You may find it easier to use a pre-machined brass ring, but you will still need a section of the ⅛" round to connect the ring to the stem band.

Shoe-irons, which are the protective strips fastened to the bottom board, and which run along the underside of the boat from bow to stern, should be made from lengths of 1/16" or ⅛" thick rectangular brass. Grant's design used 1/16" thick galvanized iron shoes. Our boats employ ⅛" thick brass for added durability, but at the cost of increased weight.

You will need three shoe-irons, each one slightly less than 15' long, so plan to purchase three 12' lengths and three 3' lengths. If possible, you should try to find these at a local industrial supply company, to avoid the high shipping costs for such long items. Many modern-day guideboat builders choose to use hardwood rather than metal for their shoe-irons, as did Willard Hanmer and possibly other nineteenth and early twentieth century builders. Given that these shoe-irons have the potential for taking the most wear of any other component of the boat, you should consider the kind of use your boat will receive. If you anticipate heavy wear on the shoe-irons, you might be better off using brass as opposed to hardwood.

To make the ferrules or bands that are attached to each end of the carrying yoke, you will need a small section (4" to 6") of 1¼" inside diameter thin-wall brass sink drain tubing. We purchased a longer piece, however, on which we filed saw teeth on the edge of the excess to use to size the ends of the yoke arms. You can purchase this at most hardware or plumbing supply stores. This kind of drainpipe is usually only available with chrome plating, but with a little emery cloth and some elbow grease you will be able to remove the chrome plating and achieve a highly polished brass finish.

Finally, purchase a small tube of waterproof silicone sealant. Because you will be fastening all of your brass

work into wood, a little dab of sealant on each screw ensures a waterproof seal. This not only prevents moisture from getting into the wood, but it also provides a little extra holding power for the screws.

A good alternative to the bewildering array of silicone sealant tubes available in home centers and hardware stores is aquarium sealant. You can purchase this at any pet supply store. The tube is much smaller, less messy, and you do not need a special applicator as you do with the larger tubes. It is also completely waterproof. Another method sometimes used by both amateur and professional builders is to dip the screw threads in varnish just before the final installation.

A FEW WORDS ABOUT BRASS

Different species of wood have qualities that make them more suitable for certain kinds of woodworking. For example, spruce is strong and bends quite easily after being steamed or heated, making it ideal for laminating guideboat ribs. As with different species of wood, different brass alloys also have different properties. Alloy 260 has very high ductility, more than any other type of brass. It is used for general fabrication and forming processes. Alloy 353, also known as engraver's brass, is a strong, hard material with good machinability. Alloy 360, or free machining brass, is the most common, and produces minimal tool wear in most fabricating applications. Finally, Alloy 464, or unleaded naval brass, offers high corrosion resistance in salt water and is ideal for marine hardware. It is also quite expensive.

Often you cannot obtain the length, thickness, and shape of the brass you need from available grades, but, for our purposes, you will need only the 260 and 360 alloys. Pricing is reasonable, and they are readily available. You should be able to find what you need at local industrial supply companies, or you can purchase brass from suppliers listed in Appendix 5.

MAKING THE STEM CAPS

With the exception of Grant and Parsons, traditional guideboat builders chose not to use stem caps on their boats, leaving the top of the stem band finished at the level of the gunwales. The way a stem was finished

151

often became part of a builder's signature. Grant's stem caps were nickel-plated and had a limber hole drilled through into the under-deck space to allow water to drain out when the boat was turned over. Our boats are fitted with the limber holes, but we chose a polished brass finish rather than the historically accurate nickel plating. Polished brass is aesthetically pleasing, but you can certainly consider nickel plating as an option.

Although the stem caps on the *Virginia* add a touch of refinement to the boat, their main purpose is functional: protecting the stem and deck from wear. When a guide lifted the boat onto his shoulders for carrying, he would often raise one end and rest the other on the ground while he positioned the carrying yoke on his shoulders. Guides also lowered the stern to the ground when stopping to rest. When carried on the shoulders, the trailing end of the boat is close to, and frequently strikes, the ground (Figures 16.3a and b).

Figure 16.3a
William Held of Cazenovia, New York carries his 1903 Grant guideboat.

The stem cap is not difficult to make but requires some patience to bend and fit. Chapter 10 showed how to shape the top of your stems to correspond to the shape shown in Gardner's Plates XI and XIV. The profile of each stem top should be identical.

First, make sure the transition from the deck center capping strip to the stem is fair with no bumps or dips. The transition joint from the flat deck cap strip

to the top of the stem should be flush. The next step is to transfer the profile of the top of the stem to a bending form or jig, which you will then use to shape the brass to the same profile as the stem. The easiest way to do this is to simply hold a piece of paperboard or poster board on the side of the stem and trace the profile to it. Then cut out the profile, place it back over the stem, and make sure it fits accurately. Then use the profile to shape the jig.

Figure 16.3b
The stem cap protects the deck when the trailing end of the boat is set down.

Figure 16.4 illustrates a simple but effective bending jig. It is made from a piece of 1-by or 5/4-hardwood cut to the profile of the top of the stem. Trace the poster board profile onto the wood, and cut the profile using a band saw or jigsaw.

Figure 16.4
Bending the stem cap.

Now cut a piece of ⅛" thick brass, ¾" wide and approximately 12" long. Simply slicing off a strip from the edge of the 12" x 12" raw stock is fine.

Now comes the fun part: shaping the flat piece of brass you just cut to match the stem top. In order to do this you must first soften the brass by annealing it. Heat it over a gas burner or with a torch until it begins to turn a dull red. It is not necessary to make the brass glow bright red—in fact, if you do, you will likely melt it. Make sure that whatever heat source you use, you have adequate ventilation and no combustibles nearby.

Holding the piece with pliers while wearing a pair of leather gloves makes the hot brass easier and safer to handle. Make sure the section of brass that will receive the most bending receives the greatest concentration of heat. Remove the brass from the heat source and immediately plunge it into a bucket of cold water. Clamp the brass to the bending jig, making sure it is straight and aligned with the jig. Because the brass is so pliable at this point, you should be able to bend it and force it to the desired shape without much pounding.

Do not try to accomplish too much at one time. Work the piece slowly, and reanneal it if it is difficult to bend. The idea here is simple; you want the brass strip to take the shape of the jig. Ideally, there should be no gaps between the brass and the jig surface. Pound as needed, but use a small block of wood as a cushion instead of pounding directly on the brass with the hammer, or use a wooden mallet.

While hammering or pounding, be careful not to hit the edges of the brass strip. Any deformity incurred now will have to be filed smooth later. Keep working the brass, reannealing as necessary, to achieve the desired shape. Bending the ⅛" brass to the relatively small radius at the top of the stem will cause the outer edge to raise or curl slightly. You may simply sand this off with the disk sander or file it.

When you have completed the shaping on the jig, you will need to trim the ends to the appropriate lengths

so the piece fits neatly and tightly over the stem. Place the stem cap in position on the stem and mark the lower end for trimming. Make sure you cut the bottom edge of the stem cap square, so that it sits neatly in the recess cut in the top of the stem. The front surface of the stem cap should be flush with the front of the stem. This is important, because the stem bands will overlap the stem caps.

Hold the stem cap in position, and using the story stick you made in Chapter 13, mark the location of the screw and limber holes. You may now trim the trailing end of the stem cap about ½" to ¾" beyond the mark for the screw hole. Drill a ⅛" hole in the center of the stem cap, and countersink it to accept a #5 flat head brass screw. Drill a 7/32" limber hole and slightly break the sharp edge with the countersink. Do not drill the screw holes in the front of the stem caps; you will drill them when you fit the stem bands.

Finish the stem cap by filing all edges smooth. Take extra care to bevel or round off the edges to achieve a smooth finished appearance. After filing, work the brass with progressively finer grades of emery cloth. Finally, using polishing compounds and a buffing wheel on a grinder or in an electric drill, buff the brass to a mirror-smooth finish (Figures 16.5 and 16.6).

You will install the stem caps along with the stem bands.

153

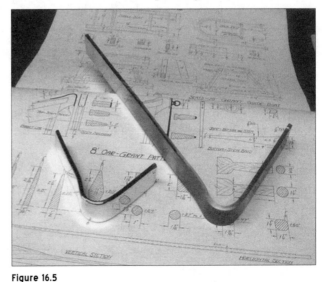

Figure 16.5

Completed and buffed stem cap (left) and initial bend (right).

Figure 16.6
Top view of completed and installed stern stem cap.

MAKING THE STEM BANDS

Stem bands, or "bang irons" as they are sometimes called, serve both an aesthetic and functional purpose. They certainly add to the boat's refined appearance, but more importantly, they protect the stems from the nicks and dents that invariably occur from banging into docks, rocks, submerged tree stumps, or even other boats.

You will make the main section, or narrow portion, of the stem bands from ¼" square Alloy 360 brass. The best guide for making the stem bands is Plate XIV. Plate VI gives you another perspective, but is not as helpful. You should study both of these drawings carefully to get a good feel for the design of the stem bands. Be aware that the drawings show a groove in the inside surface of the stem bands, which fits over the matching edge of the stem. Grant did this to save weight and we did not attempt it here.

Note that the top of the band is ⁷⁄₁₆" wide, but tapers down to ¼". This taper actually conforms to the finished edge of your stem, which may be slightly more or less than ¼". Aesthetically, it is better for the stem bands to be slightly narrower as opposed to wider than the stem itself. Functionally, of course, there is no difference. You should also note that the wider, rounded top of the band overlaps the stem cap, which has been recessed into the stem, by approximately 1⅝" (Figures 16.7a and b).

Figure 16.7a
Stem cap installed (stern). Notice the stem cap recessed into the stem.

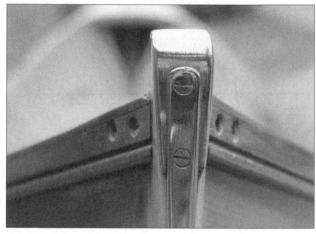

Figure 16.7b
Stem band overlapping the stem cap.

Keeping this in mind, you are ready to measure for the length of the stem band. However, before you take this measurement, you have a decision to make. Notice the drawing of the triangular piece in Plate XIV labeled *BOTTOM-STEM BAND*. This is actually the bottom section of the stem band, and on the original *Virginia*, it is not a separate piece. However, on our boats this *is* separate from the stem band. It is much easier and less expensive to shape, bend, and apply the band in two separate sections than it would be to try to do it in one piece. If done correctly, nothing is sacrificed; the pieces can be braised or simply butted together. We will describe the process for making this bottom piece later.

You must decide where you wish the main section of the stem band to end. You may decide to end it at a point close to the bottom, but where the stem is still ¼" wide. Alternatively, you may choose to go a little further and end the main section where the stem begins to widen out (Figure 16.8). This is the choice we made. It involves a little extra work in finishing, because you need to hammer the stem band flatter and wider toward the end to fit with the wider stem section and to match the leading edge of the bottom stem band section.

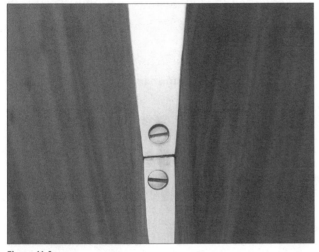

Figure 16.8
Bottom stem joint.

After you have decided where to end the stem band, go ahead and take the measurement. Make sure you flex your tape rule tight against the convex edge of the stem. Even better, use a piece of string, wire, masking tape, or even duct tape to take this measurement. Place one end of the tape where you want the top of the stem band to be, run the tape down to where you want the bottom of the band to end, and cut the tape about 2" longer than the actual measurement. The additional length will allow for corrections in case you overwork the brass while shaping the flared top end, which will result in a crack. The actual length will be determined later after you shape the top end and bend the band to fit the stem. Do not worry about locating screw holes yet.

Once you have made all the marks, take the tape off, and stick it directly on the ¼" square brass stock. Cut the brass to length and remove the tape.

Begin work by knocking off the corners on what will be the front edge of each band. One way to do this is to clamp the band in a vise and work a section at a time. You can also clamp the band to the edge of a piece of 1-by stock mounted on your workbench or in a vise (Figure 16.9). Using a file, take off the corners and round off the front edge of the band. Start by using a coarse file, and finish with a finer one. A small carbide scraper is also quite effective, removing curls of brass shavings rather than filings. Next, work the rounded edge with successively finer grades of emery cloth. Do not worry about filing the top and bottom ends of the band because you will need to flatten them first.

Figure 16.9
Rough shaping the stem band.

If you examine the drawing of the top of the stem band in Plate XIV, you will see you need to widen the ¼" square stock to approximately ⁷⁄₁₆". To do this you must anneal the square blank and pound it with a hammer over an anvil, steel plate, or solid piece of lumber (a fat log section standing on end also works well). This is not difficult but it does require a bit of patience. If you do not anneal the brass sufficiently it could actually crack or shatter. For this reason, you should try a test piece or two first to get a feel for it.

Heat only the section you need to hammer out. Remove the brass from the heat source and immediately plunge it into a bucket of cold water. Lay it flat on the anvil, steel plate, or log and begin to hammer. You

155

will get a feel for exactly how hard you can pound on the brass. As you pound, you will notice the brass begin to dent and expand. To prevent chipping, remember to avoid hitting the edges of the brass. If you are using Alloy 360 brass, you should not have a problem.

Do not attempt to flatten out the sections in one try. Your initial blows with the hammer will be effective in flattening the annealed section, but the pounded area will harden rather quickly. When the brass resists further flattening, stop pounding and re-anneal. You will need to repeat the annealing process a few times before you achieve the correct width. Keep checking the top and bottom sections of the band against the corresponding sections on the stem to make sure you have flattened or widened them sufficiently.

Also, as you pound the brass, pay attention to the fact that at this point you are trying to achieve a smooth taper on the sides as well as on the front edge of the stem band. Finish the top section by filing flat, removing all dents, scratches, and other tool marks. File in a manner that achieves a smooth taper on the sides as well as on the front, where the transition takes place from the rounded edge to the flattened edge. File the top of the band as well to achieve the rounded top, and with a fine-cut file, round the edges of the flat section (Figure 16.10). Do not worry about the bottom flat section yet; you will need to wait for the band to be fit to the curvature of the stem before you can finish it.

Once you have the sections flattened, it is time to bend the bands to fit the stem. Take a close look at the stems. You will notice that the sharpest bends occur near the waterline, and again as the stem transitions to the underside of the boat. For the most part, ¼" brass stock will bend easily, but in order to prevent breakage, you should anneal it. It is also important to note here why we have not yet drilled screw holes into the bands. The screws you will be using require ⅛" holes.[1] If you pre-drill the holes, you will have only ¹⁄₁₆" on each side of the hole, greatly increasing the risk of breaking the brass if there were a bend near a hole.

Shaping the curve of the stem band directly over the actual stem is possible, but may be awkward. It is helpful if you can clamp the band to the stem, and hammer it here and there to get a near-perfect fit. We cut a bending form from 2-by stock, using the stem pattern to define the curve of the outside of the stem on the form. We held the form in a vise while we shaped the stem band, as shown in Figure 16.11. The bending form need not be full length, since the upper portion of the stem band is essentially straight. It is important to get the blank band aligned on the form, however. You can do this by transferring an arbitrary reference mark from the stem pattern to the bending form, and aligning it with a similar mark on the stem band blank.

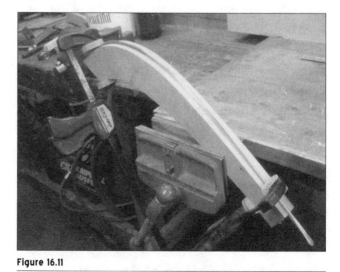

Figure 16.11
Bending the stem band over a separate bending form.

You can bend the upper portion of the band without annealing. With the band on the form, take note of where more bending is needed, and anneal that area.

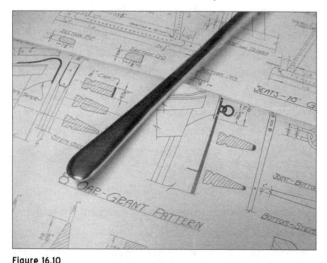

Figure 16.10
Top of stem band shaped and given a preliminary buffing.

156

The entire lower end will require annealing to shape the sharper curve there.

This is a trial and error procedure; keep bending and fitting until the stem band fits the form as close as you can get it, but do not worry about a perfect fit yet (Figure 16.12). When you permanently fasten the bands to the stems, you will find that as you tighten the screws or nails the band gets pulled into place, virtually eliminating any gaps you might see now. Thorough annealing will soften the brass so that some additional fine bending by hand will improve the fit. Light hammering with a wooden mallet or steel hammer cushioned with a piece of scrap wood struck on the end grain while the band is clamped to the form can also help.

Figure 16.12
Stem bands bent to the correct curve, awaiting bottom end shaping and fitting.

Now that you have the stem band fitted to the stem, you can finish off the bottom flat section. Anneal and flatten the end if you have not already done it. File as needed to match the tapering width of the stem, and finish as you did with the top section. If you will be using the bottom transition piece between the end of the stem band and the bottom shoes, the thickness of the end of the stem band should be ⅛".

MAKING THE PAINTER RING AND STAPLE

To make the painter ring and staple (the U-shaped connector that attaches the ring to the stem band), you will need a length of ⅛" diameter brass round. The brass should bend easily without heat, but if it is

difficult to bend, you should anneal it. For the staple, bend a 10" to 12" piece of the brass around a ⅝" rod or bolt mounted in a vise (Figure 16.13). You do not need a piece this long, but the extra length makes it easier to handle. Try to bend around the portion of the bolt without the threads to avoid scratching the brass. You may need to over bend slightly to achieve what you want, which is to have the ends approximately ⅜" apart on center. Cut the ends off, but keep the length of the resulting staple at about 2" to 3".

Figure 16.13
Bending the brass around a ⅝" diameter rod to form the painter ring staple.

To make the painter ring, wrap a long piece of the ⅛" brass around a ⅝" rod, dowel, or bolt. Cut the ring out, align the cut ends, and solder or braze it shut. Clean it up with small files and buff. One of our machinist friends actually cut the ring shown in Figure 16.16a on a lathe. If you do not have access to a metal lathe (or a good machinist friend!), you might consider buying a ring. You may also decide to leave the ring off altogether.

INSTALLING THE STEM BANDS

After buffing them to a mirror finish, you are now ready to attach the stem bands permanently to the stems. Refer again to Figures 16.7a and b and to Gardner's Plate XIV. Notice there are two screws at the top of the stem band, along with the painter ring that is attached only to the bow stem band. Clamp the stem band firmly to your workbench or in your vise, and drill two ⅛" diameter holes exactly in the center of the ⁷⁄₁₆" wide section of the band as shown in Plate XIV.

157

To insure that your drill bit does not stray, start each hole with a sharp metal punch. Drill slowly and make sure you hold the drill straight. You might find it easier to drill these holes using a drill press. Next, countersink the holes so that the flat head of a #5 x 1" brass screw will be flush with the surface of the band (Figure 16.14a). Follow the same procedure to drill one hole on the flat section at the bottom of each stem band, except size the hole and countersink for a #6 x ⅞" flat-head brass screw (Figure 16.14b).

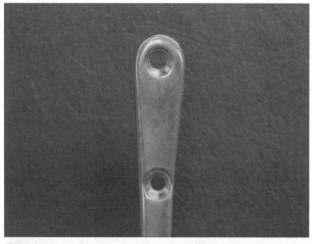

Figure 16.14a
Top of stem band.

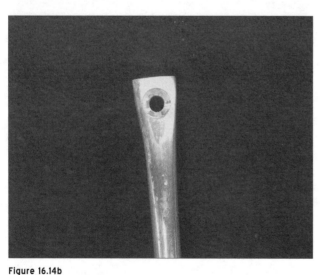

Figure 16.14b
Bottom of stem band.

On the bow stem band, drill two additional ⅛" diameter holes to accept the staple. As you can see from Plate XIV, these holes are centered between the two holes you drilled previously, and are approximately ⅜" apart on center to match the width of the painter

ring staple. Follow the same procedure as above, but do NOT countersink these holes. Turn the stem over and drill a *slight* countersink on the backside of these last two holes. The reason for doing this will become clear shortly.

Although the Grants nailed the stem bands on the *Virginia,* we recommend #4 x 1" oval-head brass screws for better holding power. You may use nails, however, in the interest of historical accuracy, and we indeed used them on one of our boats. Other than the top two screws on the band, and the first nail that is visible on the section of the stem band illustrated in Plate XIV, Gardner's drawings did not give a clear indication of the placement of these fasteners. We do know, however, from Gardner's count of tacks and screws used in the *Virginia,* that the Grants used five nails to fasten the bands to the stem. With this in mind, the placement of the screws is up to you.

Put the stem band on the stem, taking care to align the top with the pencil mark on the stem, and tape it in place. Press the band against the stem and try to get a feel for where the screws should be placed. If you bent and fit the stem properly, you need not be concerned with placing the screws in order to close any gaps between brass and wood. Nevertheless, keep this in mind as you space the screw locations out along the stem, and try to achieve a symmetrical and aesthetically appealing placement. An additional screw (or nail) to close a gap would certainly be fine as long as you can make the overall spacing consistent. Clearly indicate each location on the band with tape or a marker.

Because you have rounded the stem bands and bent them to shape, drilling the screw holes presents a problem. Drilling into a smooth and rounded surface increases the risk that the drill bit will stray off its mark. And given that you must center the hole on a ¼" wide band, your margin of error is essentially zero. You can easily solve this problem with a simple drilling jig. Cut a ¼" wide, ⅛" deep groove lengthwise into a piece of 1" to 2" wide, ⅜" thick hardwood. Cut the block to a length of approximately 1" to 2". Drill a ⅛" diameter hole exactly in the center of the groove. Make sure the hole you drill is not angled.

Now, place the grooved block over a scrap piece of ¼" brass stock. If the block does not fit tightly over the brass, wrap it with a single layer of tape and try again. Clamp the block in place with a small spring clamp and drill a ⅛" hole into the brass (Figure 16.15). Remove the block. If the hole is not centered exactly on both the front and back edge of the band, make another block. Keep trying until the hole is perfectly centered.[2]

Figure 16.15
Stem drilling guide clamped to stem.

Align the drilling jig over each mark on the band indicating where you want a screw to go. Use tape again if needed to achieve a tight fit. Clamp the jig on and drill the hole. Do this for each of the holes in each stem band, taking care not to change the shape of the bands as you drill. Next, countersink each hole to accept a #4 x 1" oval-head brass screw.

To nail the stem bands on, you will use a slightly different approach. The top and bottom screw holes are drilled as described previously, and the layout for nail hole placement is the same as for screws. Rather than drilling into the front of the stem, however, drill through from the back of it. A ¼" groove is cut in a piece of 1-by stock of sufficient dimension to be clamped to a drill press table, with the groove centered under a ¹⁄₁₆" drill bit. Place the stem band in the groove and just barely start a hole at the appropriate

location. Then examine the start hole to be sure it is centered. If a correction is necessary, start a new hole very close to the first. When the start hole is satisfactorily centered, continue drilling the hole through.

The staple attaching the painter ring may be soldered to the stem band or peened over from behind. The first step is to cut the staple to about ⅝" to ¾" long. Remove the burrs and clean any oxidation from the mating surfaces with a fine emery cloth. Spread a little soldering flux in the holes in the stem band and on the ends of the staple. Place the painter ring over the staple and insert the ends into the stem band holes, pushing them through until about a half-inch remains. You may use silver or regular soft solder to fasten the staple. Gentle heat from a propane torch is sufficient to melt the solder and make the bond. When the piece has cooled, trim the excess from the inside of the stem band. Clean up the outside using anything that works—a fine wire wheel on the bench grinder, small wire brush, emery cloth, file, etc. When the joint is clean, it may be buffed.

To attach the staple and painter ring without soldering, place the painter ring over the staple and push the ends through the two ⅛" holes spaced ⅜" apart at the top of the bow stem band. Push the ends in until there is about a ¼" to ⅜" space between the face of the stem band and the inside surface of the connector. Cut off the ends of the connector but leave approximately ⅛" to ³⁄₁₆" protruding beyond the back side of the stem band.

Now place the stem band in your vise or between two blocks of wood in a way that allows you to peen over the ends of the staple to sit flat in the depressions you countersunk on the back side of the band. Do this by hammering the ends until they flatten out just enough to create a lip on the brass round so it will not pull back out through the holes. You may need to stabilize the connector in your vise to keep it from moving while you peen the ends. Installing the painter ring and its staple in this fashion prevents the bow ring from being pulled out of the stem band.

159

You can now rub the stem band down with emery cloth, starting with a coarse grade, if needed, and working through to a fine grade. Again, take care not to change the bent shape of the bands too much, although you will need to make final adjustments upon installation. If you have a buffing wheel installed on your bench grinder, you can do the final polishing of the brass now. If you are using a drill-mounted buffing wheel, you can wait until you have installed the stem bands to do the final polishing.

If no treatment were applied to the brass at this point, within a year or less it would be tarnished, especially if the finished boat is kept outdoors or was left with the fingerprints of too many loving caresses. To preserve its luster, wipe it clean with a rag liberally wet with paint thinner to thoroughly remove the wax from the buffing compound. When clean and dry, spray it with a clear lacquer such as Krylon. Let it dry completely before mounting.

PUTTING IT ALL TOGETHER

Now that you have the stem caps, stem bands, and painter ring made, you are ready to install them permanently (Figure 16.16a). Working with the boat upright, start by placing one of the stem caps over the stern stem. If the fit is not perfect (i.e., gaps in the curved sections), try placing a long piece of duct tape over the cap and pull down on it. This should flex the cap into a tighter fit. Fasten the tape to the sides to hold the cap in place. Drill a 5⁄64" pilot hole and fasten the top of the stem cap to the deck with a #5 x 1" flat head brass screw with a little dab of silicone sealant or varnish on it. Wipe off any silicone residue before it has a chance to dry.

Next, place the stern stem band against the stem cap, taking care to achieve the proper overlap. Tape this in place. Mark the location of the holes on the stem cap, and drill 1⁄8" clearance holes through the stem cap. Do not drill these holes into the wood. Instead, drill 1⁄16" pilot holes into the wood (5⁄64" if your stem is made of hardwood), and insert two #5 x 1" flat-head brass screws dabbed with sealant. Wipe off the excess.

Working from the top down, tape the stem in place at each hole location to insure the band's tight fit against the stem. Check to make sure you have not positioned the stem band too far to the right or left on the stem. Drill a 3⁄64" pilot hole (1⁄16" for hardwood) into the stem at each screw location. Insert a #4 x 1" oval-head brass screw dabbed with sealant and screw in place, taking care not to over tighten the screws.

Figure 16.16a
Completed bow stem band and painter ring.

Figure 16.16b
Painter ring on a 100-year-old Grant guideboat.

Before moving on to the next screw location, double check that you have positioned the stem band correctly and it fits tight to the stem. Small gaps will disappear as you tighten the screws. The last screw inserted in each stem band is on the bottom flat section of the band. However, do not install this one until you put on the bottom sections of the stem bands. Repeat this process for the bow stem. Make sure the painter ring staple is not loose once the stem band is fastened to the stem cap. If it is, you may need to place a thin brass shim behind the band, or hammer the ends of the connector a little more to fill the depressions created by the countersinks.

If you choose to nail the stem bands on (except for the two upper screws and one bottom screw), you should pre-drill the nail holes if you used a hardwood outer stem. The nails we used were #18 x ¾" brass escutcheon pins, predrilled with a #60 drill bit (0.040"). Small countersinks for the heads of the escutcheon pins can be carefully drilled before the pins are driven home, allowing the pins to mount flush with the stem band surface.

MAKING AND INSTALLING THE BOTTOM STEM BAND SECTION

Now that you have the stem caps and main stem bands installed, you need to cut, shape, and install the bottom sections of the stem band. Refer to Gardner's Plate XIV for a sketch of this section. Turn your boat upside down. Cut a piece of poster board approximately 3" wide by 8" long. Butt one edge of the poster board against the bottom edge of the main stem band, and tape it in place. Mark the underside of the poster board so it conforms to the shape of the stem and hull and cut out the profile you just marked. Place it back on the bottom board, making sure the narrow end butts tightly up against the bottom edge of the stem band. Now, make a mark on the wider end (toward amidships) of the poster board template approximately 3½" from the stem-to-bottom board joint. This mark indicates the back or wide edge of the bottom section, and it should measure approximately 1½". Repeat this process for the other end of the boat.

Cover a section of the ⅛" thick sheet brass with masking tape (this makes it easier to draw on the brass). Trace your templates onto the tape and cut the pieces out on the band saw or with a jigsaw. File the edges smooth but do not bevel or round off the front (narrow) and back (wide) edges. Make sure the front edge

butts squarely against the bottom edge of the main stem band. File if needed to achieve a tight, neat joint. You may have to bend the piece to conform to the curve from the bottom board to the stem, but if necessary, anneal the brass first. Use emery cloth to achieve a fine finish, but save the polishing until after you have installed the pieces on the boat.

Again using Gardner's Plate XIV as a reference, drill ⅛" holes for the three screws on the wide edge, and one hole approximately at the joint of the stem and bottom board. Countersink these four holes to accept #5 x ⅞" flat-head brass screws. You will also need to drill a ⅛" hole at the narrow end of the bottom stem section where it meets the main stem band. Countersink this hole for either a #4 or #5 flat-head brass screw. The size of the screw depends on where this edge sits on the stem. If it is on a narrow section of the stem (¼" width), use a #4 screw. Otherwise a #5 screw will work.

Once you are satisfied with the fit and finish of the pieces, install them permanently, remembering to use a little sealant on each screw. At this point, you can put the last screw in the bottom of the stem bands where they join to the pieces you just installed. Finish the pieces with the buffing wheel and a little polishing compound (Figure 16.17).

161

Figure 16.17
Bottom stem section installed.

INSTALLING THE SHOE-IRONS

The shoe-irons are the simplest of the brass accoutrements to install on your boat, but because of the number of screws required, may take you the most time. Begin with the center shoe-iron. Make sure the ends of the ⅛" thick, ½" wide brass strips are cut 90° to their sides. If not, file them square.

Drill a ⅛" hole on each end, and in the center of the first brass strip, approximately ½" in from the ends. Next, drill ⅛" holes every 3" or so (Figure 16.18), taking care to center them on the strip. Countersink all of these holes to accept #5 x ½" flat-head brass screws. Starting at one end of the boat, butt the strip up against the center of the bottom stem band piece. There is no need to pre-drill the pine bottom board. Using a nail or scratch awl, make a small pilot hole and install the first screw. Be sure to apply a little sealer to this and each remaining screw.

Figure 16.18
A simple drill press jig for drilling equally spaced and centered holes.

Before installing any additional screws, install the remaining strips. Make sure the last one you install fits tightly, and squarely, between the next to the last strip and the edge of the bottom stem section on the opposite side of the boat. Before screwing these strips in place, sight down the length of the boat to make sure they are centered in a fair line along the bottom board. Once you are satisfied with the fit and appearance of the strips, fasten them into place, but check frequently to make sure they remain centered and fair. If necessary, tape the strips into place before you install the screws.

The procedure for installing the side shoe-irons is the same. However, the ends of the strips that butt against the bottom stem pieces, and to each other on

curved sections, must be filed to a slight angle. This is necessary because the side strips are applied in a manner that conforms to the oval shape of the outside of the bottom board (see Figure 16.19). The outside edge of these strips should be located where the bottom board and siding meet. However, as you install the strips, make sure you achieve a fair curve from one end of the boat to the other. This may require that you align one or more sections of the strips slightly to the inside or outside of the bottom board's edge. This is not at all difficult to do, as the brass strips will flex very easily from side to side. If you shaped your bottom board correctly, achieving a fair curve on the side strips should not be a problem.

Figure 16.19
Shoe-irons installed. Notice how the edge-irons conform to the shape of the bottom board.

It is not necessary to polish the shoe-irons with emery cloth and polishing compound, as they are not visible when the boat is turned right side up or in the water. However, if you have gotten used to the beautiful appearance of finely polished brass, by all means, go ahead and polish them!

SIDING PROTECTORS

To protect the portion of the inside hull directly behind the yoke cleats from being damaged or worn by the ends of the yoke, small brass plates are installed (Figures 16.20a and b).

The siding protectors are illustrated in Gardner's Plate XII, however, we believe some of the dimensions shown are incorrect. You will need to cut two sections of 0.020" thick brass to a dimension of 1½" by 1¾", not 1½" by 1¼" as is drawn in Plate XII. Shape each piece as shown in the illustration by rounding its bottom edge and by bending a ⅝" section (not ⅜" as shown) along its top edge. This narrow "lip" wraps around the sheer strip and outwale. Note that a ⅜"-dimensioned lip would have provided insufficient purchase for fastening into the gunwale. As shown in Figures 16.20a and b, drill a small hole at each edge of the ⅝" wide section, and three holes in the section that will fit on the inside of the hull. Position the plates behind the yoke cleats as shown, and fasten with #2 flathead slotted brass screws. Make sure you coat the screw threads with sealant.

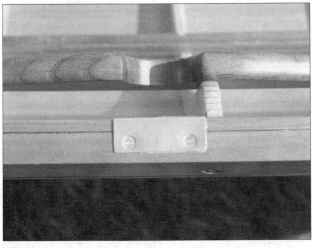

Figure 16.20a
Top view of yoke protectors. These simple brass plates prevent any side-to-side movement of the yoke from damaging the finish or the cedar strips.

Figure 16.20b
Side view of yoke protectors.

YOKE FERRULES

A complete discussion of how to make the brass yoke ferrules (Figure 16.21) is included in Chapter 17.

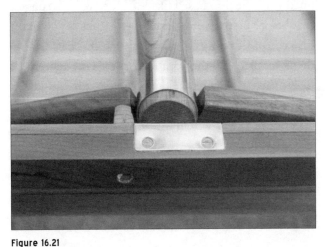

Figure 16.21
Yoke ferrule.

ROWLOCKS AND ROWLOCK PLATES

John Gardner provides illustrations and dimensions for rowlocks and rowlock plates for the *Virginia* in Plate XII. (Gardner called them "plates" while Dwight Grant and others called them "sockets" or "straps.") Producing these items is beyond our capabilities as metalworkers, so we opted to purchase them in complete sets. They are available from the suppliers listed in Appendix 5 for approximately $200, and include four plates with mounting screws, two rowlocks, and two stainless steel pins. As received, the rowlock plates showed tool and grinding marks and benefited immensely by buffing (Figure 16.22). Paint thinner can be used to remove the buffing compound residue. An old toothbrush helps here.

163

Figure 16.22
Buffed (top) and "as-received" (bottom) rowlock plates.

Gardner's Plate XII also shows the correct positioning of the plates on the outwales. You will need forty #7 x ¾" flat- or oval-head brass screws if none are supplied with the purchased plates.[3] However, we suggest that before permanently fastening the plates you make sure the positioning works well for your boat. Clamp them in place at the locations shown in Plate XII. Insert the oars, sit in the appropriate seat, and take a few strokes (if it is warm enough, you might want to try this in the water). Do this at both rowing locations. If you are satisfied with the feel, go ahead and permanently fasten the plates (Figures 16.23a and b). Make sure you drill the appropriate size pilot holes and apply a little sealant to each screw.

Figure 16.23a

Rowlock plate positioning for center seat rowing (rib locations marked for clarity).

Figure 16.23b

Rowlock and oar in place.

BUILDER'S NAMEPLATE

The last item you might consider attaching to your boat is a nameplate—a small and sometimes decorative piece of metal that identifies the craft's builder. Grant did not use them, as they certainly were not a requirement on a workboat, but your heirloom is quite a different story. You can easily purchase a nameplate at an engraving shop, but given the craftsmanship that has gone into building your guideboat, a handcrafted plate is an appropriate way to finish it off. Be sure to keep it simple yet attractive—we have seen nameplates bordering on the garish, with the name of the builder, designer, where and when built, etc., all engraved on plastic!

Figures 16.24 a, b, and c show three different nameplates, all made of brass and cut with either a band saw, scroll saw, or fretsaw. Whichever method you choose, make sure you install a suitable blade for cutting brass, and please remember to wear eye protection whenever cutting metal.

Before you begin, decide if you want your nameplate installed on the deck center capping strip or on the coaming. This is an important decision because it determines how wide the nameplate can be. For example, locating the nameplate on the deck center capping strip restricts the width of the plate to the width of the centerpiece where it will be fastened. If you choose to locate the nameplate on the coaming, you are not as restricted by width (although you may want to double check the height of the plate before you cut it!).

Once you have addressed your options, you can begin to fashion the nameplate. If your design is simple, you will not need to do much cutting or shaping. A more complicated design will require a little more work. We will illustrate the process used to cut the nameplate shown in the photo in Figure 16.24a.

This particular plate is an exact reproduction of one found on a guideboat built in the early 1900s by Parsons and Company in Old Forge, New York. Begin with an appropriately sized piece of brass. Place

Figure 16.24a
Builder M. J. Olivette. This nameplate is an exact reproduction of one found on an early 1900s Parsons & Co. boat built in Old Forge, New York.

Figure 16.24b
Builder John Michne.

Figure 16.24c
Builder Dick Millet.

masking tape on the piece to facilitate the drawing of the design. In this case, we placed a thin paperboard template on the taped surface and traced with a sharp felt tip marker (Figure 16.25). We drilled ⅛" screw holes next and cut the piece on a scroll saw using a 41 teeth-per-inch metal cutting blade. A band saw also

works well here, but if the nameplate has intricate curves, you will need to take more "nibble" cuts and do a little more filing to smooth the edges. Cut slowly, making sure to leave the line as you proceed (Figure 16.26). After you have finished the cut, remove the tape, and file the edges of the nameplate

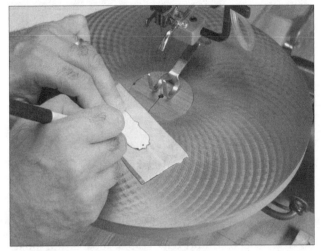

Figure 16.25
Marking template on taped brass.

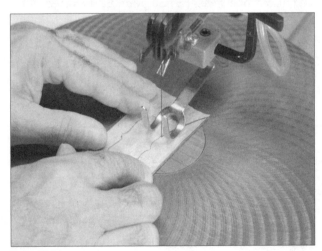

Figure 16.26
Scroll sawing the nameplate.

165

smooth. You can do the final finishing with emery cloth and by buffing to a mirror finish.

After you have the nameplate engraved, carefully position it on the coaming or deck center capping strip (Figure 16.27), and secure it in place with round-head screws coated with sealant. As you do this, stop to take note of the look of pride on your face reflected in the nameplate.

Figure 16.27
Nameplate mounted on deck centerpiece.

SOME WEIGHTY WORDS

One of the most frequently asked questions when we take our boats out is "How much does it weigh?" Estimates vary, but based on the weight of a standard length Grant boat of around 80 pounds with the center seat, backrest, and oars lashed aboard, our boats would be slightly heavier. By actual measurement, one of our boats weighed 80 pounds; the other closer to 85 pounds. We made the measurements with the oars, backrest, and center seat removed, much as we would carry our boats to a launch area. Our boats are heavier than the traditional boats because of the fiberglass, the epoxy, and, contributing most of the extra weight, the heavy brass bottom shoes.

Most modern users of a boat that he or she built with great and loving care would likely not carry it from one lake to another single-handedly. The longest carry would be from the parking lot to the shore. Boat weight is then not much of a concern, but weight reduction seems to border on an unrealistic obsession when the building of strip-built canoes and kayaks is discussed. Ounces are shaved here and there during their construction, most of the time with little significant effect on the weight of the final product. Grant and other guideboat builders seem to have accomplished all of the weight reduction possible by the 1890s, the years Durant says that guideboat design had reached its most refined stage.

Weight reduction in a modern reproduction strip-built guideboat, while not impossible, is difficult to achieve to any significant degree. Substituting ³⁄₁₆" thick strips for the design ¼" strips would not achieve much reduction, since the strips represent only a fraction of the weight of the completed boat. The spruce ribs are comparable to sawn ribs, and the seats, decking, and other trim offer little opportunity for additional reduction. The fiberglass and epoxy are significant contributors to the weight of the boat, but their elimination could seriously compromise the boat's integrity. However, we opted to use a 4 oz. cloth as opposed to the common 6 oz. used in ribless boats.

Perhaps the only place where noticeable weight reduction is possible is in the bottom shoe irons. We opted to make these from ½" wide brass ⅛" thick. Substituting a similar dimension of ash for the two or three brass strips would measurably reduce weight. There would be trade-offs, of course, mostly having to do with bottom shoe abrasion. However, hardwood bottom shoes, which Willard Hanmer sometimes used, should last many years, given care in launching and recovery of the boat, together with light recreational use rather than the daily use these boats were originally built for.

1 Nails may also be used to attach the stem bands, as on the original Grant boats. Mounting the stem band with nails will be described in a later section.

2 If you have access to metal machining equipment, or to someone who does, you can make a similar jig from a piece of steel and possibly achieve an even greater degree of accuracy (See Figure 16.15).

3 We have found that the head sizes of the screws noted by John Gardner for fastening the rowlock plates are too large to fit neatly into the countersinks of commercially available plates. If the rowlock plates you purchase come with screws, you should not have a problem. Otherwise, you might need to increase the size of the countersinks on the plates to allow the screw heads to fit flush.

CHAPTER 17
STANDARD AND OPTIONAL EQUIPMENT

In this chapter, we describe how to build oars, a paddle, and a carrying yoke. We also describe how to install footplates to protect the ribs, and how to build a floor grate, which is the way we prefer to protect the ribs and the bottom board.

OARS

Guideboat oars are typically 8' long for 16' boats and are commercially available as reproductions of the Grant oars detailed in Plate XIV, but making your own is not difficult and certainly less expensive. The basic procedure is to trace an oar pattern onto a suitable plank, rough-cut the blank, and then detail it to the final dimensions.

Draw the pattern from Gardner's data in Plate XIV. Either a full-length pattern or two short patterns may be used. The full-size pattern may be somewhat cumbersome and requires an 8' piece of material, but will accurately represent the oar shape over its full length.

In the case of shorter patterns, make the handle and blade end patterns separately. Place them on the plank at the correct distance apart and draw straight lines to connect them. Final refinement of the design shape and dimensions is done after the blank is rough cut. We opted to use the short patterns (Figure 17.1). We do not recommend using a pattern for the side profile, since its long and narrow shape is quite delicate. Direct layout on the blank is not difficult, and is preferred.

As shown in Figure 17.1, the patterns should have centerlines and the profile lines as shown in Plate XIV. The inboard terminations can be somewhat arbitrary, since the layout is measured from the outside ends.

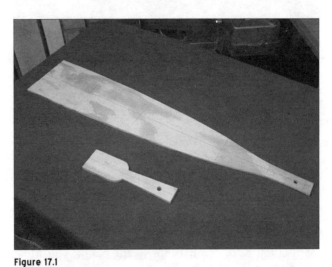

Figure 17.1

Short oar patterns on ¼" plywood.

The choice of wood for traditional guideboat oars was generally soft maple, with spruce sometimes used for shorter oars for shorter boats. Once again, availability of suitable stock may limit the choice of wood. We found that basswood was readily available in plank sizes and quality suitable for making oars. Since we did not plan on the heavy use typical of the early workboats, the choice of basswood seemed reasonable and appropriate. We know of one recently strip built reproduction *Virginia* where the builder routinely uses basswood oars for recreational use.

Whatever wood is chosen, it must be straight grained, and free of defects. Laminated oars are sometimes made where the shaft runs the length of the oar, and blade halves of the same wood species are glued on before shaping. Although there is a potential for artistry using contrasting woods with this type of construction, such ornamentation is definitely out of place on a guideboat and we strongly discourage its use.

Durant states that a pair of oars can be made from a single plank 2" thick, 6" wide, and 12' long. We found that a 10' long plank, a full 6" wide and nominally 2" thick was quite suitable. The outlines of the oars on the plank are slightly skewed, and careful layout is required. The ends of the blades are centered, but the grip ends are offset slightly so that both oars fit the plank (Figure 17.2).

Figure 17.2
Oar pattern layout on a 6" wide plank.

Before you trace the patterns to the plank, you must carefully draw centerlines. The centerlines are not exactly parallel to the center axis of the plank, so that both oars will fit. We need to locate the end points of each oar so that the centerlines can be drawn and the patterns accurately placed.

Referring to Figure 17.3, make a mark at each end of the plank, centered across the width. Now measure 21" in from each end and 1¼" in from the edge, and make a mark. These are the points marked A on Figure 17.3. Connect the A points to the center marks on the opposite ends of the plank. These are the centerlines. Check the layout by placing the outboard end of the grip pattern at point A, and the wide end of the blade pattern 8' away, aligning both patterns with the centerline. Lightly trace the patterns, and repeat for the second oar.

All of the tracings should fit the plank with no interference or overlap. Make any adjustments as necessary, and finally trace each pattern with a dark soft pencil. Connect both ends with straight lines,

outlining the oar. The taper of the shaft will not quite be as designed, but is sufficiently accurate for rough cutting. The layout should look like Figure 17.4.

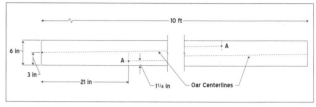

Figure 17.3
Oar layout sketch. (Drawn by Rob Axelson.)

Figure 17.4
Two oars laid out on a 10' plank.

You may now cut the oar blanks from the plank. A band saw would seem to be the tool of choice here, but we do not recommend handling and guiding such a large work piece on the typically small band saw table. We found that a coarse tooth blade in a portable jig saw cut the relatively thick plank with ease (Figure 17.5).

Figure 17.5
Oar blanks cut from the plank.

The shape of the shaft may now be refined to correct for using the short patterns. With the oar lying flat, draw lines across the shaft at the profile locations shown in Plate XIV. Using the measurements shown in the profiles, make marks equal distances from the centerline to lay out the width at each location. Be sure to note the deviation from a straight line at the 72" area where you will mount the rowlock. The width of the loom from the 72" mark to the grip is wider than the main portion of the shaft. Connect these marks and cut away the waste, staying slightly outside the line. Smooth the cut with a block plane, oscillating sander, etc. This surface is nearly finished, requiring only beveling and final sanding, so it should be made flat and straight.

The side profile of the oar is next, where the blade thickness is established. The shaft thickness will also be refined. Mark the profile lines on the side of the blank, establish a center point on each line, and lay out the thickness as you did above. Connect the marks as shown in Figure 17.6a. Note that you can easily copy the profile lines from the blade pattern.

Figure 17.6a
Side profile layout.

A ½" band saw blade with 3 teeth per inch will easily cut the side profile. Be sure to keep the cut outside the line, and clean up the rough-cut surface with a block plane: no need for a furniture surface here, just smooth enough for easy drawing of the blade profile lines. These lines will be planed off during the shaping operation, but they are useful here in the initial stages.

Figure 17.6b
Rough cut.

The blade profiles in Plate XIV show a blade surface with a raised center spine, tapering the length of the blade in a sort of rolling bevel. Lewis Grant designed a jig to machine hollow or concave surfaces on either side of center, leaving an attractively curved raised spine. Such a jig would be useful in a production shop, but for the amateur builder, shaping the concave blade surface by hand is not difficult.

First, plane the blade to a rolling bevel between the centerline and the side profile line marking the outer edge of the blade surface. This operation should produce a blade surface with cross sections as shown in the Plate XIV profiles. You can use a Pro-Prep scraper with a curved blade to hollow out the spine, together with a sharpened gooseneck scraper. Both scrapers should be freshly sharpened, or they may chatter. Final shaping can be done by carefully using the edge of a random orbit sander, tilted so that just the edge of the disk contacts the work. Approach the top of the spine with care. Scraping or sanding over the crest will dull the raised effect.

Grant's jig mentioned above used a circular saw blade fed across the oar so that the blade scraped off the waste. We can approximate the same shape by making a template with a 7¼" diameter, and using it to gage the progress of the shaping. Figures 17.7a and b show the tools and completed blade.

169

Figure 17.7a
Tools and template for shaping the spine.

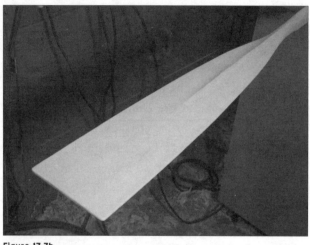

Figure 17.7b
Completed blade.

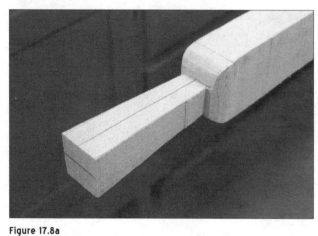

Figure 17.8a
Rough shape of the oar handle.

Shaping the grip is next. This is a straightforward operation, consisting of cutting the rough shape of the handle, rounding with any convenient tool, and sanding it smooth. If you make the carry yoke semicircle

template with a 1¼" diameter as described below in the "Carving a Carry Yoke" section, you may use it to draw a circle on the end of the handle to guide the shaping (Figures 17.8a and b).

You can conveniently bevel the edges of the shaft with a router. Before doing the actual cutting, locate the rowlock pin holes and mark an area 1" on either side.

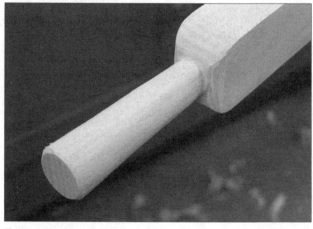

Figure 17.8b
Rounding the oar handle.

Be careful not to cut the bevel in this area (Figure 17.9). Soften the bevel so that it flows smoothly into the round portion of the shaft as the blade is approached, and round over the blade edges by sanding. Trim the blade to length if required, and soften the corners.

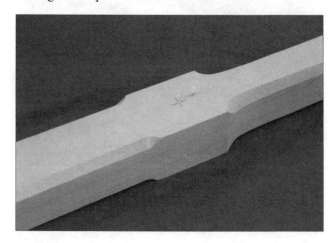

Figure 17.9
Bevel detail at rowlock mount.

Three or four coats of varnish complete the oars. It is common practice not to varnish the grip, ostensibly to prevent blisters during extended periods of rowing.

PADDLES

Why on earth, you might be thinking, do we need a paddle for a guideboat? This is a good question, and the answer is not so obvious until you find yourself having to propel your boat with only one oar (yes, they can break!).

Dwight Grant included a paddle with every guideboat he sold, but the paddle more than likely served a purpose other than being a "spare tire." In fact, because the working guideboat was used for "jacking"[1] deer at night and for approaching wary trout on remote ponds and lakes, guides needed a way to quietly, and slowly, propel the craft through the water. The paddle was perfect for this. In addition, in the course of traveling across/through the woods, guides had to take their boats through narrow channels connecting one body of water to another. Oars were too unwieldy as the channels were often not much wider than the boat itself.

As one might expect, paddles over time have been lost or broken, and one rarely finds them with old guideboats. Made of soft maple (preferred by Dwight Grant), spruce, ash, and cherry, the paddles were of a simple design, but their handles varied from the plain to the ornate.

If you decide to build a paddle, we encourage you to experiment with different designs. However, since we want to maintain historical accuracy as much as possible, we will describe the process for building the Grant paddle illustrated in Gardner's Plate XVI.

As is typical with all of John Gardner's measurements, he recorded the dimensions of the paddle precisely. However, it is doubtful the Grants (or any other builders, for that matter) intentionally constructed paddles with the degree of precision apparent in Plate XVI. For Grant to plan a paddle with design dimensions as remarkably precise as 64ths or even 32nds of an inch seems unlikely. Rather, this is probably the way the dimensions worked out, and Gardner simply recorded them as such. Keep this in mind as you refer to Plate XVI to build your own paddle. Adhere to the dimensions if possible, but accuracy to within a 64th of an inch is not necessary. Perhaps what is most important in the construction of the paddle is that it feels comfortable in your hands.

Having said that, we can begin. Start by making a set of full-sized patterns for the paddle using Gardner's measurements in Plate XVI (Figure 17.10). Make one pattern for the top profile and one for the side. You will also need a pattern for the end of the handle. You certainly can make a paddle without these patterns and simply transfer the measurements onto the wood blank, but the method we describe requires you to redraw the side profile after the top profile is cut out. Using a pattern will save time and will result in consistent measurements.

Figure 17.10
Two-piece, full-size paddle patterns. The small oval-shape pattern is for the handle end.

There are two specific areas in Gardner's drawings that deserve extra attention. One is the horizontal line drawn from the +12" point on the blade to the +29" point where the blade and shaft meet. This horizontal line indicates the presence of a spine that helps to stiffen the paddle. The other area is the diamond-shaped cross section of the shaft shown at the +29" measurement. This is the high point of the spine, which gradually decreases as you progress outward toward the blade tip. Be sure to work this spine on both sides of the paddle as you shape it.

Decide what kind of wood you will use to make your paddle and obtain a clear board free of twists, knots, or checks. The paddle we describe here is made of soft maple, typically the Grants' choice. The board should also be surfaced on all four sides. The length of the paddle is just over 5', so if you can find a ten-footer, you will have enough to make two paddles. Whatever length you end up with, the finished dimensions should be approximately $1\frac{7}{8}$" thick and minimally, $5\frac{1}{2}$" wide.

If not yet done, cut the board to length. With your try-square, check to see if both edges of the board are at 90° angles to the face. If not, joint the edge so they are. This is important for cutting the side profile on the band saw; if the edges are not perpendicular to the face, the board will go through the band saw at an angle, resulting in an inaccurate cut.

Next, draw a centerline along the full length of all four edges of the board. Then, draw a centerline down each of the two narrow ends, effectively dividing the board in half. Extend these centerlines up onto the face of the board to accommodate the top profile pattern (Figure 17.11). These centerlines will serve as references for locating the patterns on the board.

Figure 17.11
Centerlines drawn on the edges and ends of the board. Vertical lines on the ends are extended on to both faces of the board.

Position the side profile pattern on one edge so that the tip of the paddle blade aligns with the end of the board. Also, be sure the centerline running the length of the pattern aligns with the centerline on the edge of the board. Trace the pattern onto the wood (Figure 17.12a).

Carefully cut out the side profile on the band saw (Figure 17.12b), cutting about $\frac{1}{16}$" outside of the lines.[2]

Figure 17.12a
Tracing the side profile pattern onto the board.

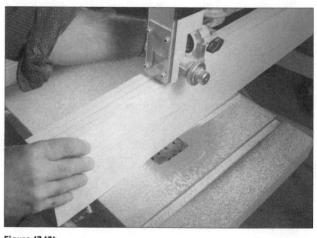

Figure 17.12b
Cutting out the profile at the band saw.

The reasons for cutting out the side profile first are ones of safety and accuracy. Doing so gives you a wider surface on which to cut out the top profile. If you were to cut the top profile first, there would be little surface area left to stabilize the piece as you run it through the band saw to cut out the side profile. This differs from the approach used for roughing out the oars, where the flat profile is cut before the sides. Cutting two oars from the same plank, along with the weight of the plank, are the considerations there.

Position the handle end pattern on the handle edge of the board, and trace it (Figure 17.13a). Next, position the top profile pattern on one face of the board. As with the side profile pattern, make certain the end of the paddle blade pattern aligns with the edge of the board and the centerline on the pattern aligns with the centerline on the face of the board. Once the pattern is correctly positioned, trace it onto the board (Figure 17.13b), and be sure to mark the +12", +29", and +30" lines for the later shaping of the spine. Repeat this on the opposite face of the board. Take the board back to the band saw and cut out the top profile, again cutting about ¹⁄₁₆" outside of the lines (Figure 17.14).

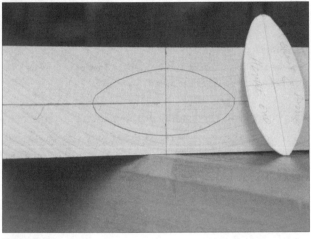

Figure 17.13a
Handle end profile.

Figure 17.13b
Tracing the top profile.

Although it is not required, you might wish to retrace the side profile on both edges of the blank, positioning and aligning the pattern exactly as before. This may make shaping the paddle a little easier. At the very least, clearly mark the location of the +12", +29",

and +30" lines on both faces of the paddle blank to aid you in shaping the spine. Your paddle blank is now ready for shaping (Figure 17.15).

Figure 17.14
Cutting the top profile at the band saw. When cutting out profiles, be sure to leave the lines!

Figure 17.15
Paddle blank, ready for shaping.

If needed, begin by smoothing out the rough edges created by the band saw cuts by passing the paddle blank across the drum or disk sander (Figure 17.16). Sand only to the lines!

Working the paddle to its final shape is pleasant work, and creates a large pile of shavings every woodworker

173

finds appealing. Even children love a good pile of wood shavings![3]

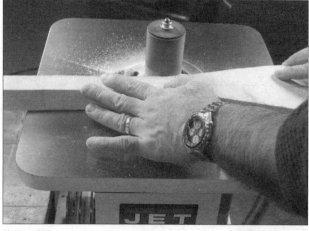

Figure 17.16
Any rough edges that may have resulted from sawing out the paddle blank can be smoothed out at the sander.

We find that shaping the shaft of the paddle works best using a concave spoke shave along with the more typical flat-blade model (Figure 17.17). Keeping the blades razor sharp will allow you to remove the thinnest shavings, resulting in a minimal amount of finish sanding.

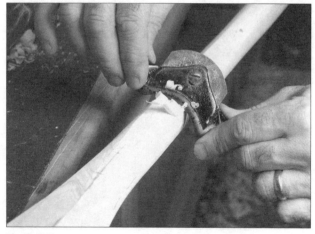

Figure 17.17
A rounded (concave) spoke shave makes for quick and efficient shaping of the paddle shaft.

The blade of the paddle can be shaped first with spoke shaves and a block plane and finally, if needed, with a random orbit sander. Take care when shaping the blade to work on the stiffening spine, which begins at the +29" line and gradually lessens until it flattens out at the +12" location. Work from the centerline out to

the paddle edges (Figure 17.18), and continue redrawing the centerline if needed to keep it as a reference.

Figure 17.18
Raise the spine by planing out from the center of the blade toward the edge. Redraw the centerline if it is planed away.

Keep checking the paddle for symmetry as you continue to shape it. As you sight down the shaft, the blade should look symmetrical on both sides, and the shaft should have no discernable bumps or indentations. Also, continually check the feel of the shaft in your hands and remove any rough spots or "out-of-round" sections.

Finally, shape the handle with a sharp chisel, spoke shave, or rasp (or all of the above), and sand smooth. As with the shaft, make sure the handle feels comfortable in your hands. If desired, you can make the blade faces concave from the raised spine out to the edges, similar to the oar blades.

Sand the paddle smooth (Figure 17.19) and finish with three or four coats of marine varnish. Then sit back and imagine yourself quietly paddling your guideboat along the shores of a remote Adirondack pond. Better yet, go ahead and do it!

FOOTPLATES AND FLOOR GRATES

It was standard practice for most guideboat builders to fit their boats with thin sheets of brass or copper, bent over the ribs, and tacked or nailed in place (Figure 17.20). These thin plates protected the ribs and the bottom board from damage caused by the

174

friction of the rower's boots. Typically, two sets of plates were installed, one for the middle-seat rowing position, and one for the bow. As illustrated in John Gardner's Plate XII, the two sets of plates on the *Virginia* were positioned at bow-end rib station 0[4], and at stern-end rib station 3.

Figure 17.19
The completed paddle, ready for varnishing.

Figure 17.20
Middle position footplate on a 1904 Grant guideboat. Note the placement of tacks and escutcheon pins for fastening the plate to the ribs and bottom board.

If you choose to make the footplates, the process is fairly simple. They can be cut easily with a utility knife, a pair of tin snips, or even at the band saw or scroll saw. All that is required is a sufficient quantity of 0.020" thick brass, and a template for each plate. You will first need to measure the width of the bottom board at each position, and then create a template for each plate from construction paper or poster board. The plate dimensions are evident in Gardner's drawing; all you need to determine is the

appropriate bottom board width. Once you have a satisfactory template, simply transfer it to the brass and cut it out.

Installing the plates involves some form fitting up and over the rib feet. Fasten each plate to the bottom board with 34 brass or copper tacks and to the tops of the rib feet with 36 escutcheon pins.

We chose not to install footplates in our boats. One reason is that we have seen too many boats with significant rot under the footplates, or weakened or chipped sections where the plates have been nailed to the ribs. Water that finds its way under the plates can sit for prolonged periods. With so many tack holes present, the water can seep into the wood, eventually weakening the bottom board.

The second reason is perhaps more practical. The bottom board and the rib feet are subject to significant wear and tear, either from shoes and boots,[4] or from the dragging or dropping of gear. Thin metal plates placed at only two locations protect the ribs to which they are attached, but do not provide adequate protection overall while boarding and carrying gear. We have added a removable grating to the bottom of our boats that not only provides good protection for the bottom board and ribs, but also keeps shoes and gear dry. It would be much simpler to make a new floor grate or replace slats than it would be to replace or repair the ribs and/or the bottom board.

175

While floor grating was considered unnecessary added weight, it was not unknown in some early twentieth century guideboats. For example, Grant's boat number 11, built in 1904, is shown in Figure 17.21 with a floor grate. Floor grates were added to Grant and Parsons boats sold to summer residents at the Adirondack League Club, Big Moose, and the Fulton Chain of Lakes; boats that could be carried but were not. No guide would have coped with the extra weight of a grate.

Durant mentions floor grating only briefly, and Gardner's drawings of the *Virginia* have no information detailing it. The only guidance we had for building a floor grate was the picture in Durant (Figure 17.21). By carefully examining the slat width, location, and spacing in the picture and making some educated guesses, we were able to build the grate shown in Figure 17.22.

Figure 17.21

Grant's boat number 11 of 1904. (Courtesy of Adirondack Museum.)

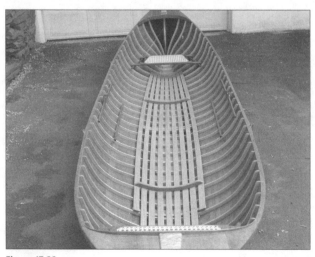

Figure 17.22

Grant-style floor grate.

The wood we chose was western red cedar, which is ideal for a grate since it is light in weight, straight grained, and does not require a finish in this application. We made the foot braces from cherry, which is much harder and will wear better than cedar.

CONSTRUCTING THE FLOOR GRATE

The floor grate consists of nine slats 1¼" wide and ⅜" thick, screwed to support cleats with #6 x 1" brass screws. The cleats serve to hold the assembly together, but also position and help to maintain the grate at the proper location on the bottom board. They are cut to fit the bottom board and rib profiles at the center rib 0, forward rib 6, and aft rib 8, with additional cleats at the forward rib 1 and aft rib 3. These two additional cleats are shown, albeit faintly, in the Durant photograph, but that boat is only 14' long. Our reproductions of the *Virginia* are 16' long, so the positions of the additional cleats were chosen to best stiffen and strengthen the assembly. Choose the placement of the two additional cleats carefully so that they do not interfere with the screwing on of the foot braces. The center cleat at rib 0 is doubled, with a cleat placed on each side of this rib.

Cut the cleats from solid stock using patterns for each location. To make a pattern, begin by measuring the width of the bottom board at rib 6 (used here as an example). Draw a line of this exact length on a blank piece of poster board, and mark its centerline. Next, position the pattern for rib 6 on this line so that the heel-end of the rib foot lines up exactly with the left end of the line (Figure 17.23). Trace the pattern, extending your lines up from the heel about 6". Flip the rib pattern over and repeat the process, this time aligning the heel with the right end of the line (Figure 17.24).

The tracing for the rib 6 cleat should look like the one shown in Figure 17.25a. Cut out the pattern with a sharp knife, leaving the sides a little long (Figure 17.25b). Place the pattern on the bottom board against rib 6 and make sure its contours match the sides of the hull. The top edge of the pattern should be even with

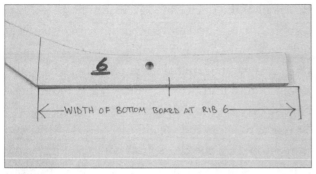

Figure 17.23

Tracing the rib pattern to make the left side of a floor grate cleat. Note the centerline, which will be useful for later alignment of the slats.

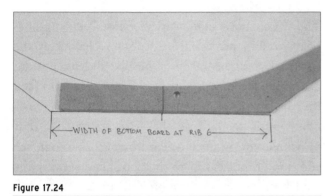

Figure 17.24

Simply flip the rib pattern over to trace the right side of the cleat pattern.

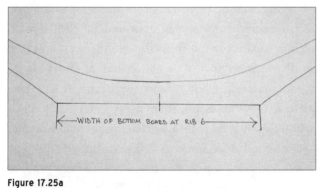

Figure 17.25a

Full cleat pattern, ready to be cut out.

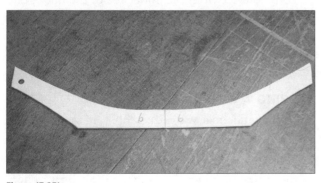

Figure 17.25b

Pattern cut out.

the top edge of the rib feet. If it is not, correct the pattern or retrace it until you have an appropriate fit. Make similar patterns for the other rib locations, and check their shape against their respective ribs.

Trace the patterns onto 1-by stock, cut out the cleats using a jigsaw or band saw, and sand off any saw marks. Do not trim the ends of the cleats just yet; the final lengths of the cleats will be established after the slats are mounted. Once all of the cleats are cut (remember, you need two of the 0 cleats), place them in position on the bottom board in preparation for laying out the slats. The two end cleats are positioned inboard of their respective ribs, and the two rib 0 cleats straddle the rib.

The three center slats are longest, at nearly 10'. Position a slat to run centered on all of the cleats, with the ends hanging over the two end cleats and their respective ribs. Do not cut the slat to exact length just yet—trimming will be done later. Drill a lead hole and drive a screw through the slat into one of the rib 0 cleats. Hold both rib 0 cleats against the rib feet and drive a screw into the other cleat. This positions the slat and the two rib 0 cleats (Figure 17.26). Hold the remaining cleats against their respective ribs and screw the center slat to the cleats the same way.

Figure 17.26

The rib 0 cleats straddle the ribs.

177

The separation between the slats varies along their lengths, but by using temporary spacers when installing the slats, the variation is consistent. Install the next slats on either side of the center slat by using a piece of ¾" thick scrap as a temporary positioning spacer between the slats at the rib 0 position, and then a ¼" spacer at the ends. Drive screws into the remaining cleats where the slat lies, but hold the cleats against the ribs while doing so.

Install the remaining slats the same way, but cut their lengths progressively shorter at the stern end. Before you install each new outside slat, cut it shorter than the previous slat by the distance between two ribs. Trim the ends of these slats so that they cover the last rib at their ends, as seen in Figures 17.22 and 17.27a. The forward ends of the slats are all trimmed later to the same length, extending just over rib 6 (Figure 17.27b).

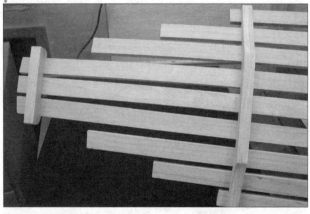

Figure 17.27a
Aft end of floor grate.

Figure 17.27b
Forward end.

When all of the screws are driven and the assembly is complete, carefully remove it. If the cleats were held tight to the ribs during assembly, the fit may be quite snug. Our grate resulted in a press fit, which also serves to hold it in place. If your grate is too tight, it may be necessary to thin one or more cleats slightly. Trim the forward ends of the slats neatly even, and trim the ends of the cleats flush with the edge of the outermost slat. You may round the ends of the cleats over for a neat appearance.

FOOT BRACES

The reason brass footplates were installed on guideboats was to protect the ribs from chafing as the rower's feet rubbed against the ribs and the bottom board, predominantly during the pull stroke. In fact, the ribs serve as a brace for the rower's feet, which naturally push forward as the oars are pulled, thus providing for more efficient rowing. Without the addition of foot braces to the floor grate, rowing the guideboat becomes a bit more difficult.

Two braces must be installed on the floor grate, one at rib position 3 on the stern-end of the boat to accommodate rowing from the middle seat, and one at rib position 0^4 on the bow end of the boat to accommodate the bow rowing position (see Gardner Plate XII). Once again, there are a variety of ways to install foot braces, including making them adjustable. Our method is to simply fasten a contoured length of wood at the appropriate position on the floor grate at these rib positions (Figure 17.28). We screwed the braces into place from the underside of the floor grate using brass screws. Before installing yours, check to make sure the location provides for the comfortable positioning of your feet while rowing.

CARVING A CARRY YOKE

Since the guideboat was a carry boat, it would not be a guideboat without the carry yoke. The guide working alone without one would be limited in his travels to the water in which he launched the boat. There would be no way he could single-handedly carry the boat around rapids or over land to the next lake, except perhaps by dragging it—not recommended in the rocky confines of the Adirondacks. The yoke permitted the guide to overturn the boat, balance it on his shoulders, and carry it to the next lake or stream.

Figure 17.28
Foot brace installed. The bottom edge is contoured to fit the profile of the grate where it is fastened.

MAKING THE TEMPLATES

Carving a yoke for your new boat is not difficult, although when you first see Gardner's drawings of a yoke in Plate XV, the technique is not readily apparent. Using the measurements in the drawings, you initially make various templates, which are then used to lay out and gauge the progress of the carving.

Begin by studying the top view drawing at the bottom of Plate XV. There is a centerline running through the arms, and another perpendicular to it marked *SECTION A*. There are two other lines on either side of the vertical centerline, similarly marked *SECTION B* and *SECTION C*. There are also lines running parallel to the arm centerline, at 1½" and 2½" out from the arm centerline. All of the lines together form a grid, on which is plotted the outline of the yoke as seen from the top. The three *SECTION* drawings above the top view show the vertical sectional profiles at the arm center, 1½", and 2½" out. The measurements shown on these profile drawings provide the information for making the templates and shaping the yoke.

The three section drawings give depth measurements at sections A, B, and C. It is convenient to make a table of these measurements and number them 1 through 9. You can then identify the corresponding grid intersections on the pattern with these serial numbers, and the height measurements from the drawings transferred to the pattern. When the hollowing out process is started, ⅛" holes are drilled in the blank at the grid intersections to the depths of the height measurements, but we will get to that later. Figure 17.29 shows the completed half-pattern.

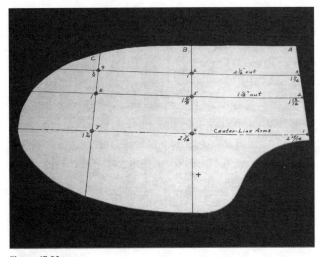

Figure 17.29
Half-pattern of carry yoke.

Using a similar technique, we can make patterns for the horizontal and vertical sections of the hollow. For the wrap-around neck cutout pattern, thinner stock is required since you must place the pattern around the curve of the yoke. The last template is one for shaping the slight taper of the yoke arms. Drill 1¼" and 1½" holes through a piece of ¼" plywood, and cut it along the center to produce half-circular templates. Figure 17.30 shows the entire set of templates.

Note the B and C templates for the outside shape of the yoke in Figure 17.30. They are split along the arm centerline, allowing for the easy shaping of one side of the yoke without interference from the side that is not yet shaped. A template for the center section (A) is not needed, and none is shown.

179

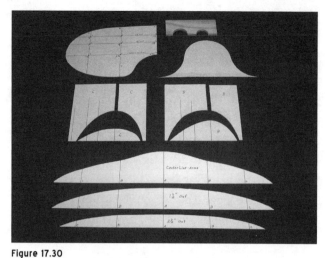

Figure 17.30
Complete set of yoke carving templates.

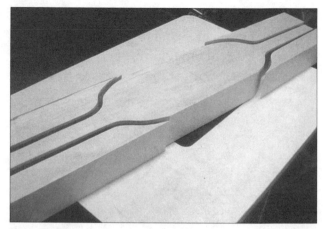

Figure 17.31a
First rough cut of overall shape.

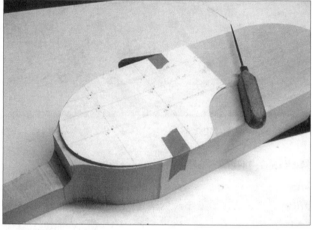

Figure 17.31b
Arms roughed out, half-template ready for marking the depth holes layout.

Figure 17.32
Drilling holes to a measured depth.

ROUGHING OUT

The traditional builders chose from a variety of available woods to make yokes, with likely considerations being the weight of the wood and the availability of a suitable blank that was not cracked. For our modern reproductions, we found that kiln-dried basswood was readily available in the required dimensions, clear, straight-grained, and free of defects.

The first step is to cut the blank to approximate dimensions, at a length 1" or so longer than required. You will trim the excess length when you fit the yoke to the hull. With the blank sized, draw centerlines on it, and the A, B, and C lines, wrapping all lines around the blank. Using the half pattern, draw the outline of the yoke, including the arms, on the blank, and rough it out with the band saw. Do not cut the neck cutout—you will do that after you have done all of the shaping (Figures 17.31a and b).

Tape the half-pattern in position on the blank and mark the nine holes at the grid line intersections using a sharp awl through the pattern. Turn the half-pattern over and similarly mark the other side. Wrap a bit of tape around the shank of a ⅛" brad-point bit, leaving exposed a length equal to the depth of the hole to be drilled. Drill the holes to the tape-marked depth. Note that the holes are symmetrical: the holes for a section on the left are the same as the corresponding holes on the right (Figure 17.32).

HOLLOWING THE INSIDE

Removing the waste from the inside is next. A handy tool for starting this is a high-speed die grinder or power woodcarving tool with a coarse carbide bit. Cut channels along the A, B, and C lines to a depth such that the drilled holes are just removed. If you had used a brad point drill bit, leave the dimple from the brad point in the bottom of the channel. This insures enough wood is left for final scraping, sanding, and adjusting with the templates. You can do some preliminary hogging out of a layer of waste with a Forstner bit, but do not drill too deep (Figure 17.33). Check your progress frequently using the appropriate template.

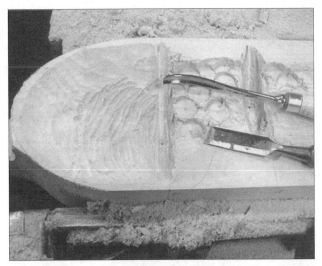

Figure 17.33
Grinding out channels to the depth of the holes. The channel on the left requires more grinding; the one on the right is complete.

Figure 17.34a
Chisels and gouges used to remove waste...

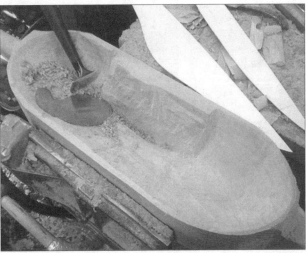

Figure 17.34b
...with scrapers used for the fine work.

181

With the channels completed to the depth of the holes, the next step is to remove the mass of wood between the channels, and smooth the inside fair (Figures 17.34a and b).

With the inside hollowed out, the arms can be rounded and work begun on shaping the outside. A spoke shave works well here, but check the diameter and shape of the arms as you proceed to insure you do not overdo it. The very ends of the arms should be left a bit larger than the inside diameter of the brass ferrules to be fitted later. The intersections of the arms with the body of the yoke are easily shaped with round Microplanes or rat tail files. Be sure that you frequently check the shaping of the outside of the body with the appropriate templates (Figure 17.35).

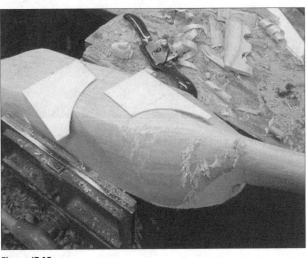

Figure 17.35
Shaping the outside.

When you have shaped the outside, give it a good sanding inside and out. You can use 80-grit paper to finish off some of the shaping details, followed by a preliminary sanding with 120-grit paper.

To make the neck cutout, tape the cutout template into position, being careful to place it on the correct side. Trace the template and carefully cut it out. Round over and smooth the cut edges. Figures 17.36a and b show the carving completed.

Figure 17.36a
Carving complete on the underside.

Figure 17.36b
Carving complete on the outside.

In Chapter 16, we mentioned obtaining a length of 1¼" thin-wall brass sink drain tubing. Now we will use it to make the ferrules for the ends of the yoke arms. Gardner, in Plate XV, showed the Grant ferrules being made of 0.020" brass. Assuming he referred to flat shim stock, we opted for the tubing, since it is already formed, harder than shim stock, and

readily available. Once we removed the chrome plating, the thickness was 0.020" to 0.022", consistent with the original.

If not already done, remove the chrome plating on a few inches of the end of the tube using successively finer grits of emery cloth. Give the brass a preliminary buffing, and cut two ferrules 1" long. Measure across the boat at the yoke cleats, and trim the yoke arms to length. Be sure the yoke will be centered, that is, the arms should be equal lengths from the center. File or sand a small chamfer on the ends of the arms. The ferrules should not yet fit on the ends of the arms, the arms having been left slightly larger in diameter than the inside diameter of the ferrules.

Using the remaining length of tubing, file small teeth around the periphery, essentially creating a hole saw. A fine-cut triangular file works very well here (Figure 17.37a). Keep one side of the file vertical as you cut the teeth so that there is a forward rake to the teeth. This only takes a few strokes for each tooth, and you will complete the tool in a few minutes. There is no need to put a set in the teeth. Doing so could make the final diameter of the yoke arm too small for the ferrules (Figure 17.37a).

Figure 17.37a
Saw teeth filed in tubing end.

Slide the saw teeth over the yoke arm end, rotating it as you work it down the arm (Figure 17.37b). Be sure to keep it going straight. Stop when you have it shaped enough to allow the ferrule to slide down the arm, with the end chamfer extending just beyond the end of the ferrule. Do not sand the shaped surface.

Figure 17.37b
Yoke arm sized with the tool.

To fasten the ferrules, roughen the inside of them with coarse sandpaper, and use a little bit of epoxy to glue them on. You may want to wait until the yoke is finish sanded, stained, and varnished (or whatever finish you choose) before gluing the ferrules on. It would also probably be best to give the ferrules a final buffing and coating with a clear spray lacquer before gluing (Figure 17.38).

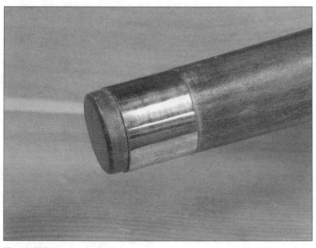

Figure 17.38
Completed yoke arm, yoke stained and varnished with satin varnish.

1 Jacking, or jack lighting, was the stalking of deer at night as they fed on water lilies or waded along the shores of lakes or ponds. From the stern seat, the guide would quietly paddle the guideboat close to shore while the "sport" would sit in the bow ready with his rifle. The jack light, or lantern, was set on the bow deck with the light cast toward the shore, leaving the boat's occupants in the dark. Mesmerized by the light, the deer would stand motionless, affording the hunter an opportunity to make the kill. The outlawing of this practice in 1897 contributed to the decline of the guideboat as a means of hunting deer.

2 If you do not have access to a band saw, you can work the side profile by hand using a draw knife along with a hand plane and spoke shave.

3 A conversation with the present owner of the Grant house and shop in Boonville, New York, revealed that, when Lewis Grant was building boats after his father Dwight passed away, the child in the house next door regularly came over to play in Lewis's pile of shavings.

4 One can only wonder what might have been the expression on a guide's face when a woman passenger climbed into his boat with sharp-heeled shoes!

183

CHAPTER 18
GUIDEBOAT CARE AND MAINTENANCE

Not long ago at a wooden boat show in the central Adirondacks, an older man was admiring one of our boats. He carefully took in the lines, gently touched the hull in several different places with his weathered hands, and caressed the stems as if they were finely carved statues. He made only one comment, perhaps directed more at guideboats in general than at the boat he was admiring. "Art forms!" Those were the only words he uttered before he walked away.

We are certain the boat you have built by following our instructions will bring you similar comments. The Grants and others builders were craftsman who didn't consider themselves artists. Yet, few people with an appreciation for wooden boats will argue with that man at the boat show that the Adirondack guideboat is an art form in its own right.

An object that produces such a reaction deserves to be well cared for and maintained. We trust that if you have come this far, you made a conscious decision to build an heirloom-quality boat; one to which you have given a great deal of time and attention. You more than likely made this decision fully aware of the responsibilities of wooden boat ownership. No wooden boat should be neglected, regardless of how it is constructed. In this chapter, we discuss responsible ownership of your hand-crafted wooden boat, including transporting; fixing scratches, nicks, dings and other damage; revarnishing and repainting; brass and seat cane maintenance; long and short-term storage; and periodic upkeep.

TRANSPORTATION

We have transported our guideboats in various ways, including roof racks, trailers, and in the back of a pick-up truck. While there is no "best way" to get your boat from here to there, each method has its advantages and disadvantages. The best method for you will depend on your vehicle and your individual travel needs.

The use of roof racks is a common method for transporting canoes and kayaks and can work just as well for guideboats. However, getting an unwieldy guideboat on top of a car is a bit more difficult, especially if you have to do it yourself. On smaller cars, the racks might not be spaced far enough apart to prevent the boat from rocking back and forth.

The problem we have with transporting a wooden guideboat on roof racks has more to do with potential gunwale damage than anything else. Transporting with roof racks requires the boat to be overturned so the gunwales rest on rails that are either round or flat, and typically no more than 1" in width or diameter. Thus, the surface area on which the gunwales make contact with the rack is relatively small.

Regardless of how securely you tie down the craft, driving over a rough road or hitting the occasional bump or pothole will cause the boat to bounce on the rails, which can leave unsightly dents or depressions in the gunwales. If you transport your guideboat on conventional roof racks, at least pad them adequately to minimize or prevent gunwale damage.

We once saw an innovative transport method where a guideboat was bolted to a rack on top of a car. A wood framework had been securely fastened to the stock roof rack; the inverted boat rested on gunwale pads with bolts through the oarlocks and framework secured with a nut.

Trailering the guideboat (Figures 18.1a and b) is an alternative to car-top transportation. Unless you already have a trailer that can be used or adapted for the guideboat, the added expense of purchasing one may be prohibitive. The trailer shown in Figure 18.1b is a lightweight, galvanized boat trailer that was adapted to carry not only the guideboat, but also the floor grate and the oars (Figure 18.2). Manufactured by Oldencamp Industries and sold under the Magneta name, it has been adapted for use as a dedicated guideboat trailer. With extra-long, 2" square tubular rails, it can easily transport two guideboats, and can be used to carry canoes and kayaks.

Figure 18.2
Floor grate and oars fastened to trailer.

However, because the setup shown also requires the craft to be transported upside down, the potential still exists for gunwale damage. Trailers, in fact, will bounce around a great deal, so the railings must be adequately padded and the craft must be securely fastened. The only acceptable tie-downs in this case are nylon straps with ratcheting mechanisms (Figure 18.3), and we recommend these regardless of how you transport your boat.

Figure 18.1a
One method of trailering a guideboat.

Figure 18.1b
Another method of trailering a guideboat. The trailer shown here was modified to also carry the oars and floor grate.

Figure 18.3
Ratcheting tie-down straps. Note the padding under the ratchet mechanism to protect the finish from marring.

Another option is a lightweight (95 pounds), all-aluminum trailer manufactured by Trailex. The company's model SUT-200-S trailer, which can double as a launching dolly, will transport a single guideboat, canoe, or kayak in the upright position (Figure 18.4). It uses a special rubberized aluminum suspension to eliminate virtually all road bounce. One advantage of trailering the guideboat upright is the ability to store

Figure 18.4
All-aluminum, lightweight Trailex SUT-200-S trailer allows for easy handling and upright transport of the guideboat.

Figure 18.6a
The boat is tied down using ratcheting straps just behind the cab...

gear in the boat and since the craft is positioned for launching, you can avoid having to lift the boat from an upside down position to get it in the water.

Trailering the guideboat right side up is much better and can virtually eliminate any potential for gunwale damage. However, you should empty any rainwater that accumulates during transport as soon as possible.

Figure 18.5 shows another method of transporting the guideboat that works well for pickup truck owners. Simply rest the guideboat on the bed of the truck and tie it down with straps in two locations (Figures 18.6a and b) to keep the craft from moving around. On trucks with longer beds, the lowered tailgate provides sufficient surface area such that the boat will be in no danger of flopping around. Shorter bed trucks may warrant the use of a hitch extension (Figure 18.7).

Figure 18.6b
...and at the rear end of the truck.

Figure 18.7
Hitch extenders, like this Extend-A-Truck II made by Darby Industries, are good for transporting a guideboat in a short-bed pickup truck.

187

Figure 18.5
For short trips, a guideboat can be transported in the back of a pickup truck.

We would be remiss if we did not mention that good old-fashioned ingenuity plays an important role in how best to transport your guideboat. One need only attend a boating event featuring guideboats to see the many different variations on how best to transport these craft. You should not be afraid to experiment with different methods or to adapt your roof racks or trailers to best fit your individual needs.

Finally, regardless of how you transport your guide-boat, make sure you take some simple precautions. Use adequate tie-downs, such as ratcheting straps, and check them frequently during transport to insure they remain tight. Take extra time to pad areas where straps or ropes contact the wood. Make sure all roof racks, trailer connections, nuts and bolts, etc., are securely fastened, and make sure trailer tires are in good shape and have adequate air pressure. The same rule that applies when using power tools applies here as well: Safety First!

REPAIRS

Most repairs to your guideboat, should they become necessary, will involve replacing loose screws, replacing broken seat risers, repairing scratches in the varnish or paint, or repairing more serious damage to the hull or trim work. No one knows the intricacies of your boat as you do, and the skills that got you this far will get you through any repairs.

REPLACING LOOSE OR MISSING SCREWS

Should a screw become loose (or turn up missing) for any reason, or otherwise need replacing, the hole should first be plugged with a dowel or a piece of matching wood. If possible, redrill the hole. Then insert a dowel coated with glue. If sawing the dowel flush with the surface is not possible, use one that will not protrude above the surface. Once the glue is dry and the dowel is secure, drill a new pilot hole and reinstall the new screw.

REPLACING SEAT RISERS

In all likelihood, you will need to replace one or more seat risers at some point. The risers, although thin, can withstand a substantial amount of weight. However, wood being what it is, a crack may develop as a result of undue stress or because of the wood weakening over time. Also, there are limits to how heavy a person can be to sit on a guideboat seat and not break it or the cleats.

Luckily, replacing a riser is not difficult. Before you remove the broken riser, make light pencil marks (or use tape) to note the location for the new riser. After removing the broken riser, drill out the holes using a ⅛" bit. Take care to not drill too deep; you do not want to drill into the hull! Insert glue-coated dowels into the holes, and tap them in place securely. After the glue has dried, trim the dowels flush and sand the area smooth. Revarnish as needed. You can now install the new seat riser just as you did the original one, taking care to maintain the original measurements. Remember to coat the screws with sealant.

SCRATCHES AND DENTS

Normally, you can buff out surface scratches on a varnished hull using a medium- or fine-cut automotive cleaner, similar to what you used to achieve the high gloss finish on your hull (refer to Chapter 15). First, go over the scratch with Meguiar's #1 medium-cut cleaner. Follow this with #2 fine-cut cleaner, and then with #9 swirl remover. Finish up with #26 Hi-Tech yellow wax.

If this does not remove the scratches, and they are not deep enough to have scratched the fiberglass, clean the area around the scratch and remove all wax residues with paint thinner. Using a fine brush, apply just enough varnish to fill the scratch. If needed, wet sand and polish the area to restore the original glass-smooth surface. Refer to Chapter 15 again if necessary.

Scratches that penetrate the varnish and damage the epoxy layer require a bit more work. Deep scratches (Figure 18.8) will bruise fiberglass cloth, manifesting the damage as white streaks or blotches. After sanding off the varnish, you may apply epoxy to try to eliminate the wound, but such treatment is generally not successful and the scratch will remain visible under the new layer of epoxy. The best way to eliminate deep scratches is to carefully sand off the fiberglass and expose new bare wood. A patch strip of fiberglass is then laid up with epoxy, the edges feathered out smooth, and the entire patch sanded and revarnished.

Repairing damage to the wood must be evaluated on a case-by-case basis. Certainly, you should replace any severely splintered, crushed, or broken wood. Cracks in the stripping can generally be repaired by working unthickened epoxy into the crack after first removing enough fiberglass to expose the crack. Putting pressure on the crack to cause it to flex slightly will work the epoxy into the fault. When the epoxy has cured, add a patch of fiberglass as described above.

Figure 18.8
These deep scratches on a canoe bottom can only be repaired by sanding off the cloth and laying in fiberglass patches.

From time to time, it may be necessary to revarnish the oars, paddle, and yoke. Seat frames may also become abraded, the ribs and bottom board scratched or dented by sand, debris, or sharp items, or the hull bruised by run-ins with errant rocks, trees, or other objects. The possibilities are endless! Always clean the area to be revarnished and lightly sand before recoating. If possible, use the same varnish as in the original application.

Occasionally, a section of trim will get a dent or ding that does not tear or cut the wood fibers, and may not even break the surface of the varnish. This frequently occurs on the top edge of the gunwales, either from transporting the boat on roof racks, or from whacking it too hard with an oar blade or shaft. Should this happen and you find the dent unsightly, there is a simple technique to remedy the problem. First, sand or scrape off the varnish around the dent. Place a moistened paper towel over the dent and press a moderately hot iron on it. Do not let the iron sit too long

on the paper towel. Keep touching the iron to the wet paper towel directly over the dented area. The warm moisture will begin to raise the compressed wood fibers. Be patient and you will find that unless the dent was too severe, it will virtually disappear. Allow the wood to thoroughly dry and then revarnish it.

REFINISHING A PAINTED HULL

Keeping a painted hull looking new is similar to keeping that new truck looking like it just left the showroom. The difference is there are no little tubes or bottles of touch-up paint for your boat. The chances are very good that you have some paint left over, though, and it has been well sealed and can be reused.

Minor scratches on the hull can be touched up with the leftover paint and a fine artist's brush. For repairing a major scratch, some preparation is in order. The area around the scratch should first be cleaned of any dirt or grime, and then the area wet sanded with a fairly fine paper, such as 220- or 400-grit. Wipe the area clean and allow it to dry well, then paint the sanded area. More than one coat may be required.

For a complete refinishing job, remove the brass, clean and wet sand the entire hull after any required repairs, and continue as described in Chapter 15. The brass could probably benefit from repolishing.

SEAT CANE MAINTENANCE

If you caned your seats with plastic caning, there is not much you need to do other than to periodically clean the caning with mild soap and water.

For naturally caned seats and backrests, all you will need is a little periodic care and attention to insure long life and serviceability. Avoid leaving caned seats exposed to the hot sun for long periods or in hot, dry, sunny rooms or near heaters, as the caning will dry out and become brittle. Over time, this exposure will result in cracking. When not in use for an extended period, remove and store your caned seats in a cool, dry location, out of direct sunlight and away from the elements.

189

If you plan to keep your boat outside for prolonged periods (which we do not recommend), remove the seats and store them out of the sunlight or cover them. We have found that the best way to maintain natural caning is to periodically spray or coat it with a mixture of 1 part boiled linseed oil to 2 parts turpentine or mineral spirits. We like to spray a thin coating on the front and back surface of the cane, let it soak in for a few minutes, and then wipe it off with a soft cloth. If the cane is dirty, you can first brush it clean with a bristle brush of some kind. A simple vegetable brush, used to clean dirt off fruits and vegetables, works well.

The caning on your seats will need periodic tightening, especially if the seats are used frequently. Caning will stretch or sag under stress and over time, and the sag will remain. It is common, for example, to see caned chairs with noticeable depressions in the caning. These depressions occur because the caning is no longer able to flex and in effect, loses its resiliency.

To retighten the cane and remove the depression, turn the seat over and place a towel dampened with warm water on the underside of the cane. You can also wet the underside with warm water and a sponge. Either way, it is important to do this on the underside since the cane has a natural glossy coating on the topside that will prevent it from absorbing moisture.

If you used a dampened towel, allow it to remain on the cane for about an hour; then let the cane dry overnight at room temperature. As it dries, the cane should restore to its original tension. If there is still some sag in the seat, you may need to loosen the cane and pull it tight. Make sure you do this with the cane moistened to prevent breakage.

It is very important to retighten the cane when you first notice it sagging. If you wait too long to retighten it, you increase the likelihood of breakage because the cane will begin to wear against the edge of the seat or the strands will break in the center. If that happens, you will need to re-cane the entire seat!

Do not varnish or lacquer natural caning. Doing so seals the cane and prevents it from breathing and absorbing the moisture necessary to keep it from drying out.

STORAGE

Keeping your boat looking new greatly depends on how it is stored. During the rowing season, you may keep it at the camp on the lake ready for a morning row or at home to be trailered to the lake. If you keep it at the camp, do not leave it in the water tied to the dock or partially pulled up on shore. The finish coatings recommended in Chapter 15, while fully acceptable for day use, are not designed for continuous immersion below the water line.

Once out of the water and safely on shore, invert the boat to prevent water accumulation. Simply laying the inverted boat on the ground can present problems where the bow and stern or gunwale touches the ground. Prolonged contact with the ground can lead to rot, and the brass stem caps will not only lose their shine, but may even corrode. Simple supports, like boards placed between a couple of rocks or concrete blocks, will safely keep the boat off the ground. While the paint or varnish provides protection from damaging UV rays, why tempt fate? We advise a shady storage spot out of direct sunlight.

Off-season storage presents other challenges. While heated inside storage is the ideal for fiberglassed boats, few are fortunate enough to have that kind of available space. Certainly, the shop where you built the boat would provide not only storage, but also facilitate leisurely maintenance in preparation for next season. Unheated indoor storage is perfectly acceptable, even preferred for non-fiberglassed wooden boats (Figure 18.9), but lacks the comfort for off-season maintenance. Many people who trailer their boats to the lake keep them on their trailers, with any tiedown straps released. Once again, storage of the boat on its trailer inside a garage is preferred.

Though outdoor winter storage is a last resort, there are things you can do to protect the boat. Remove anything that is not permanent, like the center seat and floor grate. Also remove the bow and stern seats; they may need a bit of cleaning and sprucing up. Sheltered storage is a plus, like under a shed roof or porch (Figure 18.10). It may not keep all of the snow and ice off, but protection from falling branches is a good idea. You may cover the inverted boat, but if you do, you should not place it where the sun may cause damage to the finish from localized spring heating. We have not tried shrink-wrapping as practiced by commercial boat storage services, but this might also work.

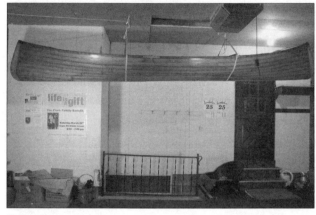

Figure 18.9

This 100-year-old guideboat, owned by the Clark family in central New York, spends its idle time in an unheated garage. A simple pulley system is used to raise and lower the boat and to keep it securely in place. Spreader bars are employed to keep the straps from exerting too much pressure on the hull.

Figure 18.10

Note the canoe stored off the ground. A good washing in the spring and the boats were ready for use.

If the boat is stored uncovered during winter (Figure 18.11), melting snow will leave a residue that must be removed on get-ready day. A mild car wash detergent and sponge does the job, followed by a hose rinse.

Figure 18.11

Not the best way to store boats, but these came through the winter needing only a good washing.

CLEANING BRASS

Brass will tarnish from handling and exposure to the elements if it has not been coated as described in Chapter 16. A periodic cleaning with a nonabrasive liquid brass cleaner like Brasso (Figure 18.12) is all you need to keep your brass work (we like to call it boat jewelry) looking bright and shiny. In the off-season, coat the brass with a protective film of oil or WD-40 to prevent tarnish. Alternatively, you may spray the brass with a clear lacquer such as Krylon, available in spray cans.

Figure 18.12

Brasso, available in hardware and grocery stores, is an excellent, nonabrasive liquid cleaner for brass and other metals.

A FINAL CONSTRUCTION NOTE

More than one boat builder has questioned our method of fiberglassing only the *outside* of our boats. These builders are comparing our guideboats to ribless canoes and kayaks that require fiberglass both inside and outside to form a strong laminate in the absence of ribs.

191

Another, and perhaps more serious, concern is the interior waterproofing of hull designs like ours, in which fiberglass and epoxy are present only on the exterior of the hull. We used a brushed-on epoxy and/or varnish and/or paint to seal and waterproof the inside of the hull. The perceived weakness here lies in the notion that as the hull flexes while in use, the epoxy and paint or varnish seal at the joints between the ribs and hull stripping can crack and admit water into the joint between them. Once moisture gets into this area, it may soak into the unprotected hull planking under the ribs. The outer covering of fiberglass and epoxy inhibits drying so that after a few years, the hull will blacken and rot, and the outer fiberglass sheath will delaminate. Of course, old traditional guideboats soaked up a lot of water. Their owners, in most cases, would simply let the boats dry out over the winter and paint everything again, readying the boat for another year of use.

We believe the concerns are unwarranted, but also not without merit. First, we should note that the spacing of the ribs at approximately 5" provides for an *extremely* rigid hull, with virtually no flexing under all but the most severe conditions. Virtually all of today's strip-built boats (canoes, kayaks, and some guideboats) are ribless. The elimination of ribs, or the use of ribs spaced far apart (as is the case with some builders), opens the door for quite a bit of hull flexing, which naturally leads to the problems noted above.

We have recommended both varnishing and epoxying for finishing the interior of our boats. If you apply these finishes properly with a sufficient number of coats (five coats of varnish over at least two coats of slow-setting epoxy), rotting will not be a problem. We also recommended the epoxy gluing of the gunwales and decks precisely to prevent problems from moisture and rot. These are areas where flexing or movement *will* occur, and where water penetration *can* be a problem. By taking the precaution to epoxy-glue these sections to begin with, you will minimize future problems.

In a strip-built boat hull, the fiberglass provides strength while the epoxy bonds the cloth to the wood

and provides waterproofing. The varnish or paint protects the epoxy from UV radiation degradation while contributing to the overall aesthetics of the craft. Severe flexing still makes it possible to break an epoxy seal, which would result in water making its way through the fiberglass/epoxy barrier into the wood. Ribbed construction minimizes or eliminates this flexing. So, in our view, the primary protection against water penetration is still the epoxy/varnish coating.

Our experience is limited only to tried and true marine paint and varnishes. If you are planning to use anything else, you should make sure it is compatible, preferably by contacting the product's manufacturer.

After spending a few hundred hours building an heirloom, you will want to treat it with care. Your boat will probably not be used to transport "sports," their game, duffel, or passengers for long distances in the manner of the old-time Adirondack guides. Treat it with respect, and your handcrafted guideboat will remain the classically beautiful heirloom you built it to be.

AFTERWORDS

THOUGHTS FROM JOHN MICHNE

After the boat was finished and taken for a shakedown cruise, I began to reflect on just how it all came about. I suppose I can say it started a few decades ago on a visit to the early Adirondack Museum. I found myself taken by the classic lines, delicate structure, and fine craftsmanship of the first Adirondack guideboat I had ever seen. I was a woodworker and had just recently built a plywood boat and so I lingered, perhaps too long for the impatient little girl by my side.

I was fascinated studying the craft's intricate array of tacks and screws used in joinery I was totally unfamiliar with. Awakened from my reverie by a tug from a daughter wanting to move on, I silently vowed that someday I would build a boat like that.

That little girl at my side in the museum grew up and left the nest along with her siblings, and I hadn't yet built a guideboat. Retirement found me relaxing by the shore of an Adirondack lake one beautiful day, when the young son of that little girl paddled in from the lake in a rented aluminum canoe. "C'mon, Grandpa, hop in!" was all I needed to hear.

Now mind you, I had never been in a canoe before. I have shot the rapids of the Hudson Gorge in a small rubber raft, sailed and power boated, spent a month at sea, and dove in a research submarine to Davie Jones' locker over two miles down to the bottom of the Atlantic. But I had never been in a canoe. Not being one to ignore the opportunity for a learning experience, I quickly found out one does not hop into a canoe. After a good laugh and the retrieval of my wet grandson from the shallow water, we were on our way.

Canoeing was fun that day. Since in retirement I intended to do a lot of camping in the Adirondacks, building a canoe could fill my need for a small manageable camp boat. A search on the Internet brought a long list of possible sources of information, and I soon found myself in a canoe builder's forum. With some apprehension, I posted a question and got a quick response.

A few weeks later, with the garage converted to a boat shop, construction of a cedar stripped canoe was well under way. It was indeed a learning—and a yearning—experience. The mental picture of that boat in the museum kept coming back to me. Could I build a guideboat this way, from cedar strips, epoxy, and fiberglass? More research. Yes, I could. I just about memorized the drawings in a copy of Kenneth Durant's book, which had become dog-eared as I searched out answers to questions about details.

193

I built the boat—a ribless cedar stripped version of Grant's *Virginia*. In profile and performance, the boat was an Adirondack guideboat. But something was lacking. I didn't have that exhilarated feeling of having built a boat like the one in the museum. It was at a small boat festival in Inlet one rare warm Adirondack spring day where vendors of boats and boating paraphernalia were demonstrating their wares. Nestled among all of the plastic, Kevlar, and fiberglass kayaks and canoes, there it was. An Adirondack guideboat similar to mine, but evoking that feeling my boat had failed to do all this time. Cedar stripped, beautifully finished, but it had RIBS! I was in love.

Over the years that I had been building canoes and that first guideboat, I remained active (and still am) on the forums and my web site dedicated to helping first-time builders avoid the problems I ran into while building boats. A casual mention of an Adirondack guideboat brought an email from another builder who had just completed building a fully ribbed cedar stripped guideboat. The correspondence with Mike Olivette continued, and when I mentioned that I would be starting a new guideboat as soon as I finished the canoe I was working on, the idea and the partnership for this book was forged. After nearly 1,000 email exchanges (and still counting), the book is done.

Along the way from that first Adirondack Museum visit to the finished boat and book, there were those that helped, inspired, and fed my fires of enthusiasm. The little girl who was with me that day at the museum is now Mrs. Lisa David, mother of my wet grandson, Cory. My first contact with anyone in the modern boat building community was the responder to my first posted question, Mac Buhler. Mac was instrumental in guiding my initial efforts, even though we had never met. When my first canoe was finished, we did get together for some paddling on the Housatonic River.

Help and guidance building that first ribless guideboat came from Ken Wallo. Ken's answers to my questions really got the project going, and were a significant contribution to my successful completion of the boat. While building my boats, Mac, Ken, and I kept in touch via almost daily emails. Our group soon grew with the addition of Larry Crook, Lou McIntyre, and Ross Leidy, who all contributed their collective expertise to my early boat building efforts.

Working with Mike Olivette was as smooth and pleasurable as could be. Certainly, Mike's enthusiasm rubbed off on me when from time to time I got stuck on a detail of building or writing. His eagerness, along with his effort to ferret out key contacts and provide construction details that I had no idea of, was instrumental in the successful completion of the project.

I didn't have the slightest idea how to duplicate Grant's brass work until Mike showed me how it was done. On my first guideboat, I used simple canoe stem banding material. That improvisation certainly contributed to that emotionless feeling about my first guideboat. We both look forward to next season, the Adirondack Museum's "No Octane Regatta" every June, and building more boats.

So now the boat is done, the book is on the shelf, and the shop is all cleaned up. What next? Building small boats is a most pleasurable addiction, and my craving for more shop time is well underway to being satisfied. Another Grant design boat, number 11 made in 1904, is framed on the stock plank. I must make a confession here—the picture of a framework at the end of Chapter 7 is actually of that boat. It will be traditionally planked with the Grant lap, screws, and copper tacks, without fiberglass and epoxy, and photographed extensively during construction. After that, I think I'll look for a spruce stump....

John Michne
Clifton Park, NY
April 17, 2005

AFTERWORDS

THOUGHTS FROM MICHAEL J. OLIVETTE

Being an Adirondack guide for nearly twenty years, and a woodworker for most of my life, the idea of having my own guideboat seemed to me to be a foregone conclusion. I began to look into purchasing one a number of years ago, and quickly realized two things: I would not be able to afford a traditionally built guideboat, new or original, and I did not want to settle for a less expensive, and correspondingly unappealing (at least to me), fiberglass version.

Then it hit me. If I'm such a good woodworker, why not prove it. So I set out to build my own guideboat. I meticulously researched the craft and its history, spoke to as many people as I could, and finally started up a three-year love affair that continues to this day. I gave serious consideration to building my first boat in the traditional manner—with beveled planks, spruce-stump ribs, and thousands of copper tacks.

A bad back made worse by hand-cutting and assembling a timber frame cabin a few years earlier solidified the decision to forego the digging of spruce stumps. The cost to purchase ribs cut from spruce stumps was prohibitive, and I reminded myself that I was trying to save as much money as I could. In addition, I really wanted my first boat to come out right, so I decided to use cove and bead cedar strips instead of the more difficult, but not impossible, method of using beveled planks. I have no regrets.

John and I differ on various aspects of the boat's construction, mostly a result of the different experiences and perspectives we bring to the process. What is important is that there is no best way to build a guideboat. Just as with the traditional builders, there are different ways to accomplish the same task. As

long as the end result does not compromise the performance, quality, or lines of the finished product, we hope you were encouraged to add your own special touch in building your boat.

Many people were either directly or indirectly involved in this project, and are deserving of my gratitude. A heartfelt thank you to my boat-building mentor, Bill Fuller, of Dewitt, New York. Without his kind and patient assistance and untiring ability to answer my many questions, my woodworking skills would never have been manifested in guideboats.

I would also like to thank the many people who were there for me to bounce ideas off, help me work through various problems, or just lend a hand or ear when needed. Thank you to good friends and fellow woodworkers John Dzioba and Rob Axelson (who, upon seeing my first boat nearly complete, exclaimed, "You really should write a book about this!"). A special thank you to Betsy Kennedy of the Cazenovia Library for allowing me to talk guideboats to anyone who will listen, and to William Held and John Hunter, both of Cazenovia, who allowed me to take photographs of their Grant guideboats. Thank you to Bill Schaeffer and Jim Carncross, who told me if anyone could build a guideboat, I could. Thanks to Pete Habla, a true artist with wood, who helped me realize I could build anything I wanted to. And thanks, as well, to Ed Vespa, for keeping me "above water."

My two daughters, Lindsay and Jaime, deserve a special note of gratitude for lending helping hands during boat building, and especially for allowing me to focus so long and hard on this project. For my parents, Marie and Pat, who waited a very long time for this, this book is for you. And finally, I offer a special note of gratitude to John Michne. John's attention to detail and his expertise in so many aspects of boat building are truly exceptional. We could not have been a better team. And, finally, thank you to Allen Fannin. Rest in peace my good friend. I will dearly miss you!

We are indebted to Diana Biro for her meticulous editing of an earlier draft of this manuscript. A particular debt of gratitude is due Mrs. Helen Durant, for graciously permitting us the use of John Gardner's drawings, and also to Craig and Alice Gilborn, for helping to obtain that permission. Thanks to Ted Comstock, Adirondack historian, for his expert help with our references to the guideboats and builders of the past. Finally, we are indebted to Hallie Bond, Curator of Boats at the Adirondack Museum, for the Foreword to this book, and for her knowledge, dedication, and commitment to boating in the Adirondacks.

John and I would like to express our special thanks to our publisher, editor, and friend, Nick Burns. Nick's enthusiasm for the project and editing skills smoothed over a lot of rough spots. The book is better for his effort, and we sincerely thank him for it.

Michael J. Olivette
Cazenovia, New York
April 23, 2005

196

APPENDIX 1

JOHN GARDNER'S DRAWINGS OF THE ADIRONDACK GUIDEBOAT *VIRGINIA*

Built in 1905 by Lewis and Floyd Grant in Boonville,
New York

(Courtesy: the Kenneth and Helen Durant Collection,
Adirondack Museum, Blue Mountain Lake, New York)

PLATE I

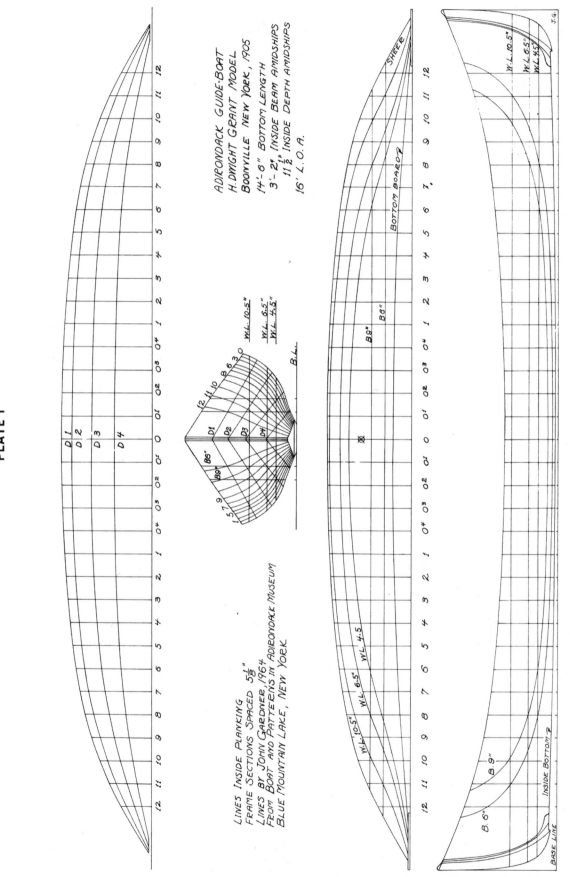

ADIRONDACK GUIDE-BOAT
H. DWIGHT GRANT MODEL
BOONVILLE NEW YORK, 1905
14'-6" BOTTOM LENGTH
3'-2" INSIDE BEAM AMIDSHIPS
11½" INSIDE DEPTH AMIDSHIPS
16' L.O.A.

LINES INSIDE PLANKING
FRAME SECTIONS SPACED 5⅛"
LINES BY JOHN GARDNER, 1964
FROM BOAT AND PATTERNS IN ADIRONDACK MUSEUM
BLUE MOUNTAIN LAKE, NEW YORK

PLATE II

Offsets — 16' Grant Guide-Boat.   Inches and Thirty-Seconds.

	Stations	0	0¹	0²	0³	0⁴	1	2	3	4	5	6	7	8	9	10	11	12	STEM
HEIGHTS ABOVE BASE LINE	Sheer	12-0	12-1	12-3	12-6	12-10	12-14	12-22	13-0	13-10	13-23	14-6	14-25	15-16	16-12	17-17	19-0	20-20	25-12
	Bottom	0-16	0-16	0-16	0-17	0-18	0-19	0-20	0-21	0-23	0-25	0-28	0-30	1-2	1-6	1-11	1-16	1-22	—
HALF-BREADTHS	6" Buttock	1-8	1-9	1-10	1-11	1-13	1-16	1-21	1-26	2-1	2-11	2-23	3-11	4-9	5-21	7-20	10-11	15-12	21-16
	9" Buttock	2-8	2-9	2-11	2-12	2-16	2-21	2-26	3-1	3-10	3-24	4-10	5-7	6-15	8-10	11-2	16-17	—	19-15
	Sheer	19-0	19-0	18-30	18-27	18-20	18-14	18-2	17-22	17-4	16-23	16-3	15-10	14-13	13-7	11-24	9-24	7-9	0-13
	Bottom	4-10	4-9	4-8	4-6	4-4	4-1	3-28	3-24	3-19	3-11	3-4	2-26	2-16	2-4	1-22	1-8	0-26	—
	10.5" Water L.	18-15	18-15	18-11	18-7	18-0	17-23	17-9	16-20	16-9	15-21	14-28	13-27	12-18	10-26	8-19	6-4	3-28	0-13
	6.5" Water L.	16-2	16-2	15-30	15-26	15-19	15-10	14-27	14-10	14-25	12-31	12-1	11-24	9-2	7-0	5-0	3-14	2-5	0-13
	4.5" Water L.	13-26	13-26	13-22	13-17	13-9	12-31	12-15	11-29	11-10	10-12	9-11	7-28	6-10	4-26	3-15	2-14	1-17	0-13
DIAGONALS	Diagonal 1	20-12	20-12	20-9	20-6	19-31	19-23	19-10	18-30	18-13	17-27	17-4	16-6	15-1	13-19	11-24	9-16	6-31	0-15
	Diagonal 2	18-2	18-2	17-31	17-28	17-22	17-16	17-6	16-26	16-13	15-26	15-5	14-8	13-7	11-21	9-28	7-30	5-27	0-15
	Diagonal 3	13-23	13-23	13-21	13-19	13-15	13-10	13-2	12-25	12-17	12-1	11-16	10-22	9-24	8-15	7-2	5-18	4-1	0-16
	Diagonal 4	8-14	8-14	8-13	8-12	8-9	8-5	8-0	7-27	7-20	7-10	7-0	6-16	5-27	5-3	4-6	3-8	2-9	0-17

Diagonal 1	19-0 Above B.L.	From C.L. on W.L. 10.5	14-20	on W.L. 6.5 — 21-19
Diagonal 2	15-18 Above B.L.	From C.L. on W.L. 10.5	7-13	on W.L. 6.5 — 13-7
Diagonal 3	11-16 Above B.L.	From C.L. on W.L. 4.5	8-22	on B.L. — 14-8
Diagonal 4	6-26 Above B.L.	From C.L. on W.L. 4.5	2-27	on B.L. — 8-12

Offsets Measured Inside Plank — Inside Bottom and from the Bearding Line on the Stem.

J.G.

PLATE III

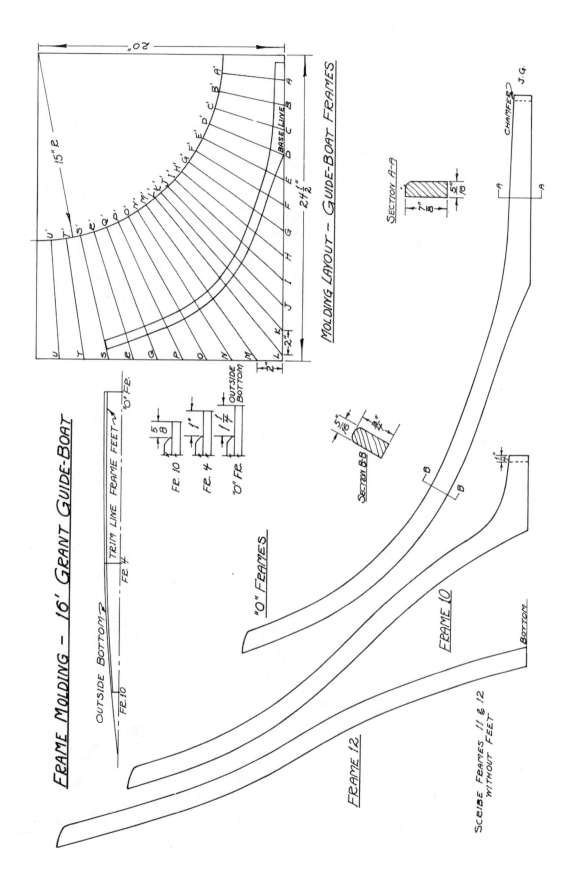

FRAME MOLDING – 16' GRANT GUIDE-BOAT

OUTSIDE BOTTOM
TRIM LINE FRAME FEET
"O" FR.
FR. 4
FR. 10

FR. 10   5/8
FR. 4   1"
"O" FR.   1 1/4"   OUTSIDE BOTTOM

"O" FRAMES

SECTION B-B   5/16"   3/4"

MOLDING LAYOUT – GUIDE-BOAT FRAMES

20"
15" R
BASE LINE
24 1/2"
2"
2"
A' B' C' D' E' F' G' H' I' J' K' L' M' N' O' P' Q' R' S' T' U'
A B C D E F G H I J K L M N O P Q R S T U

SECTION A-A   7/8"   5/16"

A   CHAMFER   J.G.
A   A

B   B
1/4"

FRAME 12

FRAME 10

BOTTOM

SCRIBE FRAMES 11 & 12
WITHOUT FEET

PLATE IV

J.G.

MEASUREMENTS — MOLDING LAYOUT — GUIDE-BOAT FRAMES FROM GRANT PATTERNS — INCHES AND THIRTY-SECONDS

DISTANCE ON LINE	AA'	BB'	CC'	DD'	EE'	FF'	GG'	HH'	II'	JJ'	KK'	LL'	MM'	NN'	OO'	PP'	QQ'	RR'	SS'	TT'	UU'
FR. 0 OUTSIDE	B.L.	B.L.	B.L.	B.L.	6-18	6-27	7-8	7-22	8-5	8-16	8-24	8-31	9-6	9-11	9-13	9-12	9-10	9-10	9-14	—	—
FR. 0 INSIDE	4-10	4-18	4-30	5-12	5-24	6-3	UNIFORM 3/4″ MOLDING														
FR. 1 OUTSIDE	B.L.	B.L.	B.L.	B.L.	6-17	6-25	7-5	7-20	8-2	8-13	8-22	8-29	9-4	9-8	9-9	9-8	9-7	9-7	9-11	—	—
FR. 1 INSIDE	4-10	4-17	4-30	5-12	5-23	6-1	UNIFORM 3/4″ MOLDING														
FR. 2 OUTSIDE	B.L.	B.L.	B.L.	B.L.	6-15	6-22	7-2	7-16	7-28	8-7	8-15	8-21	8-28	8-31	8-30	8-31	8-28	8-28	9-0	—	—
FR. 2 INSIDE	4-10	4-17	4-30	5-11	5-20	5-30	UNIFORM 3/4″ MOLDING														
FR. 3 OUTSIDE	B.L.	B.L.	B.L.	B.L.	6-13	6-19	6-30	7-9	7-21	7-31	8-6	8-12	8-18	8-21	8-19	8-21	8-16	8-16	8-18	—	—
FR. 3 INSIDE	4-10	4-17	4-30	5-10	5-18	5-26	UNIFORM 3/4″ MOLDING														
FR. 4 OUTSIDE	B.L.	B.L.	B.L.	B.L.	6-12	6-17	6-26	7-5	7-16	7-25	7-31	8-4	8-9	8-11	8-10	8-8	8-5	8-3	8-3	—	—
FR. 4 INSIDE	4-11	4-17	4-30	5-10	5-18	5-24	UNIFORM 3/4″ MOLDING														
FR. 5 OUTSIDE	B.L.	B.L.	B.L.	B.L.	6-9	6-12	6-20	6-30	7-7	7-15	7-21	7-26	7-31	8-1	8-1	7-31	7-28	7-25	7-24	—	—
FR. 5 INSIDE	4-11	4-17	4-29	5-8	5-15	5-20	UNIFORM 3/4″ MOLDING														
FR. 6 OUTSIDE	B.L.	B.L.	B.L.	B.L.	6-7	6-7	6-13	6-21	6-29	7-4	7-9	7-14	7-19	7-21	7-21	7-19	7-16	7-13	7-11	—	—
FR. 6 INSIDE	4-11	4-18	4-30	5-8	5-10	5-13	UNIFORM 3/4″ MOLDING														
FR. 7 OUTSIDE	B.L.	B.L.	B.L.	B.L.	6-3	6-0	6-0	6-6	6-14	6-21	6-26	6-30	7-2	7-4	7-5	7-3	7-1	6-31	6-31	—	—
FR. 7 INSIDE	4-11	4-18	4-30	5-8	5-8	5-6	UNIFORM 3/4″ MOLDING														
FR. 8 OUTSIDE	B.L.	B.L.	B.L.	B.L.	5-28	5-18	5-16	5-18	5-22	5-27	5-31	6-2	6-7	6-9	6-9	6-9	6-6	6-6	6-7	—	—
FR. 8 INSIDE	4-10	4-17	4-29	5-5	4-31	4-23	UNIFORM 3/4″ MOLDING														
FR. 9 OUTSIDE	—	B.L.	B.L.	B.L.	5-19	5-2	4-26	4-24	4-25	4-27	4-31	5-2	5-5	5-6	5-8	5-10	5-10	5-11	5-14	—	—
FR. 9 INSIDE	—	4-20	5-0	5-7	4-22	4-7	UNIFORM 3/4″ MOLDING														
FR. 10 OUTSIDE	—	B.L.	B.L.	B.L.	5-6	4-13	3-30	3-22	3-19	3-17	3-18	3-19	3-21	3-23	3-24	3-25	3-24	3-25	3-26	3-30	4-6
FR. 10 INSIDE	—	4-19	4-31	5-0	4-8	3-17	UNIFORM 3/4″ MOLDING														
FR. 11 OUTSIDE	—	No	Foot	B.L.	4-25	3-22	2-31	2-16	2-8	2-3	2-0	1-30	1-29	1-27	1-26	1-25	1-24	1-23	1-25	1-29	2-6
FR. 11 INSIDE	—	No	Foot	B.L.	4-15	3-6	2-10	1-23	1-11	UNIFORM 3/4″ MOLDING											
FR. 12 OUTSIDE	—	No	Foot	B.L.	1-3	0-29	0-25	0-20	0-16	0-12	0-8	0-5	0-4	0-6	0-12						

DISTANCES FROM FRAME LINES TO ARC ON 15″ RADIUS. SCRIBE FRAMES 11 & 12 MOLDED A UNIFORM 3/4″ THROUGHOUT.

PLATE V

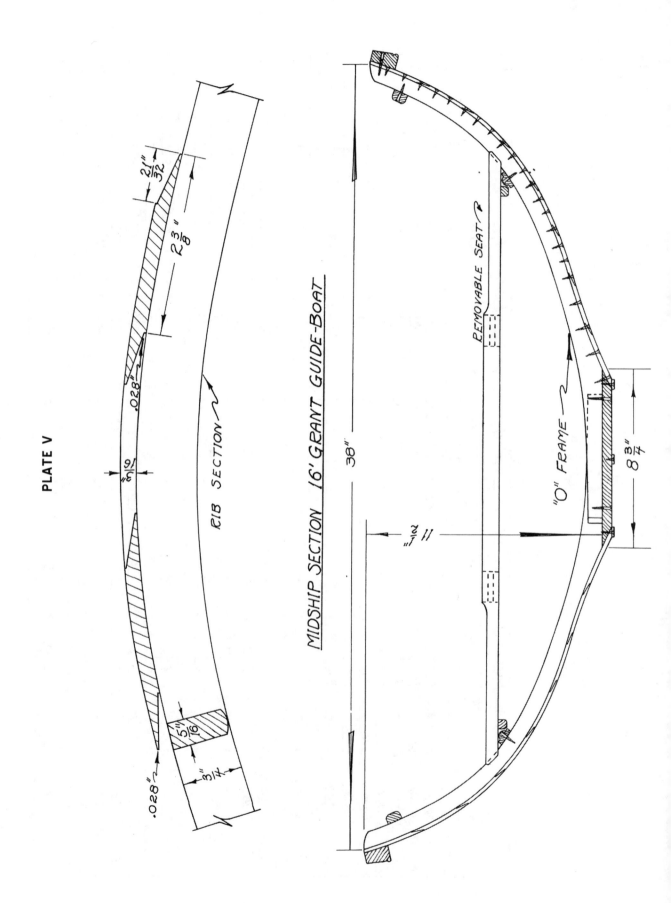

$\frac{2''}{32}$

$2\frac{3}{8}''$

$.028''$

$\frac{3''}{16}$

RIB SECTION

$.028''$

$\frac{5''}{16}$

$3\frac{1}{4}''$

MIDSHIP SECTION 16' GRANT GUIDE-BOAT

38"

$11\frac{1}{2}''$

REMOVABLE SEAT

"O" FRAME

$8\frac{3}{4}''$

PLATE VI

GRANT STEM PATTERN

SHEER 16' GUIDE-BOAT

BEARDING LINE

RABBET LINE

FRAME STA. 12

FRAME STATION 11

BASE LINE

INSIDE BOTTOM

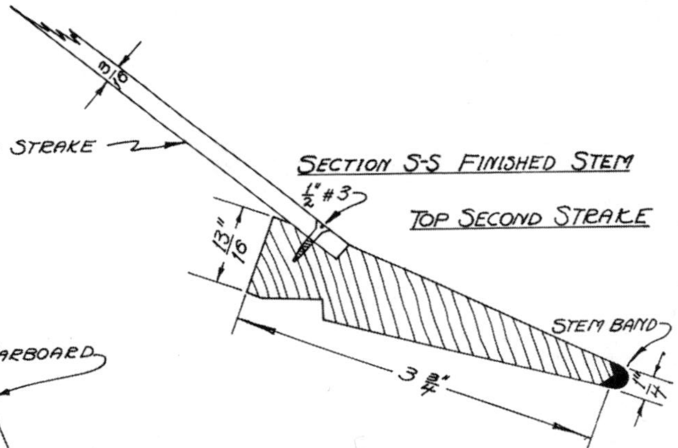

SECTION S-S FINISHED STEM
TOP SECOND STREAK

STEM BAND

SECOND STREAK

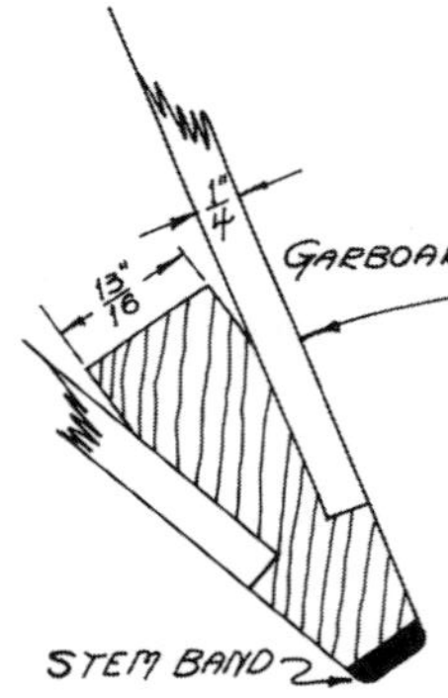

SECTION R-R FINISHED STEM

GARBOARD

STEM BAND

MEASUREMENTS FROM POINT X ON FR. STA. 12, 10" ABOVE BL												
	XA	XB	XC	XD	XE	XF	XG	XH	XI	XJ	XK	XL
INSIDE STEM	7-19	7-25	8-2	8-10	8-12	8-15	8-16	8-19	8-22	8-28	9-3	9-16
INSIDE BOTTOM	8-12	8-25	9-15	10-10	11-10	12-14	13-19	15-30	—	—	—	—
BEARDING LINE	—	—	8-29	8-21	8-18	8-17	8-18	8-19	8-21	8-25	9-0	9-9	9-23
RABBET LINE	—	—	—	9-26	9-19	9-15	9-12	9-12	9-12	9-15	9-21	9-30	10-11
OUTSIDE STEM	—	—	10-0	10-0	2-11	11-6	11-18	11-28	12-6	12-15	12-22	12-27	13-7

MEASUREMENTS FROM PERP. ON 2" PARALLELS STARTING 12' ABOVE BL							
	M	N	O	P	Q	R	S	T
INSIDE STEM	0-27	1-10	1-23	2-1	2-9	2-15	2-20	2-23
BEARDING LINE	1-4	1-21	2-1	2-11	2-20	2-25	2-30	2-31
RABBET LINE	1-23	2-8	2-18	2-27	3-2	3-7	3-11	3-13
OUTSIDE STEM	4-9	4-16	4-21	4-25	4-28	4-30	4-31	5-0

MEASUREMENTS IN INCHES AND THIRTY-SECONDS.

HORIZONTAL DISTANCE FROM FRAME 12							
A	B	C	D	E	F	G	
2 1/16"	4"	6"	8"	10"	12"	14"	
PERP. DISTANCE ABOVE BASE LINE							
H	I	J	K	L	M	N	O	P	Q	R	S	T
2"	4"	6"	8"	10"	12"	14	16	18	20	22	24	26

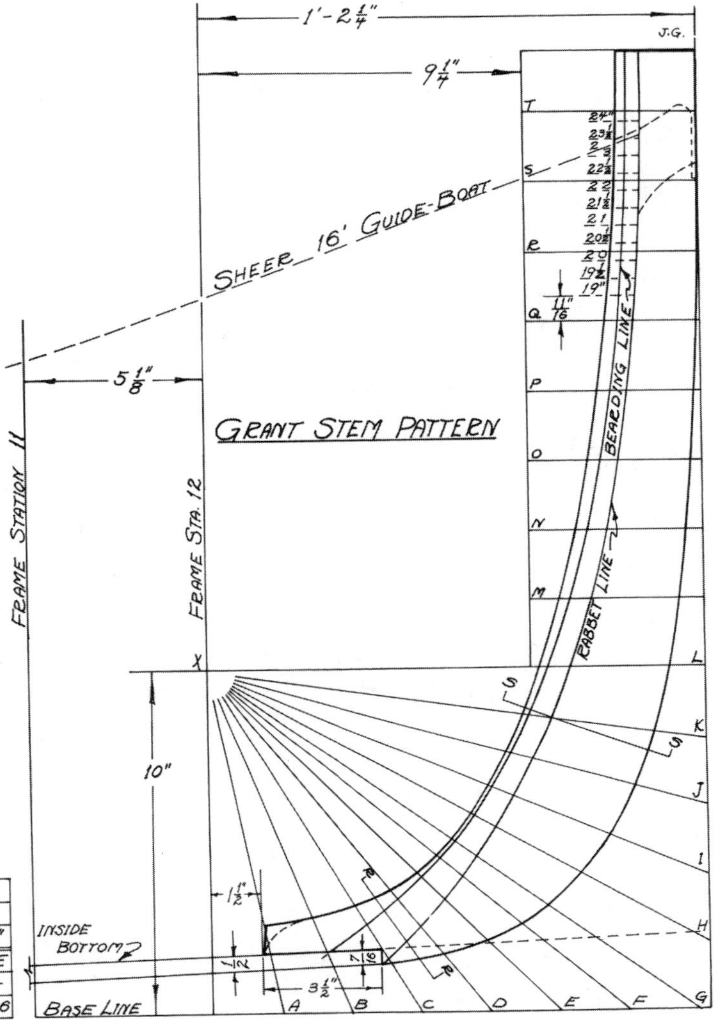

PLATE VII

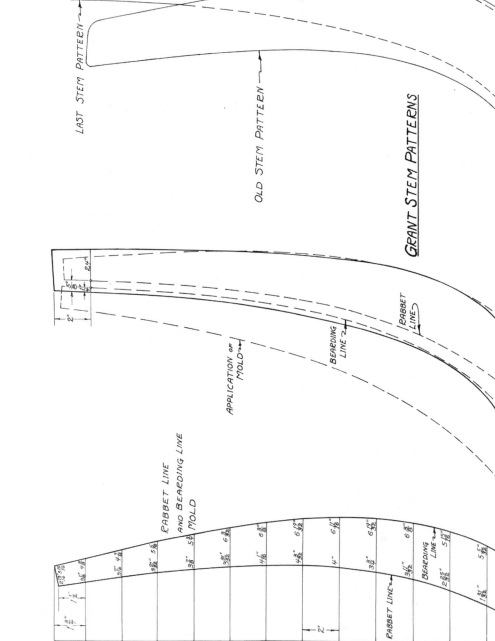

LAST STEM PATTERN

OLD STEM PATTERN

GRANT STEM PATTERNS

BOTTOM BOARD

APPLICATION OF MOLD

BEARDING LINE

RABBET LINE

MOLD

RABBET LINE AND BEARDING LINE MOLD

RABBET LINE

BEARDING LINE

PLATE VIII

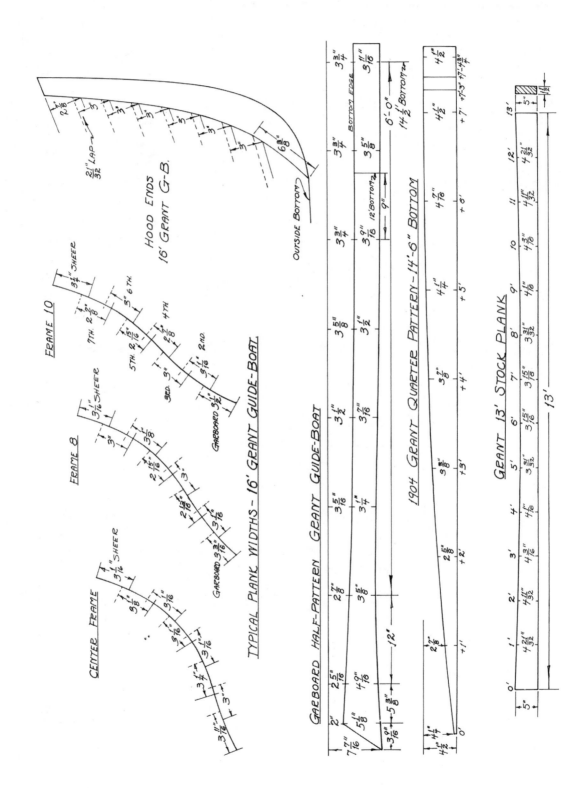

CENTER FRAME

FRAME 8

FRAME 10

TYPICAL PLANK WIDTHS — 16' GRANT GUIDE-BOAT

HOOD ENDS
16' GRANT G-B.

GARBOARD HALF-PATTERN   GRANT GUIDE-BOAT

1904 GRANT QUARTER PATTERN — 14'-6" BOTTOM

GRANT 13' STOCK PLANK

PLATE IX

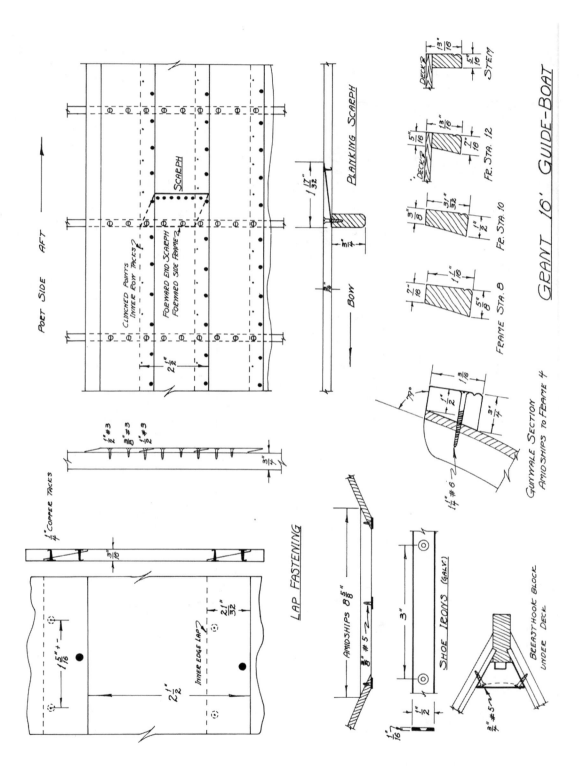

GRANT 16' GUIDE-BOAT

PLATE X

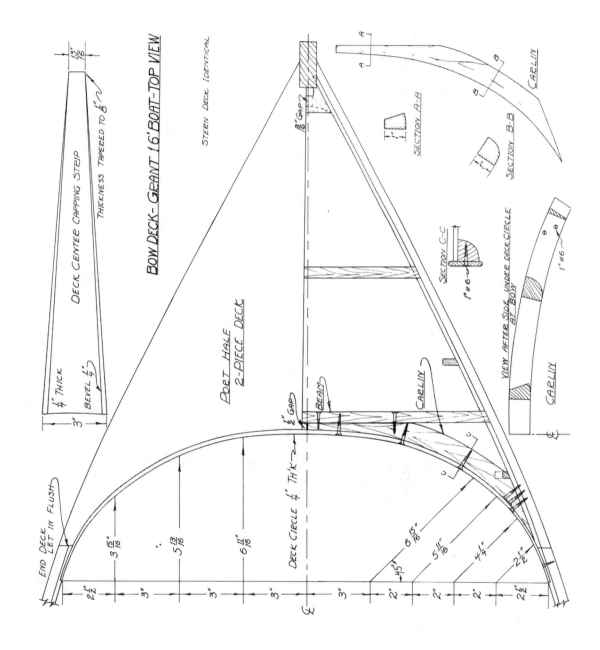

BOW DECK - GRANT 16' BOAT - TOP VIEW

STERN DECK IDENTICAL

DECK CENTER CAPPING STRIP

THICKNESS TAPERED TO $\frac{1}{8}$"

$\frac{13}{16}$"

$\frac{1}{4}$" THICK

BEVEL $\frac{1}{4}$"

3"

PORT HALF
2-PIECE DECK

END DECK
LET IN FLUSH

$\frac{1}{2}$" GAP

BEAM

CARLIN

DECK CIRCLE $\frac{1}{4}$" TH'K

$\frac{3}{16}$" GAP

$3\frac{15}{16}$

$5\frac{13}{16}$

$6\frac{11}{16}$

$6\frac{15}{16}$"

$5\frac{11}{16}$"

$4\frac{1}{4}$"

$2\frac{1}{2}$"

$2\frac{1}{2}$"

3"

3"

3"

3"

2"

2"

2"

$2\frac{1}{2}$"

$4\frac{3}{4}$"

SECTION A-A

$\frac{1}{1}$"

SECTION B-B

$\frac{1}{1}$"

CARLIN

SECTION C-C

1"#6

VIEW AFTER SIDE UNDER DECK CIRCLE
AT BOW

CARLIN

1"#6

PLATE XI

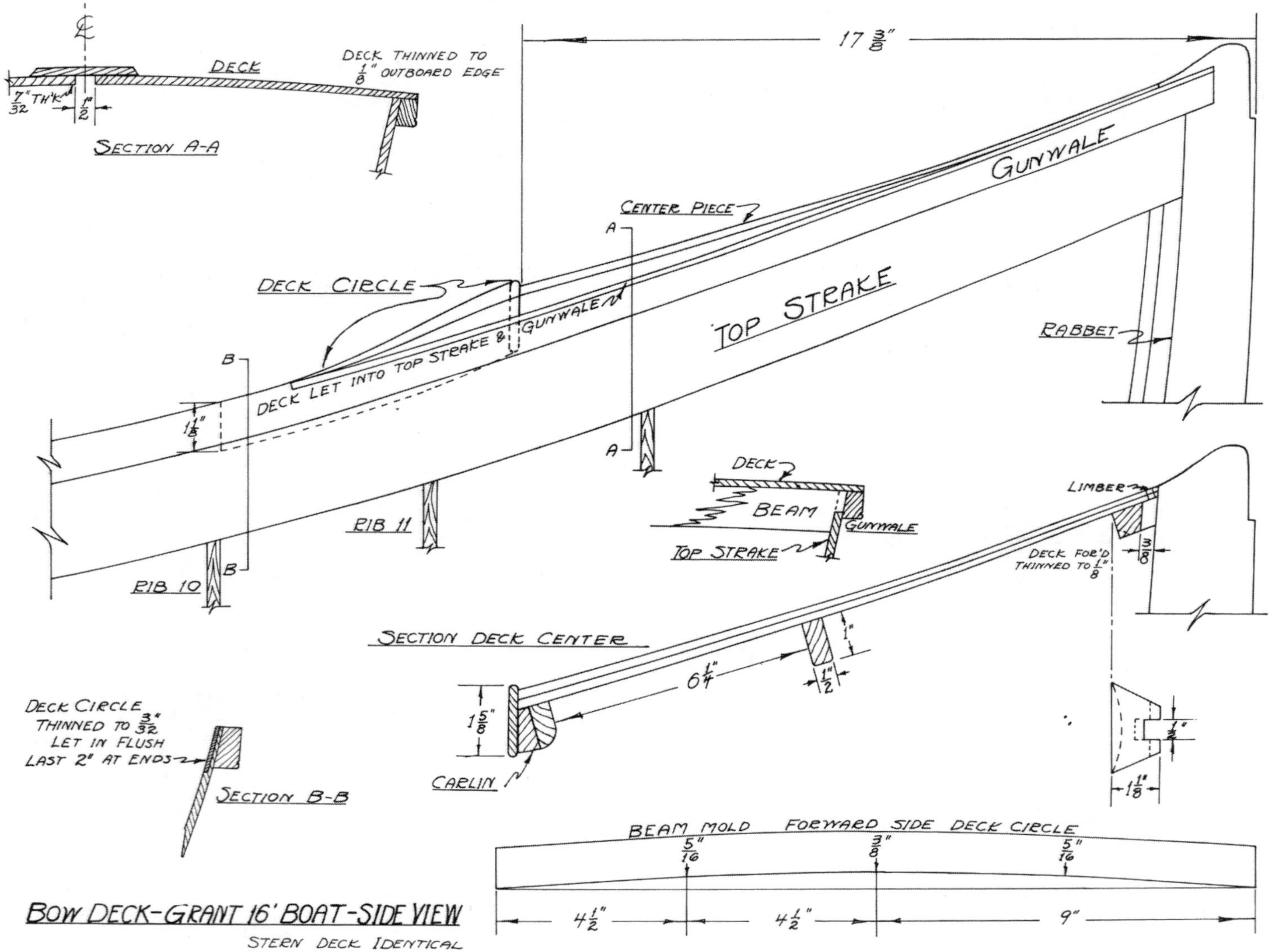

DECK THINNED TO ⅛" OUTBOARD EDGE

DECK

SECTION A-A

₤

⅞" THK
½"/32

GUNWALE

17 ⅜"

RABBET

CENTER PIECE

TOP STREAKE

DECK CIRCLE

GUNWALE

DECK LET INTO TOP STREAKE

A   A

A   A

RIB 11

RIB 10

⅛"

B   B

DECK CIRCLE
THINNED TO ³⁄₃₂
LET IN FLUSH
LAST 2" AT ENDS

SECTION B-B

LIMBER

³⁄₈

DECK FOR'D
THINNED TO ⅛

1 ½"
½"

DECK

BEAM

GUNWALE

TOP STREAKE

1"
½"

6 ½"

SECTION DECK CENTER

1 ⅝"

CARLIN

BEAM MOLD   FORWARD SIDE DECK CIRCLE

5⁄₁₆   3⁄₈   5⁄₁₆

4 ½"   4 ½"

9"

BOW DECK-GRANT 16' BOAT-SIDE VIEW

STERN DECK IDENTICAL

PLATE XII

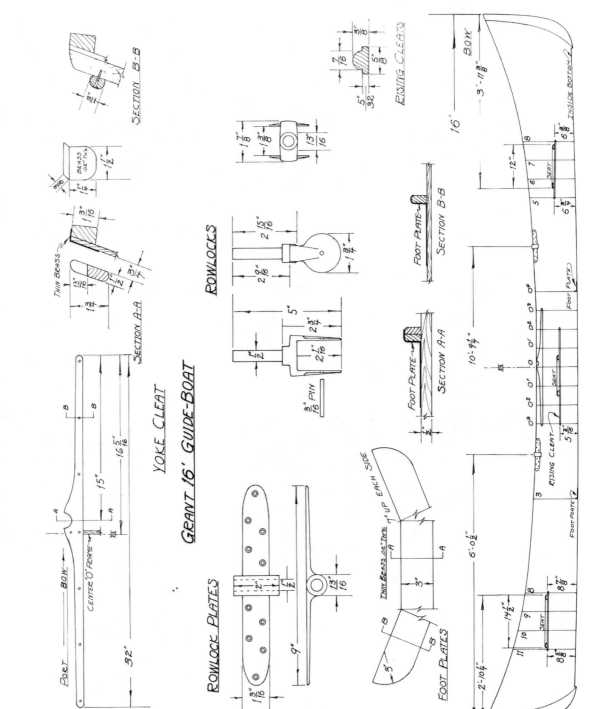

SECTION B-B

SECTION A-A

YOKE CLEAT

GRANT 16' GUIDE-BOAT

ROWLOCKS

ROWLOCK PLATES

FOOT PLATES

PLATE XIII

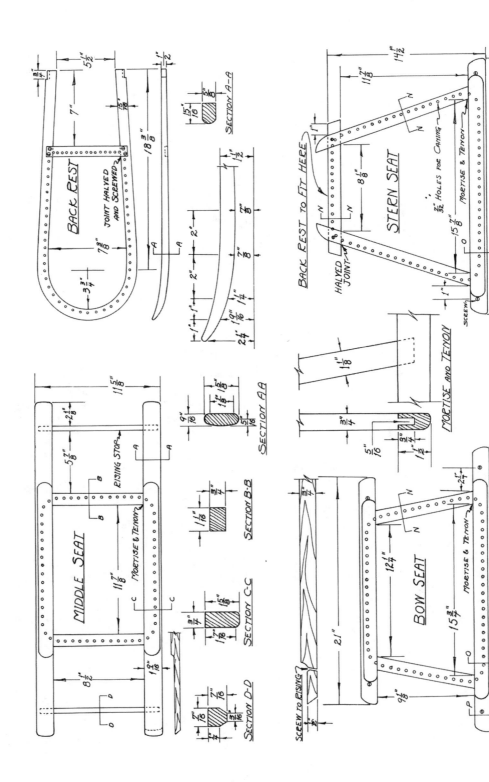

SEATS – 10' GRANT GUIDE-BOAT

PLATE XIV

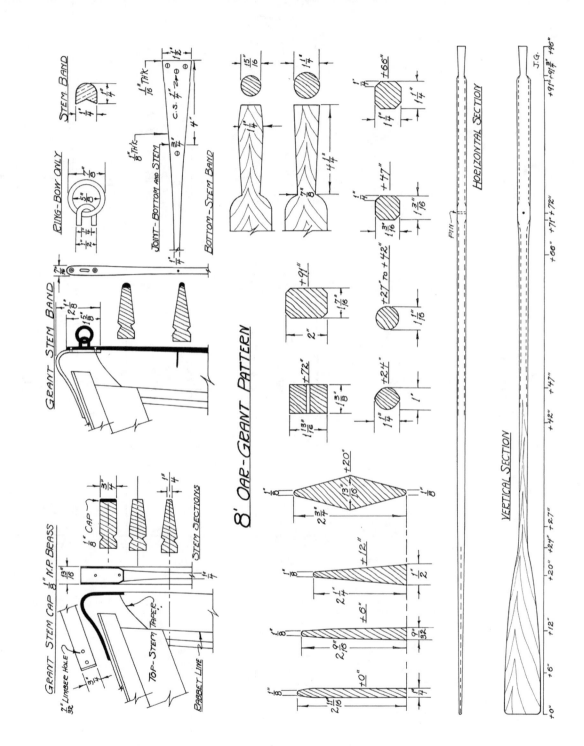

PLATE XV

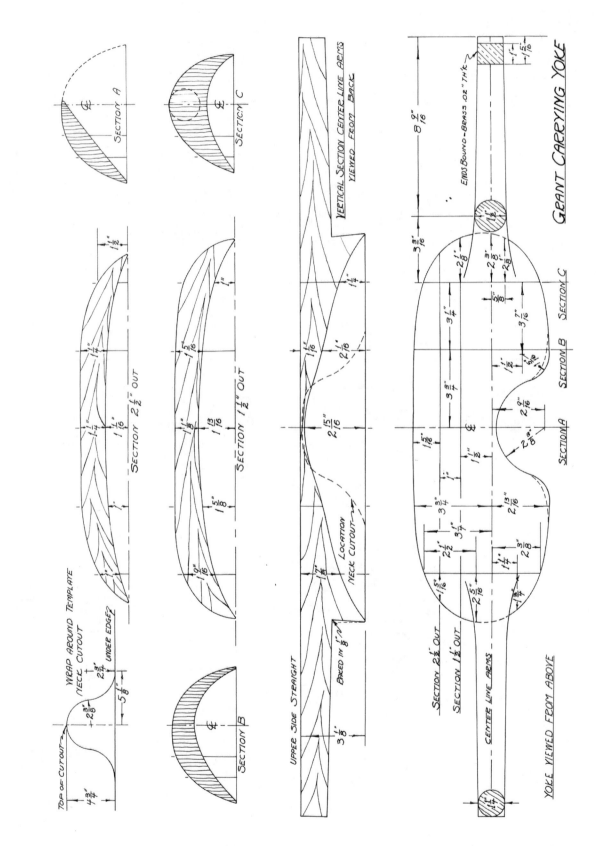

GRANT CARRYING YOKE

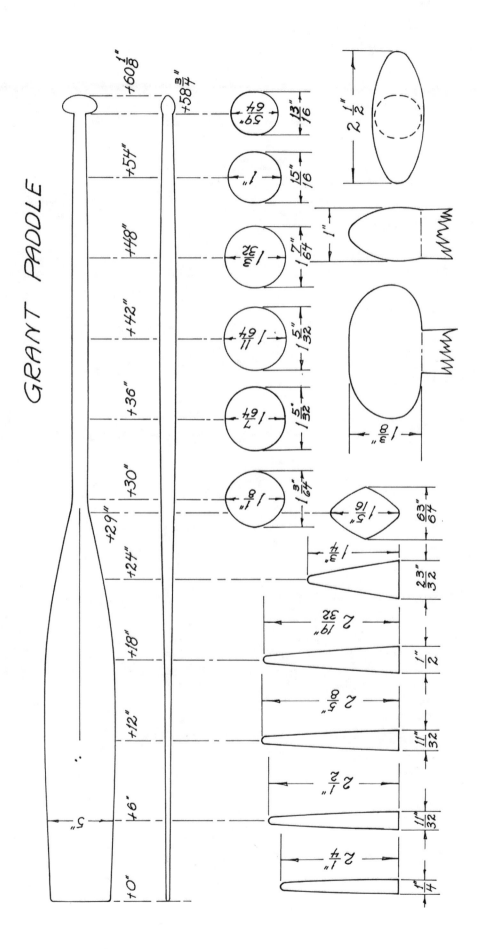

PLATE XVI

GRANT PADDLE

APPENDIX 2

SCREW SIZES AND QUANTITIES

Section A describes the sizes and quantities of screws needed for constructing the Adirondack guideboat in this book. Unless otherwise noted, the quantities are exact. To make it easier to order the necessary screws, Section B presents a summary of screw sizes and their quantities.

SECTION A

PURPOSE	QUANTITY[1]	SIZE[2]
BOTTOM BOARD, STRIPPING, AND GUNWALES		
Through bottom board into rib feet	116	#6 x 1 at toe; #6 x 1¼ at heel (58 of each)
Through stripping into ribs	878[3,4]	#3 x ½
Through siding into stems	68[4]	#3 x ½
Through gunwales into stems	8	#5 x 1
Through gunwales into cross pieces under deck	8	#6 x 1¼
Through gunwales into ribs	66	#6 x 1¼
Through bottom board into stems	4	#6 x 1 at toe; #6 x 1¼ at heel

SECTION A, CONTINUED

PURPOSE	QUANTITY[1]	SIZE[2]
DECKS		
Through deck circles into carlins	20	#4 x ¾
Through decks into gunwales	40	#3 x ½
Through decks into crosspieces	12	#4 x ½
UNDER DECKS		
Through inside blocks into siding and wale if not using epoxy only (see Gardner Plate IX)	4	#5 x ¾
Through cross pieces into carlins	8	#6 x 1
Through carlins into gunwales	8	#6 x 1
ACCESSORIES		
Through three shoe-irons into bottom board	170	#5 x ½ (for ⅛" thick shoe-irons; use ⅜" length if shoe-iron thickness is less)
Stem band into bottom of stem	4	#6 x ⅞
Stem band into bottom board	8	#5 x ⅞
Stem band into top of stem (see Gardner Plate XIV)	4	#5 x 1
Stem band into main stem	14	#4 x 1 (if not using nails)
Stem cap into deck	2	#5 x 1
Rising cleats into ribs (see Gardner Plate XII)	28	#5 x ⅞
Yoke cleats into ribs (see Gardner Plate XII)	16	#5 x ⅞
Siding protectors	10	#2 x ¼
Rowlock straps into gunwales	40	#7 x ¾
Crosspieces of back rest (see Gardner Plate XIII)	4	#4 x ½ (not specified in Gardner's drawings)
Seats into cleats (see Gardner Plate XIII)	8[5]	#6 x 1¼ slotted round head brass; except back of stern seat: 1½ flathead brass

216

SECTION B

SIZE	LENGTH	MINIMUM QUANTITY NEEDED[6]
#2	$\frac{1}{4}$	10
#3	$\frac{1}{2}$	986
#4	$\frac{3}{4}$	20
	$\frac{1}{2}$	16
	1	14
#5	$\frac{1}{2}$	170
	$\frac{3}{4}$	4
	$\frac{7}{8}$	52
	1	14
#6	$\frac{7}{8}$	4
	1	76
	$1\frac{1}{4}$	134
	$1\frac{1}{4}$ (roundhead) $1\frac{1}{2}$ (flathead)	8 2
#7	$\frac{3}{4}$	40

1 In most cases, the quantity specified is the exact number needed. Plan on purchasing extra to account for defective, lost, or damaged screws.

2 All screws are slotted flat-head brass unless otherwise indicated, and are listed as size x length.

3 Quantities listed here are close to exact.

4 These quantities are for the alternate screw pattern described in Chapter 11. If you fasten every strip to every rib, and to the stems, you will need to double these quantities.

5 If the seats and risers are built according to the dimensions in the Gardner drawings and mounted with the #6 x 1¼" seat mounting screws, the screws will penetrate the risers and expose the sharp points. We found that #6 x 1" screws were a more suitable and safer alternative.

6 Ordering screws in bulk almost always requires a minimum purchase quantity of 100. For anything but the smallest required quantity (e.g., #6 x ⅞), purchasing in bulk is more cost effective. For example, even though you need only 40, it will cost you less to order 100 #7 x ¾ screws from one of the sources listed in Appendix 5 than to purchase them individually at a hardware store. Also note that odd size screws (#3, #5, #7) typically are not stocked in hardware stores.

APPENDIX 3

WORKING WITH EPOXY

In Chapter 11, we described the process for fiberglassing your hull using epoxy. In this appendix, we devote more attention to exactly what epoxy is and how to handle it safely. We also describe a method for measuring and mixing epoxy resin and hardener that works well for us. Finally, we include a few words about cleaning up.

All of the major epoxy manufacturers listed in Appendix 5 publish extensive documentation online and in print about the topics we discuss here. If you are completely new to using epoxy, you might want to take a look at some of it. However, we have written this appendix to provide you with all the information you will need to successfully and safely use epoxy not only for this project, but also for any similar boat building you might undertake.

While much of our discussion holds true for all epoxies, please note that we use MAS products almost exclusively and some of what is described here (e.g., measuring requirements and working temperature guidelines) may apply only to that company's products. If you will be using epoxy products from another manufacturer, please refer to that company's instructions.

HOW IT WORKS

Epoxy coatings are used because of their outstanding chemical resistance, durability, low porosity, and strong bond. Epoxies consist of a resin base and a curing agent, commonly referred to as "hardener." The two components are mixed in a certain ratio, which produces a chemical reaction. The epoxy curing reaction is exothermic, that is, it produces heat as it cures, hardening the mixture into an inert, hard plastic. The rate at which the epoxy mixture cures is dependent on temperature: the warmer the temperature, the faster the epoxy cures. In fact, with each 18°F increase in temperature, the cure time will decrease by half. Conversely, the cure time is doubled for each 18°F decrease in temperature.

After the base and hardener are combined in the proper ratio, there is a working time, or pot life, during which the epoxy can be applied or used. The reaction of base and hardener proceeds most rapidly in the liquid state, but as the mixture begins to gel, the reaction slows and hardness increases. As the mixture achieves a solid state, the chemical reaction proceeds more slowly, and the mixture becomes harder and stronger as time passes. Generally the pot life will be anywhere from minutes to one hour or longer. At the end of the pot life, the mixture becomes very warm (or even dangerously hot) and quickly begins to harden. A complete cure will generally take several days, but for boat building, consider an epoxy coating fully cured after 72 hours at 77°F.

As previously mentioned, the curing process gives off a significant amount of heat. If that heat is immediately dissipated, the temperature of the curing mixture will not rise and the speed at which the chemical reaction occurs will continue at a more uniform rate. In other words, if the mixture is spread out into a thin film, the exothermic reaction will proceed more slowly than if it is confined to a smaller area like the mixing cup. For this reason, it is advisable to mix smaller rather than larger batches of epoxy resin: i.e., about 6 oz. at a time, or what can comfortably be applied within the pot life limit.

Another property of epoxy is worth mentioning. Epoxies have a tendency to yellow and lose their gloss with exposure to the ultraviolet rays of direct sunlight. After about six months of exposure, the cured epoxy begins to decay. Further exposure will cause chalking to occur and the coating will eventually disintegrate, losing all of its mechanical and protective properties. The only solution to this problem is to protect the epoxy with paint, or with varnish containing a UV protectant. We covered this subject at greater length in Chapter 15.

SAFETY PRECAUTIONS

Improper or unsafe use of epoxy products can be hazardous to your health. The primary health concern when working with epoxy systems is skin irritation, which in turn can lead to skin sensitization from prolonged and repeated contact. We know of some individuals who have had to give up boat building altogether because of health problems resulting from a failure to heed certain simple precautions.

The general rule of thumb to maintain a safe and healthy working relationship with epoxy is to keep it off you and out of you. That means preventing it from getting on your skin in any form, whether mixed, unmixed, or as dust from sanding operations, as well as preventing the sanding dust from getting into your lungs.

Any time you work with epoxy, cover your skin and wear a tight-fitting dust mask. Wear a long-sleeved shirt and long pants when working and launder the clothing after each use. Better yet, put on a Tyvek suit or a pair of Tyvek sleeves for added protection. Do not attempt to work with epoxy (including mixing and measuring) unless you are wearing protective gloves and safety glasses or goggles.

There is a debate regarding the type of glove that provides the best protection when working with epoxy. One school of thought advocates the use of latex (assuming the user does not have a latex allergy). Another suggests the use of vinyl, arguing that although latex provides good protection from biological hazards, some of the hazardous chemicals in epoxy diffuse right through it. We have not experienced any negative side effects using latex gloves. Whatever type you choose, the gloves should be disposable. There is no need to reuse gloves, and doing so may increase your risk of coming into contact with the epoxy. In addition, the use of disposable gloves means you have one less thing to clean.

Sanding epoxy produces a very fine, potentially irritating, dust. If possible, try to do the sanding outdoors. If you must work inside, some form of dust collection is an absolute necessity, and you should insure adequate ventilation in the work area. If there is no way to collect the dust, a good-fitting dust mask and latex gloves are essential (you should wear these anyway), followed by showering after sanding. Expect there to be dust all over the shop! Launder any clothing you have worn during sanding before wearing it again.

Finally, it almost goes without saying that if you have children or pets around, do NOT leave opened containers of resin or hardener where they can get at them. And be sure to eliminate epoxy residue or sanding dust from any areas to which children or pets may be permitted access.

MEASURING

To use epoxy successfully, you must accurately measure both the resin and the hardener. Since all of the hardener reacts with all of the resin to form the hard cure, any deviation from the exact ratio defined by the manufacturer is inviting trouble. An excess of one component beyond what is chemically required by the other will result in an extended cure time (if it fully cures at all) and full design strength may not be realized.

There is no solvent in epoxy in the usual sense, and epoxy should not be diluted. If you feel you must dilute the mixture or either of its components, check with the manufacturer before doing so. MAS epoxy has no solvents and requires a 2 to 1 resin-to-hardener ratio. For every 2 volumes of resin, 1 volume of hardener must be mixed with it.

The usual way of measuring epoxy is by using the pumps sold along with the epoxy. These pumps are calibrated to deliver accurate volumes of both the resin and hardener—until they start to, well, burp! For some reason, probably internal wear, after the pump delivers its volume it draws an air bubble into the pumping chamber during the return stroke. During the next delivery cycle, the pump suddenly burps the bubble, resulting in the delivery of an inaccurate volume.[1]

Another common error in measuring is counting the number of pump strokes. To make a 6 oz. batch using the 2:1 ratio, you would want 4 oz. of resin and 2 oz. of hardener. Since the MAS hardener pump only delivers half the amount of a resin pump, four strokes of resin and four strokes of hardener are required. Right in the middle of pumping, you get a phone call, the dog chases the cat up under the boat, or the UPS guy is ringing the doorbell. Even lesser distractions have caused miscounting of pump strokes. Epoxy that never hardens can result. That means scraping and removing the partially cured mess and starting over.

Pouring resin and hardener is not the way to measure epoxy. The pumps work, but are better used for dispensing only, not for dispensing a measured amount based solely on the number of pump strokes. To overcome this problem, we use a simple calibrated plastic cup that is easily made and reusable.[2]

You will need a package of 10- or 12-oz. translucent plastic cups (colored ones will not work), a fine-point permanent marker such as the fine-point Sharpie, and a means of accurately measuring 1 oz. of liquid. You will also need something to dispense small volumes. Epoxy dealers sell a variety of calibrated plastic beakers; the 50-ml. size (about 2 oz.) is ideal for measuring. You will also need some way of accurately filling the little beaker with water to the 1 oz. mark (Figure A3.1a). You can pour in most of it, but use a syringe or a plastic spray bottle to bring the level exactly up to the mark. If you use the beaker with graduation marks embossed right on the plastic, use

the fine-point marker to mark the outside at the 1 oz. mark. The embossed marking is difficult to see when the beaker has liquid in it.

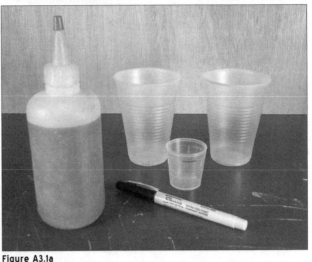

Figure A3.1a
Plastic cups, small beaker, fine-point marking pen, and glue bottle filled with water for filling the beaker. Food coloring was added for clarity.

Figure A3.1b
Calibration using two cups, one inside the other.

Now, put one empty plastic cup into a second one. Measure 1 oz. of water in the small beaker, and pour it all into the inside cup (Figure A3.1b). With the assembly sitting on a flat table, make a mark on the outside cup at the level of the water in the inside cup. Add another ounce, and make another mark. Repeat this until you have added 6 oz. Remove the inner cup, and mark the outer cup with 1, 2, etc. up to 6, starting at the first mark near the bottom, for the respective calibration marks (Figure A3.2).

Figure A3.2

Plastic cup calibrated for 6 oz.

When you measure epoxy, put a clean new cup into the calibrated cup, and pump enough resin into it (burps and all) to reach the desired mark. It may take six or seven pump strokes to get 4 oz. of resin in the cup, but you will know exactly how much resin you have, in spite of the burps. Add the required amount of hardener in the same manner.

MIXING

Mixing epoxy is another area where strict adherence to manufacturers' guidelines is required. It must be mixed thoroughly. Using a mixing stick, stir vigorously in one direction for a while, then scrape the sides and bottom of the cup, and vigorously stir some more in the opposite direction. Do this several times, so that the total mixing time is at least two minutes.

You will probably notice your mixed batch of epoxy is full of bubbles. Do not worry! Bubbles in a freshly mixed batch of MAS epoxy are normal, and they will quickly dissipate when you spread the batch on the hull (one of the myths of working with epoxy is to mix slowly to prevent the generation of bubbles).

MAS epoxy consists of the resin, and a choice of hardeners—slow, medium, or fast. The company sells other variations for special conditions, but for general use, some fast hardener along with the slow is all you need. MAS epoxy, when mixed with slow hardener, does not blush. Amine blush is a waxy coating that forms

on the surface of some brands of epoxy, and must be completely removed by washing and rinsing before applying the next coat. Using an epoxy that blushes is comparable to watching a black and white TV with a rabbit ears antenna instead of cable. There are better products. When mixed with slow hardener with up to about 25% fast added (always maintaining the 2:1 ratio), MAS still does not blush. (Using the medium or fast hardeners alone, however, will result in blush.)

The MAS slow hardener is just what it says it is—slow. It is a very comfortable epoxy for the novice, since there is plenty of time to apply a full 6 oz. batch without the danger of it starting to cure before you are ready for it to do so. This is the ideal situation for wet out, since you want a good penetration of the wood before it cures, providing a deep bond of the cloth to the hull.

Earlier we described the exothermic, or heat-producing, property of curing epoxy. If you allow the epoxy mixed with a fast hardener to remain in the relatively confined space of the plastic cup for too long, it will become too hot to handle and will very likely melt the cup (Figure A3.3).

Figure A3.3

The result of keeping the mixed epoxy in the plastic cup too long.

TEMPERATURE CONSIDERATIONS

Your shop, or the area in which you are to do the epoxy work, should be comfortable and within the range of curing temperatures and humidity recommended by the epoxy manufacturer. For clear coating using MAS epoxies, the air temperature should remain at approximately 65° to 70°F. You can warm your shop air relatively quickly, but the boat and epoxy components must also be warm. If necessary, bring the epoxy components into a warmer area the night before you start using them.

If for some reason you must do your wet-out and fill coats in cooler temperatures (below 60°F) or if you suspect the temperature will drop below 60°F soon after application, you should consider using epoxies more suitable for those conditions, such as MAS FLAG Resin and Medium hardener, but check for blush.

Using MAS epoxy with slow hardener, and with the temperature at or near 65° to 70°F and with nominal humidity, you can easily wet-out one day and fill the next. You can do a fill coat using 25% fast hardener and 75% slow first thing in the morning, and do another coat in the evening, and repeat the process the next day, for a total of four fill coats.

CLEANUP

To remove latex gloves, grab one at the cuff with your thumb and index finger and peel it off inside out. Remove the other one in the same manner and dispose of them.

If you find that you have gotten epoxy on your skin, do NOT use solvents to remove it. Not only are the solvents bad for you—worse than the epoxy is—but using them as a cleaner only helps to work the harmful ingredients of the epoxy further into your skin. Instead, first use a waterless hand soap such as GoJo, along with paper towels, to remove the epoxy. Then wash thoroughly with regular soap and water. Finally, apply a medicated skin cream to restore natural oils that may have been removed in the process.

Epoxy will drip, and newspaper is easily soaked with the uncured epoxy that later glues the paper to the floor. Cover the floor under the boat with cardboard to capture drips; do not use plastic sheeting because it may create a dangerously slippery surface. Contain any large epoxy spills that occur with an inert absorbent material such as kitty litter or sand. You should not use sawdust, wood shavings, or any other fine cellulose materials to absorb hardeners. By the same token, because spontaneous combustion can occur, never dispose of hardeners in trash containing such materials.

To clean hardened epoxy from tools or other hard surfaces, simply pop the drip off with a scraper or screwdriver. For cleaning drips that have gelled but not yet hardened, simply wash with white vinegar or isopropyl alcohol. If you must use solvents such as acetone, do so only for cleaning tools. Wear heavy, solvent-proof gloves, and make sure you have adequate ventilation. Do not use acetone on your skin or on any surface to be epoxied.

1 MAS has redesigned its pumps and now offers 4cc and 8cc versions that purportedly do not "burp." The larger size ½ and 1 oz. pumps are still available from other epoxy vendors.

2 Many thanks to Ross Leidy for suggesting the original description of a calibrated cup method.

APPENDIX 4

MAKING SCARF JOINTS

The pine planks used for siding a traditional guideboat were usually made of two pieces, joined together in a scarf joint end to end with clinched tacks. The sheer plank in the Grant boats was made of three pieces. This method of making a plank permitted the use of shorter lumber, but perhaps more importantly allowed the grain of the plank to more closely follow the curve of the sheer. When planking a boat with narrow cedar strips, the flexibility of the relatively narrow strips permits the grain to quite easily follow the curve of the sheer. Joining strips end to end in a scarf joint simply allows you to make up the required length.

As noted in Chapter 8, planks long enough to be ripped for the 18' lengths required for the *Virginia* are not readily available, nor would they be easy to transport, handle, and cut if they were. It also seems that whenever you find a long plank, it will have a defect somewhere that either renders it useless for boat building or would require cutting around, defeating the premium length. There are many more acceptable shorter planks available than there are perfect long ones. The task, then, is to build a boat from wood that is shorter than the finished boat. Recall that one of our boats was indeed built with natural full-length strips, while another one was planked with every strip scarfed together to make up the correct length.

SCARF JOINTS

In this joint, the ends of the stock to be joined are tapered to a chisel point and the mating surfaces are glued together. The pine plank scarf joints of traditional guideboats were made similarly with tapered plank ends, but were fastened together with clinched tacks. In a modern strip built boat, the joint is cut and glued together on the bench before the now full-length strip is mounted on the hull. Gluing the joint as the two strips are mounted on the hull is possible, but misalignment or a poor joint may result. The bending and twisting stresses that strips undergo require a joint that is at least as strong as the wood itself. A properly made scarf joint satisfies this requirement, and can be placed almost anywhere on the hull where a natural full-length strip would be used regardless of bend or twist.

A good scarf joint is almost invisible, and certainly does not attract the eye. When the joint is made using book-matched strips, grain and color matching can be nearly perfect. If you make the joint with raw-cut strips before any planing or milling of the bead and cove edges, the scarfed strip is virtually indistinguishable from a natural full-length strip.

To make a scarf joint, cut the ends of the strips at an angle much shallower than a simple 45° miter. The actual numerical value of the angle is not important; rather, consider the ratio of the thickness of the stock to the length of the cut. This ratio can range anywhere from about 1:6 to 1:12 for joints where the cut is made across the wide edge of the stock. In practical terms, a 1:8 scarf means that for ¼" thick stock, the length of the taper is 8 times ¼", or 2". A 1:6 scarf would have a taper length of 1½", and a 1:12 would be 3" inches long. We recommend a 1:8 scarf, which provides a sufficiently large glue surface and one you can easily cut with precision. The actual cut need not represent a given ratio exactly, but you must cut both strips to be scarfed exactly the same.

Which way do you cut the taper for the scarf? Do you cut through the narrow edge of the strip, or the wide edge? Almost without exception, scarf joints for strips, planking on traditionally built guideboats, and gunwale stock are cut across the wide edge. The resulting joint, when seen on a mounted strip or plank, is vertical or at a right angle to the length of the strip. Scarfing across the narrow edge of the stock is sometimes used for joining different colored woods for decorative purposes on canoes and kayaks. The wide scarf has a gluing surface significantly greater than the narrow scarf, which is an important consideration when the joint will be stressed, as on a curve.

MAKING THE SCARFS

Cutting the tapers on strips, either before or after milling the edges, is not at all difficult. Two important points to remember are that the strip must be firmly presented square to the cutting tool and both pieces must be cut exactly the same. The chisel edge should finish square across the strip. A disk sander with 80-grit paper and shop vacuum dust collection or a table saw with a simple sled jig can be used satisfactorily. In both cases, the disk and saw blade must be square with the worktable. In a pinch, you can mount a belt sander with some sort of jig to firmly hold the strips at the desired angle. Safety is more of a concern with the table saw, since the strips hanging off the table need to be tightly held in the jig. While surgeons have performed miracles reattaching severed limbs, it is rather doubtful that scarfing fingers back together was covered in medical school. A clamping arrangement on the sled is a must.

Figure A4.1 shows a disk sander being used to cut the scarfs. We clamped a block of wood to the table to guide the strips into the sanding disk at the appropriate angle. We first held the strip against the guide block and tight to the table, and then fed slowly into the 80-grit disk. When the chisel end is developed, stop feeding but hold the strip firm for a few seconds. When cutting action has all but stopped, keep the strip tight against the block and firm on the table and pull it to the left. This release action slides the strip

along the angled guide block and lifts the cut surface away from the disk without damage.

Figure A4.1

Cutting a scarf in a cedar strip using an angled guide block clamped to a bench-mounted disk sander.

Figure A4.2 shows the equipment required for the glue-up and includes the glue bottle, two small C-clamps, two short lengths of scrap strips used as gluing cauls, and a pencil. The glue is the same as that which we use for gluing strips together on the boat. Coat each of the two cauls with wax (candle, paraffin, bees, etc.) to prevent the glue from sticking to them. A pencil is also required, and the gluing bench surface should be clear and flat for at least a few feet on either side of the area where you will be making the joint.

Figure A4.2

Equipment required for scarfing strips.

Begin by aligning the joint—do not use any glue yet, just hold the joint together. Slide the pieces back and forth while at the same time feeling for thickness and overlap. This is difficult to describe, but once you have done a few scarf joints, it becomes quite simple. You want to get the thickness through the joint to be exactly the same as the rest of the strip. Once you have the correct alignment, make a pencil mark for alignment reference across the top (Figure A4.3).

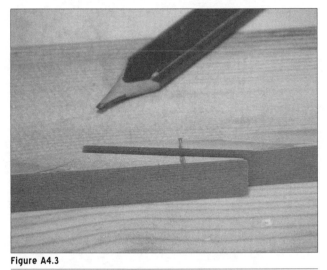

Figure A4.3
Once the joint is aligned dry, mark the top for alignment during gluing.

Now spread some glue on the cut surface of the joint: not a lot, just enough to completely wet the joint and have a little squeeze-out. Using the waxed cauls, loosely clamp the joint. Before tightening the clamps, make sure the edges of each strip are flat solid on the bench, assuring a straight joint, and the pencil marks are aligned. Now tighten the clamps to get a little squeeze-out, but do not over tighten and starve the joint (Figure A4.4).

Let the glue dry for about an hour, more or less, and remove the clamps. Clean up the joint with a quick scraping to remove any squeeze-out. If you are using strips with bead and cove edges already milled, immediately turn the joint over and clean the excess glue out of the cove before it has a chance to harden. Hardened glue in the cove will prevent the strip from fitting correctly when you mount it on the hull. You can make a simple clean-up tool from a scrap piece of beaded strip with the end cut at less than 90°.

If scarfing is done on raw-cut strips without the bead and cove edges yet applied, the strips can be sized with a thickness planer prior to milling the edges.

Figure A4.4
The scarf joint glued and clamped between waxed cauls.

SCARFING GUNWALE STOCK

The principles of scarfing thicker stock such as that used for gunwales are the same as in scarfing strips. The cuts must be square to the stock, and both cuts must be identical. The preferred glue is epoxy, mainly because of its strength and water-resistant properties.

To glue a gunwale scarf, mix some resin and hardener only, without a thickening agent. A slow curing type is preferred to allow sufficient time for soak in before excessive curing inhibits it. Spread the mixture on both pieces to be joined and let it soak in. If it all soaks in, add more. Thicken the remaining mixture with the additive of choice. Wipe off any excess soaking epoxy and glue the joint with the thickened mixture. Apply only enough clamp pressure to hold the alignment and still get some squeeze-out. Applying too much clamp pressure will force the mixture out and starve the joint, possibly leading to later failure. Rather than using flat gluing cauls as was done with strips, use the wedge-shaped off-cuts from cutting the scarf joints to direct clamping force at right angles to the joint. Be sure to wax them first.

Figure A4.5 shows a simple sled used for cutting scarf joints for gunwale stock on a table saw.

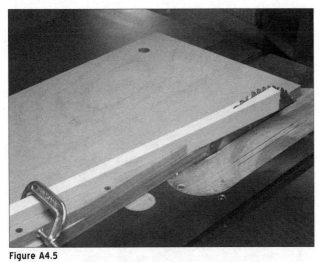

Figure A4.5

Scarfing sled for gunwale stock.

The sled base is ¾" plywood about 1' wide, so that it will span from the blade to beyond the miter gauge slot. A piece of hardwood is dadoed into the bottom to act as a runner in the miter gauge slot. The position of the slot is such that the edge of the plywood at the blade is actually a little beyond the blade. You will trim it later. A hardwood fence is positioned at the desired angle as shown, and temporarily left hanging over the edge of the base. Screws and glue hold the fence down.

When assembly is complete, place the sled in the miter gauge slot and turn on the saw. Run the sled past the blade for a final precise trim, including the overhanging portion of the fence. A strip of coarse sandpaper glued to the inside surface of the fence will help hold the work piece and prevent it from sliding. As mentioned previously, there should be a clamp on the base to hold the work piece against the fence and to keep your fingers from getting scarfed. Although not apparent in the photo in Figure A4.5, a stop on the fence prevents the sliding of the clamp into the saw blade.

APPENDIX 5

SOURCES

Listed below are a variety of manufacturers and suppliers we have dealt with directly or who are well known and respected by the boat building community. The list of suppliers and manufacturers is by no means exhaustive. Rather, it represents the companies whose products we have used extensively or who, in our experience, supply reasonably priced, quality products backed with excellent customer service. All contact information was current at time of publication. We do encourage you to patronize local businesses as much as possible!

Also listed is a variety of reference material relevant to the Adirondack guideboat, including museums, magazine articles, and books.

TOOL SUPPLIERS AND MANUFACTURERS

AMAZON.COM
www.amazon.com

CMT USA, INC.
307-F Pomona Drive
Greensboro, NC 27407
888-CMT-BITS
www.cmtusa.com

COASTAL TOOL & SUPPLY
510 New Park Avenue
West Hartford, CT 06110
877-551-8665
www.coastaltool.com

INTERNATIONAL TOOL CORPORATION
2590 Davie Road
Davie, FL 33317
800-338-3384
www.internationaltool.com

THE JAPAN WOODWORKER
1731 Clement Avenue
Alameda, CA 94501
800-537-7820
www.thejapanwoodworker.com

JESADA TOOLS
310 Mears Boulevard
Oldsmar, FL 34677
800-531-5559
www.jesada.com

KLINGSPOR'S WOODWORKING SHOP
P.O. Box 3737
Hickory, NC 28603-3737
800-228-0000
www.woodworkingshop.com

LEE VALLEY TOOLS, LTD.
P.O. Box 1780
Ogdensburg, NY 13669-6780
800-267-8735
www.leevalley.com

MLCS
2381 Philmont Avenue, Suite 105
Huntingdon Valley, PA 19006
800-533-9298
www.mlcswoodworking.com

TOOLS PLUS
53 Meadow Street
Waterbury, CT 06702
800-222-6133
www.tools-plus.com

WOODCRAFT
P.O. Box 1686
Parkersburg, WV 26102-1686
304-422-541
www.woodcraft.com

WILKE MACHINERY COMPANY
3230 N. Susquehanna Trail
York, PA 17402-9716
717-764-5000
www.wilkemachinery.com

MANUFACTURERS AND DISTRIBUTORS OF EPOXY, FIBERGLASS, VARNISH, PAINT, AND OTHER FINISHING SUPPLIES

DEFENDER INDUSTRIES
42 Great Neck Road
Waterford, CT 06385
800-628-8225
www.defender.com

EPIFANES NORTH AMERICA, INC.
70 Water Street
Thomaston, ME 04861
800-269-0961
www.epifanes.com

INTERLUX YACHT FINISHES
2270 Morris Avenue
Union, NJ 07083
908-686-1300
www.yachtpaint.com

JAMESTOWN DISTRIBUTORS (2 LOCATIONS)
Building #15, 500 Wood Street
Bristol, RI 02809

215 Third Street
Newport, RI 02842
800-423-0030
www.jamestowndistributors.com

KOP-COAT, INC.
(MAKERS OF Z-SPAR CAPTAIN'S VARNISH)
1850 Koppers Building 436 Seventh Avenue
Pittsburgh, PA 15219
412-227-2700
www.kop-coat.com

MAS EPOXIES
2615 River Road #3A
Cinnaminson, NJ 08077
888-MAS-EPOXY
www.masepoxies.com

MEGUIAR'S
17991 Mitchell South
Irvine, CA 92614
800-347-5700
www.meguiars.com

NEWFOUND WOODWORKS
67 Danforth Brook Road
Bristol, NH 03222-9418
603-744-6872
www.newfound.com

NOAH'S MARINE SUPPLY
PMB 566 1623 Military Road
Niagara Falls, NY 14304
800-524-7517
or, in Canada,
54 Six Point Road
Toronto, Ontario, Canada M8Z 2X2
416-232-0522
www.noahsmarine.com

SYSTEM THREE RESINS, INC.
3500 West Valley Highway North
Suite 105
Auburn, WA 98001
800-333-5514
www.systemthree.com

WEST MARINE
P.O. Box 50070
Watsonville, CA 95077-0070
800-262-8464
www.westmarine.com

WEST SYSTEM EPOXY PRODUCTS
Gougeon Brothers, Inc.
100 Patterson Avenue
P.O. Box 908
Bay City, MI 48707-0908
989-684-7286
www.westsystem.com

HARDWARE

JAMESTOWN DISTRIBUTORS
(see contact information above)

MCMASTER-CARR
P.O. Box 4355
Chicago, IL 60680-4355
630-833-0300
www.mcmastercarr.com

NOLAN SUPPLY
111-115 Leo Avenue
Syracuse, NY 13206
800-736-2204
www.nolansupply.com

LORY WEDOW
(HANDCRAFTED ROWLOCKS
AND ROWLOCK PLATES)
Blue Mt. Metal Arts , Inc.
P.O. Box 606
Brocton, NY 14716
315-725-2453
email: ldwedow@hotmail.com

PRE-CUT STRIPS, PLANS, KITS, AND OTHER
BOAT BUILDING SUPPLIES

THE ADIRONDACK GUIDEBOAT
P.O. Box 144
Charlotte, VT 05445
866-425-3926
www.adirondack-guide-boat.com

BEAR MOUNTAIN BOAT SHOP
P. O. Box 191
Peterborough, Ontario, Canada K9J 6Y8
877-392-8880
www.bearmountainboats.com

NEWFOUND WOODWORKS
(see contact information above)

NICK SCHADE
Guillemot Kayaks
10 Ash Swamp Road
Glastonbury, CT 06033
860-659-8847
www.guillemot-kayaks.com

OARS AND PADDLES

SHAW & TENNEY, INC.
P.O. Box 213
20 Water Street
Orono, ME 04473
207-866-4867
www.shawandtenney.com

SEAT CANING SUPPLIES

H. H. PERKINS CO.
222 Universal Drive
North Haven, CT 06473
800-462-6660
www.hhperkins.com

INFORMATION SOURCES
AND RELATED READING

MUSEUMS

THE ADIRONDACK MUSEUM
Route 28N & 30
P.O. Box 99
Blue Mountain Lake, NY 12812-0099
518-352-7311
www.adirondackmuseum.org

MYSTIC SEAPORT MUSEUM
75 Greenmanville Avenue
P.O. Box 6000
Mystic, CT 06355-0990
888-973-2767
www.mysticseaport.org

ANTIQUE BOAT MUSEUM
750 Mary Street
Clayton, NY 13624
315-686-4104
www.abm.org

MAGAZINES

BOATBUILDER MAGAZINE
Box 420235
Palm Coast, FL 32142
800-786-345
www.boatbuildermagazine.com

231

MESSING ABOUT IN BOATS
29 Burley Street
Wenham, MA 01984-1943
978-774-0906
www.messingaboutinboats.com

WOODENBOAT
WoodenBoat Publications, Inc.
Naskeag Road
P.O. Box 78
Brooklin, ME 04616
207-359-4651
www.woodenboat.com

BOOKS AND ARTICLES

Bond, Hallie E. *Boats and Boating in the Adirondacks.* Blue Mountain Lake, New York: The Adirondack Museum and Syracuse, New York: Syracuse University Press, 1995.

Durant, Kenneth. *Guide-Boat Days and Ways.* Blue Mountain Lake, New York: The Adirondack Museum, 1963.

Durant, Kenneth and Helen. *The Adirondack Guide-Boat.* Blue Mountain Lake, New York: The Adirondack Museum and Camden, Maine: International Marine Publishing Company, 1980.

Ford, Howard. "Building an Adirondack Guideboat." *Adirondack Life,* January/February, 1977 (also in *WoodenBoat,* no. 18, September/October, 1977).

Gardner, John. *Building Classic Small Craft* (2 volumes). Camden, Maine: International Marine Publishing Company, 1977, 1984.

Kahn, Michael. "A Celebration of Adirondack Guideboats." *Adirondack Life,* August, 1998.

McCarthy, Henry "Mac". *Featherweight Boatbuilding.* Brooklin, Maine: WoodenBoat Publications, 1996.

Miller, Bruce, W., and Jim Widess. *The Caner's Handbook.* Asheville, North Carolina: Lark Books, 1991.

Moores, Ted, and Merilyn Mohr. *Canoecraft: An Illustrated Guide to Fine Woodstrip Construction (2nd ed.).* Toronto, Ontario, Canada: Firefly Books, 2000.

Smith, Mason. 1987. "Adirondack Guideboat." *Small Boat Journal,* no. 57 (October/November 1987): p. 29–33.

Stephens, Robert W. 1996. (May/June). "Light Boats in the Wilderness: The Evolution of the Adirondack Guideboat." *WoodenBoat,* no. 130 (May/June 1996): p. 34–45.

Van Leuven, Susan. *Illustrated Guide to Woodstrip Canoe Building.* Lancaster, Pennsylvania: Schiffer Publishing, Ltd., 1998.

232

GLOSSARY

Several terms used to describe the building of a boat from wood, both technical and nautical, may be unfamiliar to the first-time builder or sailor. All of the definitions apply to the Adirondack guideboat. For the nautical terms, the point of reference is the boat moving in its normal direction of travel, with the observer facing forward.

aft
Toward the rear or stern of the boat.

amidships
The center portion of the boat.

athwartships
Spanning across the boat from one side to the other.

batten
A thin flexible strip of wood used for drawing or establishing smooth curves.

beam
The measurement of the maximum width of the boat, usually at its center.

bedded
Adjoining overlapping planks sealed with putty or mastic are "bedded."

beveled lap
The edges of overlapping planks are tapered to a near knife-edge such that when fastened together, the tapers mate to produce a smooth continuous surface.

bilge
The inside bottom-most portion of a boat.

book match
A method where adjacent pieces of wood cut from the same stock are fastened edge to edge, much like the pages of a book, producing a pleasing mirror image grain pattern.

bottom board
The spine of a guideboat, analogous to a keel, upon which the ribs are fastened.

bow
The front of the boat.

breast hook
A small piece, joining the bow with both gunwales.

bright
A finish on a boat that is transparent to show the grain of the wood, usually varnish.

carlins
The outermost curved deck support.

carry

The act of carrying or moving a boat over land from one body of water to another. Also referred to as portage, although "carry" is the traditional term used in the Adirondacks. Carry also refers to the physical place or location on land where one must carry a boat from one body of water to another. Such places often had names, e.g. the Marion River carry.

caul

A woodworking term indicating a piece of protective material, usually wood, used between the pressure faces of a clamp and the pieces to be glued.

cleats

See risers.

clinched

The rolling over of the end of a tack fastening planks together such that the end curves back into the wood, forming a tight joint. Also clenched.

coaming

A raised thin strip around the inner edge of the deck to deflect water.

cutwater

234

The foremost edge of the boat's forward stem.

deck

A flat or slightly curved surface between the gunwales at the bow and stern, providing shelter for storage below and also to shed water.

fair curve

A smooth curving line connecting discrete points.

fore

Refers to the front of the boat.

Fuller bit

A proprietary drill bit consisting of a tapered drill bit with integral countersink, used for drilling and countersinking pilot holes for wood screws in a single operation.

fun

The positive feeling one enjoys while building a boat.

garboard

The lowest plank, attached to the bottom board.

gunwale

The reinforced top outer edge of the hull, also known as a wale.

hull

Main part of the boat; the body of the boat without any seats, decks, oars, etc.

inboard

Facing or positioned to the inside of the boat.

kerf

The slot created by a saw blade as it cuts through wood.

lap straked

A method of fastening planks to form a hull where the top edge of each plank is covered by the bottom edge of the next.

limber hole

A small hole in the deck near the bow that allows collected water to drain when the boat is inverted.

loft
The process whereby a full-size drawing of a component of a boat is made from measurement data in a table of offsets.

oarlocks
See rowlocks.

outboard
Facing or positioned to the outside of the boat.

outwales
That portion of the gunwale positioned on the outside of the hull.

painter ring
A small metal ring fastened high on the stem to which a line (the painter) is attached.

patience
The least expensive component of a boat to which craftsmanship is directly proportional.

planking
Thin wood boards mounted on the ribs that form the outer surface of the hull.

port
The left side of a boat.

portage
See carry.

quarter sawn
Lumber sawn from a log such that the grain lines are perpendicular to the wide dimension of the plank.

risers
Thin strips of hardwood fastened to the ribs upon which the seats are supported. Also called cleats or rising cleats (Gardner).

rocker
The shallow gentle upward curve of the bottom board at the bow and stern.

rolling bevel
A bevel cut on the edge of a plank, the angle of which is constantly changing along its length.

rolling rabbet
A rabbet cut into a one-piece stem, the angle of which follows the angle of the planking or stripping, and into which the ends of the planking or stripping are fitted.

rowlock plate
A metal plate or strap fastened to the gunwale, with a socket that receives the pivoting rowlock pin attached to the oar.

rowlocks
The hardware that mounts the oar to the boat. It consists of a pivot pin through the oar that fastens a horn to the oar, with a larger pivot pin on the horn that mounts into a mating socket on the rowlock plate screwed to the gunwale. See Plate XII in Appendix 1.

scarf
A joint used to fasten the ends of two planks or strips together to increase overall length. See Appendix 4.

sheer line
The profile of the topmost edge of the boat.

sheer strip
The first strip applied to the ribs that defines the sheer line.

siding
The term used by traditional guideboat builders for planking.

spruce crook
A slab of wood cut vertically from a spruce stump, which includes the root.

squeeze-out
Excess glue forced from a joint that indicates the application of a sufficient amount of glue within the joint.

starboard
The right side of a boat.

stem
The extreme bow or stern member at which all planking terminates.

stern
The rear of the boat.

story stick
A convenient length of wood used for transferring measurements by simple marks.

strake
An individual thin plank, usually pine, used to cover the ribs of a traditional guideboat.

table of offsets
A table of measurement data that, when plotted on a set of axes, will describe the shape and lines of a boat.

trim
A boat in which the load is distributed to cause it to float level is said to be in trim.

wales
See gunwale.

wood flour
Very fine wood particles obtained from sanding operations used for thickening and coloring epoxy.

yoke
A carved block of wood that allows carrying an inverted boat on one's shoulders.

ABOUT THE AUTHORS

JOHN D. MICHNE is a retired chemist and gamma ray spectroscopist. He spent his career in nuclear and environmental radiochemistry, and has designed, constructed, and programmed microprocessor-controlled remote deep ocean instrumentation. John has written feature articles for his local newspaper, and recently wrote a series of articles on wood-stripped canoe construction posted at his website at www.michneboat.com.

John's woodworking experience dates back to the 1940s. He completed his first boat, a 12-foot plywood and fiberglass outboard runabout, built over oak framework in 1965. His more recent work has consisted of award-winning canoes and guideboats, including a canoe stripped in Honduras mahogany and trimmed in Peruvian walnut. John's reproduction of the *Virginia* as described in this book won Best in Show at the annual Northeastern Woodworkers Association Showcase 2002, judged by a distinguished panel of nationally known professional woodworkers. Other awards won at the NWA: second place in class for a cedar stripped 17' canoe, 1999; first place in class, 13' mahogany stripped canoe, 2000; Best of Show and People's Choice Award, 14' Adirondack guideboat, 2004.

John and his wife live in Clifton Park, New York.

MICHAEL J. OLIVETTE is a professor and administrator at Syracuse University. He has spent much of his life exploring New York State's Adirondack Mountains. He is a licensed Adirondack guide who, like the guides of the old days, is also an accomplished carpenter, furniture maker, and boat-builder. In the "off-season," Michael builds rustic and traditional furniture, and has built a timber frame cabin by hand, in the southern Adirondacks, where he spends much of his free time. Michael is also a field tester for L.L. Bean, Inc. A few years ago, Michael combined his woodworking skills with his love of the Adirondack guideboat and built his first reproduction of Grant's guideboat, *Virginia*.

Michael lives with his two daughters in the lakeside community of Cazenovia, New York.